DISCIPLES

Disciples

How Jewish Christianity
Shaped Jesus and Shattered the Church

Keith Akers

a p o c r y p h i l e   p r e s s
B E R K E L E Y , CA
Apocryphile Press
1700 Shattuck Ave. #81
Berkeley, CA 94709
www.apocryphile.org

Printed in the United States of America
ISBN 978-1-937002-50-3

Dedicated to the memory of
Carl Anders Skriver
(1903–1983)

Table of Contents

List of Tables and Figures

Acknowledgments

Many people helped me in the writing of this book. A number of people offered help, encouragement, conversation, and sometimes extensive comments, including Mark Sullivan, Steve Bastasch, Judy Carman, Jeffrey Bütz, John Simcox, Bob Arconti, John Plummer, James Robert Deal, Craig Todd, Rachel MacNair, Charles Vaclavik, and Steve Kaufman.

Thanks also to the people at Taylor Library in the Iliff Theological Seminary in Denver, where I did most of my research. Thanks to my wife, Kate, not only for her continual comments but for understanding that this book was important. Thanks also to anyone I have overlooked.

Introduction

First, there was a movement

A book about the disciples of Jesus would typically start with Jesus himself: first there was Jesus, then he had disciples. This book suggests a fundamentally different story: *first there was a movement, then Jesus emerged as its leader.* This movement was known to history as "Jewish Christianity"—Jews who followed both the Jewish law, as they understood it, and also followed Jesus, as they understood him, and persisted in this even after the rest of Christianity became a gentile religion.

Understanding Jewish Christianity as the source of Jesus' religion suggests a second fundamental point: *this movement held vegetarianism and opposition to animal sacrifice as central tenets.* Jesus took over the leadership of a Jewish heretical sect which affirmed the virtue of poverty, the corrupting influences of power and wealth, and the value of peace. But one integral belief of Jewish Christianity was dropped by the later church: its objections to the Jerusalem temple. Jewish Christianity saw the practice of animal sacrifice in the temple as a bloody and barbaric business. The chief business of the ancient temple was accepting the offerings of slaughtered animals. It was more like a butcher shop than a place of worship. For Jewish Christianity, Jesus gave his life when he disrupted the temple business during Passover week. Instead of animal sacrifice, they practiced an alternative ritual, baptism in flowing water, and were vegetarians.

Some two decades after Jesus was crucified, these disciples split with its most famous missionary, Paul, over the issue of vegetarianism and eating meat sacrificed to pagan idols. This sect continued its existence as a force independent both of Judaism and of the rest of Christianity for at least several hundred years afterwards. Both orthodox Jews and orthodox Christians regarded this movement as heretical, though for different reasons.

1

This book examines the claim that Jewish Christianity was not only the key group that *followed* Jesus, but also preceded and *shaped* him. It hard to tell at a distance of two millennia where Jesus ends and the movement begins, and what exactly Jesus contributed that was new. Jesus was baptized by John and took up much of the message of John's movement. But the radicalism of Jewish Christianity, as Christianity expanded into the gentile world, created problems.

The Historical Importance of Jewish Christianity

Jewish Christianity is *the* group, among the dozens of different early Christian groups, which we have to understand if we are to understand Jesus or primitive Christianity. Jesus was a Jew and all of his earliest followers were Jews. When gentile Christianity rejected Jewish Christianity, it was in fact rejecting the core of primitive Christianity.

The heart of primitive Christianity was the Jerusalem church. It was founded in the immediate aftermath of Jesus' death, and led by James, the brother of Jesus, and his successors. Paul, the great opponent of Jewish Christianity, was not a peer of the Jerusalem church and never knew Jesus outside of his visions. When Paul parted company with the church after an angry confrontation at Antioch, James took the rest of the family of Jesus, the Jerusalem church, and likely everyone who either had known Jesus or was living in Palestine at the time with him. "Even Barnabas was carried away," reports Paul (Galatians 2:13).

But scarcely more than a decade later, the great Jewish revolt against Rome completely altered the world of primitive Christianity. This revolt was brutally suppressed by the Romans, who captured Jerusalem and destroyed the temple in the year 70. While the whole world of Judaism was devastated, including Jewish Christianity, the gentile Christian churches were left untouched. Any influence of the Jerusalem church on the gentile Christian churches, or missionary effort on behalf of Jewish Christianity, was greatly curtailed or completely halted.

We don't know the exact sequence of events, but the final result cannot be doubted: a century after the destruction of the temple, gentile Christianity is widespread, while Jewish Christianity is a minor sect. The Jewish Christians dominated the primitive church before the year 70, but late in the second century the Jewish Christian Ebionites rate barely a paragraph in Irenaeus' lengthy work *Against Heresies*.

Early Christian history created an incredible diversity of believers. The most striking feature of early Christian writings (before the council of Nicaea in 325), when compared to the early writings of other religions such as Islam or Buddhism, is that so much of it is devoted to polemics against other Christians. Early church fathers such as Tertullian, Origen, Irenaeus, Epiphanius, Theodoret, Hippolytus, and others wrote massive works about and against other Christian heretics—often more than they wrote against pagans or other external enemies of Christianity. Except for allegiance to Jesus, there was scarcely any agreement over basic precepts and practice in early Christianity; even monotheism itself was in question.

How do we explain this striking and unusual diversity in early Christianity? Factionalism in other religions typically features broad similarities of doctrine and practice among competing schools of thought. This is what we see in the Sunni-Shia split in Islam or the divisions among Theravada, Vajrayana, and Mahayana Buddhists, in which all the various competing schools were similar to each other in acknowledging basic doctrines. What differences exist often center on questions of authority, or on details of doctrine or practice so obscure that they may baffle outsiders.

But where are the broad similarities in doctrine between the orthodox and the heretics in second and third century Christianity? Where are the doctrines and practices on which Irenaeus, Tertullian, and Epiphanius *agree* with their opponents—or where, for that matter, do their opponents agree among themselves?

This diversity was not the result of a strong, authoritarian church which suppressed deviant doctrines. Quite the contrary, this diversity was caused by a *lack* of authority. The Jerusalem church and Jewish Christianity should have been the authority, but the horrific outcome of the Jewish revolt against Rome (66 to 74) so weakened the church it that it effectively destroyed the church's authority, and there was literally nothing to replace it.

"Jewish Christianity" as scholars understand it today was simply the successor to this greatly weakened Jerusalem church. What followed was a century of doctrinal chaos. It was not until the Council of Nicaea in 325 CE that order was mostly restored in the church—though at a heavy cost, as we will see, to early Christian ideas. The original ideas of simple living and nonviolence had been banished to the monastic communities, and many new doctrines, such as the virgin birth and the divinity of Jesus, had been introduced which were completely unknown in primitive Christianity.

In the beginning, Jesus and all his disciples were Jews. In the end, Jewish Christianity was condemned as a heresy. Until and unless we can resolve this paradox, we cannot understand either Jesus or the movement which he led.

The Narrative of Jewish Christianity

We don't have a single continuous "story" about Jewish Christianity. What we have is a series of snapshots, showing in greater detail some aspects of Jewish Christianity, and leaving others in tantalizing obscurity. It is like a jigsaw puzzle, with some of the pieces lost, and others which could be put in different places (see Figure 1). But by piecing together what we do know, we can know a great deal: its key ideas, its likely origins, and its most palpable influences. In short, we can know its history.

In talking about Jewish Christianity, I cannot avoid talking about Jesus, but I deliberately put aside the question of the historical Jesus as much as possible, and simply address the question of the origins and history of this sect of early Christianity. Obviously there was some sort of close relationship between Jesus and Jewish Christianity, but what was it? Readers interested in more detail may want to wait until chapter 10, or look at my earlier book, *The Lost Religion of Jesus*.

In fact, figuring out what precisely Jesus *added* to the movement is trickier than initially appears, not because his followers added so much later on, but because Jesus himself may have added so little. The whole project of scholars and the religious community—to understand the religion of Jesus by going back to the presumed source, the historical Jesus—is misdirected.

We can get a better idea of the historical problem by imagining some future historians, 2000 years from now, trying to understand the American revolution of 1776. These historians are working with fragmentary records and know little more than what many Americans on the street know today about the revolution. They know, for example, that George Washington was the leader of the revolution. They also are familiar with some of the most famous "sayings" of the revolution, such as "give me liberty or give me death," or "we hold these truths to be self-evident, that all men are created equal." These historians ask, who was the "historical George Washington," and what were his teachings?

These sayings suggest an ideology of both equality and the importance of liberty. Yet none of the most famous "sayings" of the American revolution came from Washington, but from Patrick Henry, Thomas Jefferson, and others. Indeed, the only saying of Washington which many Americans could quote is "father, I cannot tell a lie, I chopped down that cherry tree," which is probably legendary.

When our future scholars discover that none of these sayings were original with Washington, they might assume that his followers distorted the message of Washington. In fact, noting the almost mythical attributes of Washington, they might doubt whether there was a historical Washington at all.

But suppose these scholars from the future had spectacular manuscript discoveries from the early twenty-first century, and found some *authentic* sayings of Washington: would this help? Even if a complete copy of the First Inaugural Address fell into the hands of our historians, they would be struck by the fact that there are so many specific invocations of divine order and only a single vague reference to "the sacred fire of liberty." They could well conclude that Washington's key insight was that "the foundation of our national policy will be laid in the pure and immutable principles of private morality." Here is proof, if any more is needed, that the views of the "historical Washington" were distorted by his followers. He was really more of a "wisdom teacher" than a revolutionary, the Confucius of America.

In fact, of course, we know that the opposite is the case. The better-known sayings of the revolution like "all men are created equal," even though they are not from Washington himself, actually reflect Washington's views *better* than an authentic saying about the "pure and immutable principles of private morality." Washington was the leader of the revolution, not the philosopher of the revolution; but even though he was not the original author of the common sayings of the revolution first articulated by Patrick Henry, Samuel Adams, Thomas Jefferson, and others, they *do* convey his basic ideas.

It would appear that the same sort of dynamic is operating in the case of Jesus and his movement. The decisive ideas of Jewish Christianity were already "in the air" at the time of Jesus. Jesus certainly promoted them and gave his life for them, but did he originate them? If we were ever to find the genuine sayings of Jesus which really *were* original with him and distinct from the movement around him, they might be misleading, just as the reference to the "pure and immutable principles of private morality" is actually rather misleading about Washington's attitude towards the American revolution.

The relationship of Jesus to his movement, I will argue, is very similar. Jesus was more the "George Washington" of Jewish Christianity, than he was like Thomas Jefferson, Thomas Paine, Patrick Henry, and the other "theoreticians" of the American revolution.

The key ideas were already there, truth ready to be proclaimed to the world. Rather than Jesus creating the community which he led (or the beliefs which he held) from scratch, the reality is more likely that the community which put these ideas into practice already existed. Who *were* those disciples of Jesus?

Figure 1. Relationships between persons and belief systems

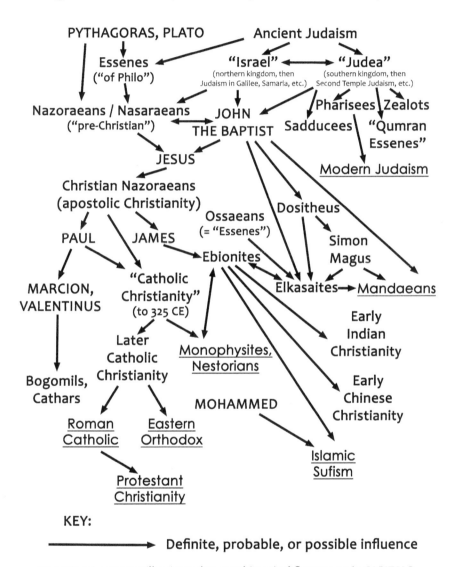

KEY:

———————————➤ Definite, probable, or possible influence

Underlined groups still exist today. Key historical figures are in CAPITALS.

WARNING: this is a very rough guide. Not all relationships are equally strong or equally probable; it is not intended to be complete. See text for details.

Part I:
The Problem of
Jewish Christianity

1. What is Jewish Christianity?

Jewish Christianity consisted of those first disciples of Jesus who continued to be loyal to the Jewish law, as interpreted by Jesus, even after Jesus' departure from the earth. Jesus was a Jew and for some time afterwards, there was no obvious split between his disciples and Judaism. But eventually Christianity separated from Judaism and became an avowedly gentile religion, except for a few groups who insisted on following the Jewish law, as interpreted by the true prophet Jesus, as the basis of their religion. *Those latter groups,* deemed heretical by orthodox Christianity, are the ones we want to talk about.

We know about Jewish Christianity through the writings of the church fathers, especially Irenaeus (second century), Hippolytus (third century), and Epiphanius (fourth century). We also have the so-called "pseudo-Clementine literature," especially the lengthy *Recognitions* and *Homilies*, which are largely Jewish Christian documents. We will discuss all of these at length later.

When exactly all these heretical Jewish Christian groups started is, of course, a tricky subject, and the answer depends on whom you ask. Orthodox Christianity, a gentile religion, goes to great length to depict Jewish Christianity as a *deviation* from the teachings of Jesus, or at least from the church.

We will argue that there is enough continuity in both leadership and in ideas so that we can meaningfully say that it was a *single, continuous, distinct movement* from at least the time of John the Baptist down to Epiphanius in the fourth century. Indeed, we can likely extend this period of time backward about a generation before John the Baptist, and a century or two after Epiphanius. Before and after that we are in more speculative territory, but even then we can speak of influences on Jewish Christianity, as well as the influences *of* Jewish Christianity.

A Movement Without a Name

"Jewish Christianity" is the unavoidable but problematic name for this movement. It is unavoidable not just by scholarly convention, but also because we don't know any single name which these disciples gave to themselves.

The Ebionites were the best known and largest of these groups. We have probably more information about the Ebionites than about all the other groups combined. But there were other groups such as the Nazoraeans, Nasaraeans, "Symmachians," Elkasaites, and various others (see Table 1–1). We will accept "Jewish Christianity" because, at least, it does convey two correct impressions: they *were* Jews and they *did* follow Jesus.

"Jewish Christianity" is a problematic term, though, because both ancient and modern writers have expectations about the terms "Jewish" and "Christian." People expect "Jewish" to signify the Jews that they are familiar with: Jews made in the image of the rabbinic Judaism which came to dominate the Jewish religion after the destruction of the temple in the year 70. Ancient writers as well as modern scholars make this assumption, and the book of Acts is the primary case in point. But "Jewish Christianity" is as different from rabbinic Judaism as rabbinic Judaism is from Islam.

"Christian" implies a viewpoint that Jesus is the Christ, and therefore many assume that this movement could not have existed before Jesus. But I will argue that groups recognizably "Jewish Christian" already existed *before* Jesus; the whole idea that Jesus exerted a decisive influence on the ideas of his movement is a prejudice of a gentile Christianity eager to separate Jesus from the "Jewish influence" of those around him. In any event, we cannot settle an empirical question ("did this group exist before Jesus?") through a definition.

The term "Jewish Christianity" also implies that the "Jewishness" of "Christianity" is a special problem, as if Christianity in its original form was not Jewish. People are surprised at the idea that *later* Jewish Christians such as the fourth-century Ebionites were closely connected to the *early* Jewish disciples such as James, Peter, and John. This sounds like an extraordinary idea which requires some sort of extraordinary evidence. But no one sees any problem in connecting any of the various *gentile* Christian groups to these first Jewish followers of Jesus, when *that* connection is the really challenging problem, historically speaking.

Ebionites	Mentioned by Irenaeus, Hippolytus, Epiphanius, and many others. Heavily influenced the *Recognitions* and *Homilies*. Name derives from *ebionim*, Hebrew for "the poor."
Nazoraeans	Name of first Christians, according to the New Testament and Epiphanius; also name of heretical Jewish Christian sect
Nasaraeans	Pre-Christian group, probably same as Nazoraeans
Nazarenes	Ambiguous: could mean resident of Nazareth, or possibly same as Nazoraeans
Notsrim	Jewish name of Jewish Christians from *birkat ha-minim*; probably same as Nazoraeans
Symmachians	Followers of Symmachus, an Ebionite, therefore actually Ebionites
Elkasaites	Followers of the book of Elxai; discussed by Hippolytus, Epiphanius; clearly related to Jewish Christianity, but may not be Jewish Christian
Sampsaeans	Another name for Elkasaites, only mentioned by Epiphanius
Ossaeans	Another name for Elkasaites, only mentioned by Epiphanius; might also be another name for "Essenes"
Cerinthians	Not a Jewish Christian group

Table 1–1. Names of Jewish Christian groups mentioned in ancient literature.

So we are saddled with an unsatisfactory term, "Jewish Christianity," and a bewildering variety of different names for individual groups.

This variety is less confusing than initially appears. Most likely, there are just two or three basic groups of Jewish Christians.

1.   We have vastly more information about the Ebionites than we have about all other groups *combined*. So for much of this book we will be talking just about Ebionites. The Symmachians are supposed to be followers of Symmachus, who was an Ebionite, so these people are really just Ebionites.
2.   There is a cluster of "N" names—Nazoraeans, Nasaraeans, Nazarenes, and *Notsrim*—which, I will argue, all refer to the same group, and which I will discuss in chapter 8, "The Nazoraeans."
3.   There is a further cluster of groups which are also actually the name of a single group: the Elkasaites, Sampsaeans, and Ossaeans. The Sampsaeans and Ossaeans, only mentioned by Epiphanius, are just different names for the Elkasaites.

There are three principles that I will defend throughout the book which are central to understanding Jewish Christianity in any of its manifestations.

1. The first disciples of Jesus were Jewish Christians.

The first disciples of Jesus were different from virtually everyone else in the ancient (or the modern) Christian world in one significant respect: they were *Jews*. They were not simply Jews by birth, but held a "Jewish Christian" ideology, which this book will elucidate. The claim that "the first disciples of Jesus were Jewish Christians" is, therefore, *not* a simple truism.

In particular, Jewish Christians remained loyal to the Jewish law. Even the canonical gospels make many firm statements about the Jewishness of the Jesus movement. Matthew 5:17–18 ("think not that I have come to abolish the law . . .") and 15:24 ("I was sent only to the lost sheep of the house of Israel") are extreme, but hardly the only, examples of this.

However, as we will see, the Jewish Christians had a rather deviant interpretation of the law, and this creates problems for our understanding of what "Jewish Christianity" is. Scholars have often tried to *define* Jewish Christianity in terms of its beliefs about the

Jewish law, and this has gotten them into trouble. Beginning in the nineteenth century, modern scholars such as F. C. Baur, Adolf von Harnack, and Albrecht Ritschl debated "Jewish Christianity" by looking at how various groups dealt with the issue of Torah-observance (Jackson-McCabe, p. 7–38).

But we can't discover the nature of Jewish Christianity through a definition. "Jewish Christianity" didn't necessarily see the critical issues *at the time* as being ones of "Torah-observance." Depending on one's idea of the Torah, the Jewish Christians may not have been loyal to the Torah at all.

Hans-Joachim Schoeps defined "Jewish Christianity" as the views of a particular group (Schoeps, p. 9). We shouldn't assume that Jewish Christians would be concerned about the same questions of Torah observance about which twenty-first century scholars, or even second-century Christians, would be concerned. It is Schoeps' approach which we will take in this book. Rather than *define* Jewish Christianity, we seek to *discover* Jewish Christianity.

Jewish Christianity resembles both Judaism and Christianity in some aspects, but other key beliefs and practices—including some of the most historically interesting—fall outside of *both* religions. Most conspicuously, the Ebionites of the fourth century had a very divergent understanding of the Jewish law and rejected much of the Jewish scripture (known to Christians as the "Old Testament," a terminology I will use hereafter) as "false texts." High on the list of these "false texts" were all the Old Testament passages relating to animal sacrifice. This bold revisionism is antithetical to *both* Christianity and Judaism in their modern orthodox forms.

We should avoid stereotyping Jewish Christianity or first-century Jews generally. Both modern scholars and early gentile Christians are prone to assume that "Jewish Christians" were just orthodox Pharisees that wanted to follow Jesus, following the descriptions of Jewish Christianity presented in Acts, and distinguish early Jewish followers of Jesus (e. g. Peter, James, and the other disciples) from the later Jewish Christians (e. g., the Ebionites).

But is there really a fundamental difference between the very first Jewish disciples of Jesus and the later Jewish disciples of Jesus (the Ebionites, for example)? Without giving away too much of the plot, it's safe to say that the differences between "earlier" Jewish followers of Jesus and "later" Jewish Christianity are much less than most Christians would suppose, and that early gentile Christians found this an extremely embarrassing point.

2. The Jewish Christians were involved in factional disputes.

There was a scandal in the early church, and to this day the church has never recovered from it. Soon, people were calling each other names, and angry words were spoken, even between the apostles. Soon, the early movement was split into differing factions.

The *later* Jewish Christian groups, such as the Ebionites, continued as if this conflict had never been resolved. They took up the cause of Paul's Jewish opponents, holding Peter and James as heroes and castigating Paul as a traitor to the cause. They preached a message of Jesus as a prophet of the eternal law of God, which included simple living, pacifism, and vegetarianism.

But there were other gentile groups, such as followers of the second-century gnostic Marcion, who took a very different course. They sided with Paul and castigated *Peter* as the false apostle. Peter and the other "Jewish" apostles had misunderstood Jesus' radical message, which Paul alone had really seen.

The book of Acts takes yet a third position: Paul, James, and the other apostles successfully resolved this controversy. Acts does not deny that problems existed, but tends to water them down. The problem, according to Acts, is a difference of opinion about Jewish ritual observance, such as Sabbath observance, kosher laws, and most especially male circumcision.

Acts has confused and misrepresented the context and the outcome of this dispute. Part of the purpose of Acts seems to be precisely to obscure the embarrassing details of this conflict, to minimize the seriousness of the dispute. So what was this dispute about, if it was not about Jewish rituals?

3. The key controversial issues were vegetarianism and rejection of animal sacrifice.

The content of the dispute is fairly clear if you lay the accounts of the different parties side by side. If you look at the *Recognitions* and

Homilies (documents heavily influenced by, if not written by, the Jewish Christian Ebionites) as well as the descriptions of the Ebionites by the fourth-century church father Epiphanius, you see that the later Jewish Christians made a big issue out of meat-eating and animal sacrifice. They are vegetarians and very much opposed to both. "I have come to destroy the [animal] sacrifices," says the Ebionite Jesus (*Panarion* of Epiphanius, 30.16.5). God never wanted to see animals killed, and so never wanted animal sacrifices, according to *Homilies* 3.45.

Paul has opponents in the early church *who are loyal to the Jewish law, who are vegetarians, and who are against animal sacrifice.* Paul asserts that meat-eating is fine, and that there was nothing wrong, in principle, with eating animals sacrificed to pagan idols: "Eat whatever is sold in the meat-market without raising any question on the ground of conscience" (I Corinthians 10:25).

Scholars have been peculiarly blind to this dispute in early Christianity. Paul's letters, the earliest documents of Christianity, lay out the views of his opponents in a straightforward way. But these same views are also present in later Jewish Christianity. These facts cannot be overlooked or explained away: they establish the common thread which links the Jewish opponents of Paul in earliest Christianity to the fourth-century Ebionites. Jewish Christianity is a group loyal to Jesus (as they understood him), loyal to the law (as they understood it), claiming descent from the first Christians, believing in simple living and nonviolence, and practicing vegetarianism and rejecting animal sacrifice.

We next turn to consider opposing concepts of Jewish Christianity as found in the ancient sources: first, what other Christians thought about Jewish Christianity, and second, what the Jewish Christians thought about themselves.

2. How Other Christians Saw Jewish Christianity

Much of our evidence about Jewish Christianity comes from the testimony of its gentile Christian opponents. To understand Jewish Christianity, we must first understand how it appeared to other Christians.

The traditional Christian view of Jewish Christianity is based on Acts. Acts has had a tremendous influence on the orthodox Christian perception of Jewish Christianity. Church fathers such as Irenaeus and Epiphanius also wrote about Jewish Christian sects. They were often far more perceptive about Jewish Christianity and noted things that don't fit into the view found in Acts; but even down to the present day, Acts exerts a decisive influence both on Christians and scholars.

The gentile Christian view of Jewish Christianity was driven by an obvious problem: Jesus was a Jew, and all of his first followers were Jews, and yet from their point of view, the Jewish Christians were heretics and the true followers of Jesus were gentile. Somehow they had to explain how this had happened.

One obvious response is to say that Jesus *himself* broke with Judaism, and there were some second-century Christians who said exactly that. Marcion and his followers were gentile Christians who formed a coherent, radical, and sweeping answer to these questions. The Jewish disciples and followers of Jesus, such as Peter, James, and John, all completely misunderstood what Jesus was getting at—which was to reject Judaism altogether. Only Paul, of all Jesus' early disciples, really understood this critical point.

The orthodox explanation of how this all happened was the book of Acts. It not only addresses the problem of Jewish Christianity, but also the explanation given by Marcion. It is a *narrative* and has a powerful psychological force even today. Acts has done *such* a good job that modern scholars often evade these problems by trying to shift the question of why the split in early Christianity happened, to a general historical question about "the break between Judaism and Christianity" (e. g. in Tabor, 2012, p. 176).

But this way of phrasing the question *already* presupposes the orthodox version of events by ignoring the split in the church itself, which *preceded* the so-called "break between Judaism and Christianity" by *decades* and was far more important to the history of the church. A fairer way of stating this question would be "how and why did one group of Christians break from Judaism, while others did not?"

The Traditional View

Acts views Jewish Christian opponents as "legalists": people who required the rituals of Judaism in all its details, as well as the moral precepts (the ten commandments and various other ethical directives in the law). It never names these opponents, except to call them "Pharisees."

Acts describes a debate in the early church between Jewish Christian "legalists" and more liberal Christians—both Jews and gentiles—who wanted to accommodate everyone. These Christian "Pharisees" (Acts 15:5) observe the Jewish law in all its detail, saying "unless you are circumcised according to the custom of Moses, you cannot be saved" (Acts 15:1).

Paul, James, Peter, and all the others agree on a solution: the gentile followers of Jesus need not convert to Judaism, they need only follow four seemingly minor regulations—they are to abstain from "what has been sacrificed to idols," from "blood," from "what is strangled," and from "unchastity" (Acts 15:29). Jewish Christian legalism is rejected: there is no requirement to be circumcised, in fact there are no requirements to observe any other Jewish rituals at all, not even the Sabbath. The writer of Acts is determined to control the narrative of this dispute and only by implication the story of the later Jewish Christian movement.

Acts nowhere suggests, by the way, that the Christian Pharisees of Acts 15 are the same as the later Jewish Christian Ebionites, but this is the impression that anyone who reads this account is left with: Jewish Christians are legalists. It has succeeded marvelously; almost all modern scholars assume that the Jewish Christianity of the second, third, and fourth centuries must be spiritual descendants of these Christian Pharisees, and therefore in some sense "legalistic," and in almost exactly the way that Acts 15 describes them.

Problems with the Traditional View

There are a number of problems with the traditional view, though, which I will quickly mention here.

1. *The New Testament can't make up its mind when legalism was rejected.* Acts 15 is not the only place where some in the early movement—including the apostles, and even Jesus himself—are described as "legalists." This raises an obvious question: did Jesus himself break with Jewish legalism, or was that left to his disciples after divine revelation?

New Testament evidence can be cited both ways. Mark 7:19 ("thus he declared all foods clean") implies rejection of the kosher laws; Jesus gets into frequent conflicts over the Sabbath; and Jesus went out of his way to disrupt the animal sacrifice business in the temple near the end of his life. All of this creates the impression that Jesus himself broke with the Jewish authorities on key questions. On the other hand, Jesus commands the leper to offer a sacrifice, Jesus says that not an iota or dot will pass from the law until all is fulfilled, and even Jesus' parents make a sacrifice in the temple after his birth.

This equivocation suggests there was an intense need to *create* a narrative about Jesus and legalism after the fact, but no clear idea of how to do it or at what place and time it would be located. These inconsistencies are not fatal to the traditional view expressed in Acts, but they do pose a significant problem.

2. *The idea of a legalistic Jewish Christianity is completely inconsistent with what we know about later Jewish Christianity.*

Epiphanius, writing in his *Panarion* late in the fourth century, describes the Ebionites as a group which is vegetarian, categorically opposes animal sacrifices and rejects the Old Testament texts which command animal sacrifice: "Nor do they accept the Pentateuch: certain passages they reject" (*Panarion* 30.18.7). The *Homilies* agree on this point, rejecting passages in which God appears as warlike, jealous, wicked, and so forth. From the Ebionite point of view, the Old Testament is a tissue of lies: "For the Scriptures have had joined to them many falsehoods against God" (*Homilies* 2.38).

From this description it is clear that the fourth-century Ebionites were definitely anti-legalistic. How can Jewish Christianity, then, be "legalistic"? We could postulate that Jewish Christianity changed over time, or that there were different groups of Jewish Christians, but each of these "solutions" in turn creates further questions. This is not an absolutely fatal objection to the picture of a legalistic Jewish Christianity, but it is a very significant problem, suggesting that Acts is trying to force the round peg of actual Christian history into the square hole of later theology.

3. *The idea of legalistic Jewish Christianity reflects concepts and images of Judaism which are from a different time and place.*

While the sort of legalism exhibited in the gospels and Acts probably did exist among Jews in the first century, it was hardly typical, and it was almost non-existent in Galilee (see chapter 4, "The Prophets, the Lost Tribes, and Galilee").

First-century Palestinian Judaism incorporated many divergent groups and individuals, some of which did not necessarily hold the Jewish law to be central to their religion in the same way that rabbinic Judaism of later centuries would. Indeed, this kind of legalism would be the exception, not the rule, in Galilee.

Even by orthodox Jewish standards, some of the views attributed to these Jewish Christians are quite extreme. What kind of orthodox Jews, either in ancient times or today, would say that you must be circumcised in order to have a part in the world to come (Acts 15:1), or that Jews should not even associate with non-Jews (Acts 10:28)? If we were talking about any *other* Galilean sect of this period, we would not conclude that it was a hotbed of temple worship—in fact, we would assume the very opposite. This is not *proof* that Jewish Christian legalism did not exist, but it is a very significant problem for the view presented in Acts.

4. The idea of Jewish Christian legalism serves the theological needs of the struggle against Marcion.

Did Jesus *himself* break with Jewish legalism, as the gospels suggest at several points? Marcion maintained *precisely* this point of view—that Jesus *did* break decisively not only with legalism, but with Judaism itself. In Marcion's view, the "Jewish apostles" such as Peter did not understand this, and it was Paul alone of the early apostles who saw this clearly and protested in Galatians against the "Judaizers."

By the second century, these gentile Christian heretics such as Marcion and Valentinus were a far more potent threat than Jewish Christianity. Irenaeus (late second century) spends the bulk of his lengthy *Against Heresies* railing against gentile "gnostic" heretics such as Marcion, while he dismisses the Jewish Christians with just a few sentences—probably a rough indication of their relative strength at this time. Jewish Christianity, as a factor within Christianity, went downhill in a hurry, from the dominant form of Christianity in the apostolic age to scarcely more than a footnote a century later.

Marcion and Valentinus epitomized a radical tendency within early Christianity to sever the cord between Judaism and Christianity completely. Marcion denied the Jewish apostles; denied the Jewish God; and denied the world created by that Jewish God. Marcion posited *two* Gods, not one—a Jewish God who created the world (the God of Moses), and the Christian God who was the highest spiritual reality (the God of Jesus). The Jewish God, a vengeful, petty deity, created the material world, but he botched the job. Marcion rejected not only the Jewish law but *the Jewish God* as well. For Marcion, Jesus never incarnated physically in the world, only *seeming* to have a physical body—the idea of the "docetic Christ" (from the Greek verb *dokeo*, to appear). Marcion pointed to the conflict in Galatians 2, as showing that Paul was opposed to Peter and the other "Jewish" apostles (Tertullian, *Against Marcion* 1.20, 4.3, 5.3).

Many other scholars have suggested that Acts is biased (see chapter 15 below). Obviously it would be in the interest of the gentile church to refute Marcion point by point, by emphasizing (1) that the "Jewish God" was the same as the "Christian God," (2) that Jesus incarnated physically, and (3) that Paul, Peter, and James all acted in harmony.

The viewpoint of Acts is *so* convenient for Christian theology that it is too clever by half. We should be asking ourselves: is this all there is to the split in the early church? A dispute about rituals, quickly resolved? That's it, nothing, no more? The mind goes blank: what other answer is even possible? Like Goldilocks and the three bears, Acts finds early Christianity neither insufficiently Jewish, but not too Jewish either. It is "just right" in its Jewishness: Jewish enough to refute Marcion, but not so Jewish that we might need to take Jewish Christianity seriously.

Jesus and his first followers *were* Jews. But many key supporting details for this picture in Acts and the gospels were likely supplied after the destruction of the temple in the year 70, when rabbinic Judaism was ascendant. The churches needed a narrative which emphasized Jesus' Jewishness, not one which gave a nuanced view of the complex diversity of first-century Judaism and pointed out that dissident Jews existed at the time. Jesus and his first followers often look for all the world *as second-century Jews* must have appeared to second-century Christians. Jesus, James, and Peter were Jews, but they and their first followers probably looked and sounded more like Jews such as John the Baptist, Honi the Circle-drawer, and Hanina ben Dosa (all of whom we will discuss later), rather than like Pharisees such as Shammai or Hillel, and *certainly* not like Caiaphas the high priest.

This doesn't *prove* that these details are wrong. But the convenience of this picture creates the suspicion that these "Jewish" details come from the *opponents* of Jewish Christianity—orthodox, gentile writers who understand the deadly threat of Marcion's theology. Marcionism had a completely different belief structure from both that of the Ebionites and the orthodox. Had Marcion's supporters become dominant within Christianity, the religious history of Europe, Asia, and Africa could have been taken in a completely different direction. Rejecting Marcion required tying Christianity to something in Judaism.

The nature of the crisis in early Christianity

The book of Acts is a remarkable document. Confronted by a basic split in the early church which in fact (as we shall see) persisted from the time of Paul to the fourth century, Acts came up with a consistent narrative that wraps most of the significant details of the early church history into a coherent narrative which explains everything and minimizes this split. Even though scholars have questioned many of the details in Acts, its overall narrative is the dominant one even today.

Later views of Jewish Christianity, namely those from the early church fathers, are somewhat more nuanced than Acts, and often report details which are actually embarrassing to the orthodox point of view. But they also seem to be under the spell of Acts; even Epiphanius struggles to fit his view of Jewish Christianity into the schema of Acts.

Having looked at the traditional Christian view of Jewish Christianity, we now ask: how did the Jewish Christians see themselves?

3. How the Jewish Christians Saw Themselves

How did the Jewish Christians see themselves?

For now, we just want to know what the theology and religious practice of the Ebionites was in the third and fourth centuries. This does not give us a perfect match, or guarantee that what we will come up with applies to the first century; we are comparing Acts on Jewish Christianity (written in the second century), with Jewish Christianity's self-image from the third and fourth centuries. But it is a good place to start, because we have a relative abundance of material about what the Jewish Christians thought from the third and fourth centuries. As we shall see, much of this applies to the second century and even gives us a broad insight into the first-century schisms which were so critical to the history of the church.

Ebionite theology is a unique and largely unexplored window into the worldview of the early Christians. To guide us, we have the commentaries of the church fathers, most especially Epiphanius, as well as the pseudo-Clementine literature: the *Clementine Recognitions*, the *Homilies of Clement*, and two short letters to James, one from Peter and one from Clement. There are brief mentions of the Ebionites in earlier church fathers such as Irenaeus (second century) and Hippolytus (third century). Other writers mention the Ebionites but add little that is new. I have summarized the evidence for 15 specific Ebionite beliefs in Table 3–1 below, showing the source for each belief I attribute to the Ebionites. In Table 3–2 below, I compare ideas which Epiphanius attributes to the Ebionites to very similar ideas in the *Recognitions* and *Homilies*, which clearly shows that this literature has a strong Ebionite influence, if they aren't in fact Ebionite documents.

How do we know these are Ebionite ideas? Can we go further than these 15 specific Ebionite beliefs? Throughout this book I will often cite Epiphanius or the *Recognitions* and *Homilies* as evidence for an Ebionite belief. While this is generally safe, it's actually not quite that simple; there are some things in these documents that do *not* belong to the Ebionites. But to avoid a lengthy digression, I have spared the reader the argument at this time. Those wanting more details on these sources and the origins of Ebionite theology should skip ahead to Part V, and then return here.

Ebionite Ethics

The Ebionites had a distinctive ethics, theology, and ritual practice. Their ethics can be summarized as pacifism, vegetarianism, and voluntary poverty or simplicity.

The Ebionites saw themselves as "the poor." Their name, *ebionim*, comes from the Hebrew term for "the poor." This name was based on the primitive communalism of the book of Acts (2:44, 4:32–35), when the entire community shared all their possessions, and they gave everything they had to the church (*Panarion* 30.17.2). This agrees with all the well-known passages in the gospels such as "blessed are the poor," and Jesus telling the rich young man to sell everything he has, give it to the poor, and follow him. It also finds a remarkable parallel in Luke 14:33: "whoever of you does not renounce all that he has cannot be my disciple."

But the Ebionites were also vegetarians and against animal sacrifice. Epiphanius relates that when he queried an Ebionite on their vegetarianism, pointing out that there was a lot of meat-eating in the Jewish scriptures, the Ebionite simply replies, "Christ revealed it to me" (*Panarion* 30.18.9). God never wanted animals killed at all (*Homilies* 3.45), and commands us to avoid dead flesh (*Homilies* 7.4, 7.8). In the Ebionite gospel, Jesus indignantly refuses to eat the Passover meat, and declares "I have come to destroy the sacrifices" (*Panarion* 30.22.4, 30.16.5). In the *Recognitions* it appears that the key reason Christ came was to destroy the sacrifices (1.54).

The *Recognitions* discuss pacifism and nonviolence in several places in contexts which are clearly Jewish Christian. In *Recognitions* 1.70–71 the Jesus movement does not resist the attacks of Saul (Paul before his conversion) on James and the others, because of their commitment to nonviolence. *Recognitions* 2.36 insists that peace is the perfection of law. *Homilies* 2.44 rejects the idea that God is warlike. All of these sound like elaborations on Ebionite ideas or stories.

Pacifism was extremely common in early Christianity, it is part of the earliest layers of the gospel, it is acknowledged as something evidently noncontroversial by Paul, and thus it is likely from Jesus himself or those closest to him. While there are heresies of all sorts and varieties, described in loving detail by the church fathers, no one describes any militarists (heretical or otherwise) in the early church, until the fourth century and Constantine's accession to power.

Ebionite Theology and Rituals
In outline, Ebionite theology was similar to orthodox theology:

1. God is the creator of everything that is.
2. Jesus is the messenger of God.
3. Jesus brings both a moral code and a warning of a future judgement.

However, the Ebionites had a peculiar twist to each of these ideas.

The Ebionites were radical monotheists. God had revealed his law fully at the beginning of creation (*Homilies* 8.10), and later especially to the Jews. For anyone willing to listen, his law and his message were accessible without recourse to priests or sacred texts. This law was not necessarily a written law; in fact, the law that had been written down, the Old Testament text, had been corrupted by "false texts" inserted by people other than Moses. Not only did the Ebionites deny "Biblical inerrancy," they held the opposite—that the so-called sacred texts were actually filled with false texts.

The Ebionites believed that Jesus was the "true prophet," referring not to the prophecies in Isaiah but to Deuteronomy 18:15–18, where Moses promises a future prophet to (in effect) resume where Moses left off—"him shall you heed," Moses warns. The Ebionites took this prophecy to refer to Jesus. An important theological detail is that Jesus is *not* God, but only God's messenger.

Moreover, Jesus, or Christ, or the true prophet (the Ebionites weren't clear on this point) had already appeared many times throughout history. Christ, in fact, appeared as Adam, and appeared bodily to the patriarchs. There was no single incarnation of the Christ; Christ is *constantly* reappearing. "Christ," in fact, is a fairly malleable term. It does not refer exclusively to Jesus; Jesus was merely the first, and others who like him "fulfill the law" are also considered to be "Christs." Unlike Luther, who posited the priesthood of the believer, the Ebionites seemed to believe in the Christhood of the believer.

Just as Jesus, in the Sermon on the Mount, says that his morality is stricter than that of others, the moral code which the Ebionite Jesus brought was much stricter than that either of orthodox Judaism or orthodox Christianity. It required pacifism, poverty, and vegetarianism, all of which were considered optional both in orthodox Judaism and orthodox Christianity, when they were not actually discouraged.

There is one all-important ritual for the Ebionites which we find in the *Recognitions* and *Homilies*: baptism. It is not the Jewish rituals (Sabbath, circumcision, etc.) which we might expect to be emphasized, but a new "Christian" ritual, that of baptism. Baptism was not a once-only ritual of introduction into the new religion, as it came to be for the orthodox, but a ritual to be practiced every day. Baptism is very important for salvation, and indeed without baptism it appears that you cannot be saved. The Ebionites also celebrated communion, or the Eucharist, but with bread and water rather than bread and wine. The Ebionites avoided alcohol, and therefore obviously would not put wine in a ritual in which they expected to participate.

According to the church fathers, Jewish Christians did observe the Jewish rituals such as the Sabbath and circumcision. But there is no unequivocal reference to circumcision or any festivals being *required* by the Ebionites either in the church fathers or in the *Recognitions* and *Homilies*. In fact, the *Recognitions* and *Homilies* explicitly reject such requirements. It is possible to fulfil God's law and will, and be a Jew in God's estimation, without being circumcised (*Recognitions* 5.34). Both Moses and Jesus have one teaching, and God accepts the Jews and gentiles who follow either (*Homilies* 8.6–7). This formulation would make all the ritual elements of the Jewish law optional. (The Elkasaites may have required circumcision, according to Hippolytus, *Refutation of All Heresies* 9.9).

Other Jewish rituals are referred to obliquely if at all. The Ebionites observed the Sabbath as holy, though they hedged their bets and also observed Sunday, the Lord's Day, as sacred as well—making them perhaps the first people in history to regard the modern "weekend" as sacred (Eusebius, *Ecclesiastical History* 3.27.5).

Ebionite Ethics and Orthodox Ethics

Ebionite morality seems much stricter than orthodox Christian ethics: pacifism, vegetarianism, voluntary poverty. Nevertheless, we do see parallels in the orthodox Christian movement, mostly among the monastic communities, who also often practiced pacifism, vegetarianism, and voluntary poverty.

What differentiated the pacifist vegetarian Ebionites from pacifist vegetarians such as, for example, orthodox thinkers like Origen, Basil, and Clement of Alexandria? For the orthodox, vegetarianism was not required at all; they followed Paul's injunctions not to judge people on the basis of what they ate (Romans 14:3). Once the letters of Paul were accepted as Christian scripture, *ethical* vegetarianism for all practical purposes became heretical, though vegetarianism continued for centuries as either an ascetic ideal (for example in many of the early monastic communities) or a health ideal (for example among many modern Seventh-day Adventists). For the orthodox, vegetarianism—when it was acknowledged—didn't have a humanitarian or ethical focus. The Ebionites believed that vegetarianism was more than just an optional way to self-improvement; it was a necessity for Godly living. Pacifism probably represented the majority view of early Christianity, both Jewish and gentile, before Constantine. Most early church writers were pacifist as a matter of course, quoting such well-known passages in the gospels as "love your enemies" in support. Justin, Origin, Irenaeus, Tertullian, Hippolytus, Arnobius, and Lactantius are examples (see *The Lost Religion of Jesus*, chapter 7).

The elimination of pacifism and simple living from Christian orthodoxy provoked quite a bit more resistance than the elimination of vegetarianism, and pacifism and simple living have never entirely disappeared as Christian ideals. However, after the council of Nicaea both of these were eliminated as *requirements*. In the end, in orthodox Christianity, the teachings of Jesus were stripped of most of the practical applications they had for his first disciples.

Conclusions

The Ebionites felt that pacifism, vegetarianism, and simple living were required by God. Their theology specifically explained why these views were seemingly eliminated from Judaism but were intended by God to be included *from the beginning* (as we will see in chapters 5, 21, and 22). The revelation from Jesus was, therefore, not something new that suddenly broke into the world, but the re-establishment of something present all along.

Table 3-1. Rough Guide to Jewish Christian / Ebionite Beliefs, according to early texts

	Paul	Acts	Irenaeus	Hippolytus	Recognitions	Homilies	Epiphanius
One God, the Creator	Yes	Yes	Yes	Yes	Yes	Yes	Yes
Jesus the "true prophet"					Yes	Yes	Yes
Jesus is not God			Yes	Yes	Yes	Yes	Yes
Christ in Adam, appears throughout history					Yes	Yes	Yes
Christhood of the believer				Yes	Yes		
The Virtue of Poverty	Yes				Yes	Yes	Yes
Pacifism, Nonviolence					Yes	Yes	
Vegetarianism	Yes					Yes	Yes
Rejection of animal sacrifice	Yes	No			Yes	Yes	Yes
Avoid Alcohol	Yes		Yes			Yes	Yes
Not eating with unbelievers	Yes				Yes	Yes	Yes
Accept Jewish Law	Yes	Yes	Yes	Yes	Yes	Yes	Yes
False Texts		No				Yes	Yes
Daily Baptism					Yes	Yes	Yes
Rejection of Paul	Yes	Yes	Yes		Yes	Yes	Yes

Paul = Romans 14, I Corinthians 8-10, Galatians 2. Acts = Acts 10:9-16, 15, 21:17-26. Irenaeus = *Against Heresies* 1.26, 5.1.3. Hippolytus = *Refutation of All Heresies* 7.22. Epiphanius = *Panarion* 30.

Table 3-2: Epiphanius' *Panarion* 30 compared to the *Recognitions* and *Homilies*

Panarion 30	*Recognitions and Homilies*
Jesus the "true prophet"	30.18.5: "They [the Ebionites] say that the Christ is the True Prophet."	*Recognitions* 5.10: "He [Jesus] therefore is the true Prophet." See also *Recognitions* 1.54, 1.57, 2.28, 2.48, 3.41, 5.13, 6.9, 6.14; *Homilies* 3.52, 3.53, 17.6. Compare *Homilies* 3.49.
Jesus is not God	30.3.1, rejection of the virgin birth; 30.16.3, Jesus the son of God from his baptism; 30.20.5, the savior is "a mere man."	*Homilies* 16.15, "Our Lord neither asserted that there were gods except the Creator of all, nor did He proclaim Himself to be God."
Christ in Adam, appears throughout history	30.3.5, Christ comes when he pleases, was in Adam, appeared bodily to the patriarchs	*Homilies* 3.20: "If any one do not allow the man fashioned by the hands of God [i. e., Adam, cf. Genesis 2:7] to have had the Holy Spirit of Christ, how is he not guilty of the greatest impiety in allowing another born of an impure stock to have it?" *Recognitions* 1.33, the true prophet appeared to Abraham; *Recognitions* 1.34, the true prophet appeared to Moses See also *Recognitions* 1.52, 2.22, 2.48, 8.59
This world given to the devil	30.16.2, this world given to the devil at the request of both Jesus and Satan	*Homilies* 20.2: "God appointed two kingdoms, and established two ages, determining that the present world should be given to the evil one, because it is small, and passes quickly away . . . ." See also *Recognitions* 1.24, 5.9, 8.55, *Homilies* 7.2, 15.7

. . . continued

Table 3-2 (continued)

	Panarion 30	Recognitions and Homilies
The Virtue of Poverty	30.17.2, they called themselves "poor" because they gave their possessions to the apostles	Recognitions 2.29: "He [Jesus] mourned over those who lived in riches and luxury, who bestowed nothing upon the poor . . . whom they ought to love as themselves." Homilies 15.9: "Possessions are sins." See also Recognitions 5.9, 7.6; Homilies 3.69, 7.4, 11.4, 12.6
Vegetarianism	30.13.5, their gospel says John the Baptist did not eat locusts 30.15.3, they abstain from meats 30.22.5, their gospel says that Jesus refused the Passover meat	Homilies 7.4: "And the things which are well-pleasing to God are . . . not to taste dead flesh, not to touch blood" See also Homilies 3.45, 7.8, 8.15, 8.19, 12.6; Recognitions 7.6
Rejection of animal sacrifice	30.16.5, their gospel says Jesus came to destroy the sacrifices	Recognitions 1.54: "the rising of Christ was at hand for the abolition of sacrifices" See also Recognitions 1.36, 1.37, 1.39, 1.64, 2.71, 4.36, 8.48; Homilies 2.44, 3.24, 3.26, 3.45, 3.52, 3.56, 7.3, 7.4, 7.8, 8.19, 9.7, 18.19
Avoid Alcohol	30.16.1, they take the Eucharist with water, instead of wine	Homilies 11.15, "According to the worship of God, the proclamation is made to be sober."

continued . . .

Table 3-2 (continued)

	Panarion 30	*Recognitions and Homilies*
Accept Jewish Law	30.2.2, relies on the Jewish law with respect to the Sabbath, circumcision, and other things	*Recognitions* 1.24, 1.26, 1.35 *Homilies* 8.10: "The only good God . . . appointed a perpetual law to all . . . which can be read by all." Others as well throughout.
False Texts	30.18.7, they "reject" certain Pentateuch sayings; they "will not believe" Old Testament passages 30.18.9, they "blaspheme" the legislation	*Homilies* 2.38-44, a long list of sayings and references to Old Testament passages which are not true.
Daily Baptism	30.15.3, Peter baptized himself daily	References to Peter bathing at *Recognitions* 4.3, 8.1; *Homilies* 8.2, 11.1
Rejection of Paul	30.16.8, Ebionites have trumped up charges against Paul	*Recognitions* 1.70-71, Saul (Paul before his conversion) attempts to murder James *Homilies* 17.13-19, Peter says visions of Jesus not as authoritative as teachings received from earthly Jesus

Part II:
Jewish Christianity
Before Jesus

_____

4. The Prophets, the Lost Tribes, and Galilee

Jewish Christianity before Jesus? Is such a thing possible? Obviously, if you *define* Jewish Christianity by limiting it to followers of Jesus, then it can't be done. But if the essence of Jewish Christianity is defined in terms of its organization, religious ideas, and practices, then clearly it is possible.

And some of the key ideas of Jewish Christianity *can* be taken back nearly a thousand years before Jesus—at least to the time of the prophets Amos, Hosea, Isaiah and Jeremiah. Hans-Joachim Schoeps concludes that "Jewish Christian antagonism toward the law of sacrifice is directly descended from statements of the prophets on this subject" (Schoeps, p. 118).

By the first century, animal sacrifice was a big business in Jerusalem. Recent archeological research indicates that the local economy was not able to provide all the sacrificial animals needed, and huge numbers needed to be imported from outside the area (Hartman, 2013). The temple powered the economy of the region as pilgrims would come from all over the world to purchase and then offer animals in sacrifice.

From Tribal Cult to Universal Religion

The very oldest Judaism (perhaps down to the time of the Judges) was probably not monotheistic. Their God Yahweh was a tribal deity rather than a single universal God ruling over the entire universe. The evolution of the concept of Yahweh from a tribal deity to a universal God was probably gradual, and during the transition phase, there was probably conflict between the concept of the tribal deity, whose usefulness was primarily in smiting the enemies of the tribe, and a universal God who was a God not just of Israel but of the entire world. In this latter case, Israel had an advantage over the rest of the world in that God revealed himself first to Israel, but ultimately this revelation was to become universal.

Historically, the sacrificial cult was likely a manifestation of the earlier, tribal concept of Yahweh. Like countless other deities in the region, Yahweh was thought to be pleased by offerings made to him and could be encouraged to smite the enemies of the tribe if the proper rites and offerings were made. The sacrificial rites of Israel broadly resembled the pagan rituals of their neighbors.

When the children of Israel first entered Palestine from Egypt after the exodus, they confronted other gods. At first there did not seem to be a conflict. The local agricultural deities (such as Baal) could be offered gifts as well as Yahweh, with both useful in the same way that the Romans would find Mars and Ceres. But then ancient Judaism went through a crisis in its relationships to its neighbors at least partially because of its religious practices. These practices were moving in the direction of monotheism, which was intolerant of the worship of other gods than the one true God Yahweh. The temple of Solomon (assuming this is historical) was built roughly around the year 1000 BCE—so clearly at this time, Yahweh was thought to be the kind of God who could be propitiated by gifts and offerings. For several centuries after Solomon, the transition to a more universal concept of Yahweh made progress. Yahweh was now thought to be interested in righteous behavior as well as offerings. Ultimately, a more universal view was adopted; Yahweh was *only* interested in the righteous behavior so you could skip the offerings altogether.

Leroy Waterman, an archeologist who helped with the Revised Standard Version translation of the Old Testament, points out a significant problem here (*The Religion of Jesus*). Even after the people turned to Yahweh, their worship included elements of Baal worship. It's as if they were still worshiping Baal, but calling him "Yahweh," so that "Yahweh" became just another name for Baal. Waterman translates Hosea 2:16 as "Jehovah [Yahweh] is our Baal," and concludes, "Israel had adopted Baalism and called it Jehovahism" (Waterman, p. 18).

Hosea is a northern prophet and is one of the first to see that the problem is not just *who* you were worshiping, so that you could stop worshiping Baal and substitute Yahweh instead. The problem was *with the worship itself*. Hosea sees that the sacrificial cult is reprehensible because it has a primitive, almost childish concept of how God operates.

"I desire steadfast love and not sacrifice, the knowledge of God, rather than burnt offerings," says Hosea 6:6, thus stating that sacrifices are not part of the worship of the true God. Jesus later quoted this very text (Matthew 9:13 and 12:7), and the Ebionites referred approvingly to this saying (*Recognitions* 1.37, *Homilies* 3.56).

Nor is the reason simply that sacrifices are superstitious or unnecessary. For the Ebionites, animal sacrifices are positively evil because they kill animals, something clearly contrary to the law of God (*Homilies* 3.45). Hosea in the ninth century BCE took this same position and foresaw the time when God would make a "covenant on behalf of Israel with the wild beasts, the birds of the air, and the things that creep on the earth," and sweep away weapons of violence "so that all living creatures may lie down without fear" (Hosea 2:18, NEB).

This is clearly an *ethical* concern for animals, not just a concern over hypocrisy. God's covenant is made *with the animals themselves* and insures their safety. The problem is not simply that animal sacrifices are being offered inappropriately or hypocritically; the practice of animal sacrifice is *intrinsically* wicked.

Amos, at about the same time, likewise denounces the sacrifices in unequivocal terms: "Even though you offer me your burnt offerings and cereal offerings, I will not accept them . . . but let justice roll down like waters, and righteousness like an ever-flowing stream" (Amos 5:22, 24). Amos then says that Israel never offered true sacrifices to God in the wilderness, but only to idols, and "therefore I will take you into exile" (Amos 5:25–27).

This is another passage which New Testament writers were clearly aware of and quoted approvingly. Stephen, the first Christian martyr after Jesus, cites Amos in his incendiary speech attacking animal sacrifice as idolatry in Acts 7 (about which more in chapter 12). Amos and Hosea present the same concept: sacrifices are not part of the true worship of God, but justice and righteousness are. God will destroy the nation which does not understand this (Amos 8:2–4).

This attack on sacrifices was followed up by the southern prophets Isaiah, Jeremiah, and Micah. Micah 6:6–8, while not condemning animal sacrifice outright, says that burnt offerings are not what God wants, and suggests that God *only* requires us to "do justice, and to love kindness, and to walk humbly with your God."

Jeremiah 7:21–22 grudgingly permits animal sacrifice, but has God *specifically* disavowing the idea that he ever commanded animal sacrifices: "But when I brought your forefathers out of Egypt, I gave them no commands about whole-offering and sacrifice; *I said not a word about them*" (7:22, NEB, emphasis added). The New International Version, incidentally, mistranslates this by inserting the word "just" so that it reads, "I did not *just* give them commands about burnt offerings and sacrifices . . ." which, of course, totally distorts the meaning.

Isaiah says:

> I am sated with whole offerings of rams and the fat of buffaloes; I have no desire for the blood of bulls, of sheep and of he goats. Whenever you come to enter my presence—who asked you for this? No more shall you trample my courts. The offer of your gifts is useless, the reek of sacrifice is abhorrent to me. (Isaiah 1:11–13, NEB)

It is true that much of or even most of the rhetoric in some of the prophetic writings is directed, in context, against the hypocrisy of offering gifts on the one hand while denying basic justice with the other; we do not want to lose sight of this. However, the sacrificial practices *themselves* are also questioned. "I have no desire for the blood of bulls, of sheep, and of he goats" (Isaiah 1:11) is stated without qualification. The question, "who asked you for this?" (1:12) does not make sense unless it is the *sacrificial cult itself* that is in question. "This" refers to the "countless sacrifices." Isaiah, like Jeremiah 7:21–22, denies (contradicting Leviticus) that God ever commanded sacrifices.

Isaiah, like Hosea, and like the Ebionites a millennium later, states an ethical concern for animals themselves. Isaiah offers the famous image of the wolf and the lamb living together in harmony, adding that "they shall not hurt or destroy in all my holy mountain; for the earth shall be full of the knowledge of the Lord as the waters cover the sea" (Isaiah 11:9).

Later on Isaiah offers the opinion that "he who slaughters an ox is like him who kills a man" (66:3)— directly equating killing animals with killing humans. What God *does* want is a higher law—justice, righteousness, breaking the bow and sword, all creatures lying down without fear. It is this higher law which is the spiritual ancestor of Ebionite thought.

There is no single point of view of "the prophets." Some of the prophets, such as Zechariah, Haggai, and Malachi, looked forward to a resurgence of the land of Israel and return of temple worship. But the rejection of the sacrificial cult, the tendency towards a universal religion, and an ethical concern for animals frequently went hand in hand in some of the prophetic writings.

The Lost Tribes of Israel

The struggle to determine whether God wanted a universal religion, sent first to the Jews, or was a tribal deity who would establish Israel as the dominant power in the region, was still undecided in the first century. This struggle was fought against a background of the rise and fall of various attempts at a national state on the part of the ancient Jews.

According to Biblical history, the united monarchy of David and Solomon was followed by a division into the northern kingdom ("Israel") and the southern kingdom ("Judea"). It is from the area occupied by the *northern* kingdom (which includes Galilee) that Jewish Christianity probably sprang.

Assyria came to dominate the northern kingdom of Israel, which later revolted against Assyria but was defeated around 722 BCE. After this conquest, at least the elites of the northern kingdom were deported and Israel became an Assyrian province. We never hear again, at least officially, from the northern elites or the ten northern tribes which represented the area subject to the Assyrian conquest.

The area subsequently known as Galilee was part of the homeland of this northern kingdom.

The southern kingdom was attacked by Babylonia and defeated in 586 BCE, with a similar result: much or most of the population was deported. But the southern kingdom got a lucky break. In 538 BCE, after Babylonia was conquered by Persia, the exiles from Judea were allowed to return to their homeland by Cyrus. It is these returning southern exiles who went on to write much of the history of ancient Israel.

So, what happened to the exiles from the first conquest of the northern kingdom by the Assyrians in 722 BCE? No one knows. The ten tribes that constituted the northern kingdom became known as the "lost tribes of Israel," and various theories have been proposed in modern times as to what actually happened to them.

The northern kingdom was likely the more important of the two before its fall (Finkelstein and Silberman, *The Bible Unearthed*). Indeed, the northern kingdom was more important even than the "united monarchy" of David and Solomon, who emerge from the evidence more as local tribal chieftains than as founders of a mighty dynasty. In contrast to the northern kingdom, there are few mentions of David and Solomon outside of the Hebrew scriptures, nor is there much archeological evidence for them or for Solomon's temple.

The bias of the Jewish scriptures, according to Finkelstein and Silberman, was simply due to the fact that it was the exiles from the fall of the *southern* kingdom that eventually wrote the history of this period. The northern kingdom had no one to write their history from their point of view. Naturally, the history that was written by those who returned from the Babylonian conquest emphasizes the importance of the southern kingdom and the temple.

How would residents of Galilee have viewed these developments? What happened to the "lost tribes of Israel," as the tribes of the northern kingdom are sometimes referred to? Wouldn't it be natural, after the fall of the northern kingdom, that many former residents—minus their elites—remained in the area, retaining some memory of primitive Judaism? Wouldn't it be natural for the inhabitants of the former northern kingdom, those who still had some memory of the pre-exile Jewish religion in the north, to regard the temple cult in the south, and the entire Jerusalem establishment, with suspicion? Might not the later residents of Galilee have been able to quote Isaiah, Jeremiah, Amos, and Hosea, all of whom had deprecating comments about the temple and the political establishment there, in support?

The Rechabites

Hans-Joachim Schoeps traces some Ebionite ideas back to the Rechabites, described in Jeremiah 35 (*Jewish Christianity*, p. 118–121). On analysis, though, it seems that only two particular Ebionite ideas are invoked: abstinence from alcohol, and the implication of a rejection of a central place of worship and therefore rejection of the temple.

Before the fall of the southern kingdom, the Rechabites are invited by Jeremiah to drink wine (Jeremiah 35). But they refuse, citing the instructions of their long-ago patriarch, Jonadab son of Rechab, who instructed his family never to drink wine or to live a sedentary lifestyle at all, but to be nomadic and live in tents. It's possible that their nomadism and their rejection of wine are connected in a straightforward economic way; nomads can't maintain vineyards.

If we go back earlier, we find in II Kings 10:15–28 a story about Jehonadab son of Rechab, presumably the same person. Evidently not a pacifist, he helps King Jehu (of the "northern kingdom") slaughter some of the followers of Ahab in Samaria. II Kings says nothing about Rechabite beliefs, but does identify Jonadab (or Jehonadab) son of Rechab as someone from the northern Israelite kingdom in the 9th century BCE. That the Rechabites are appearing before Jeremiah, in the *southern* kingdom of Judea some centuries later, shows that at least some Israelites from the northern kingdom survived the fall of the northern kingdom and continued to practice their religion.

Since the Rechabites were nomadic, they were likely suspicious of, or hostile to, any fixed place of worship. The prophets who denigrated the temple cult sometimes saw the wilderness as a holy or special place (e. g. Isaiah 40:3 and 43:19, Jeremiah 31:2, and Hosea 2:14). John the Baptist was "a voice crying in the wilderness" (quoting Isaiah 40:3) and Stephen in Acts 7:44 speaks favorably of the "tent of witness in the wilderness" in the same speech in which he compares temple worship with idolatry.

Nearly a millennium later, Hegesippus gives evidence of Rechabite sympathy with the Ebionites. When James, the brother of Jesus, was stoned in the temple at the instigation of the temple elite in the year 62 (see chapter 18), some of the priests of the Rechabites are there to protest, pointing out that James is actually praying for them: "Cease, what do ye? The just one [James] prayeth for you" (*Ecclesiastical History* 2.23.17). The Rechabites are depicted as sympathetic allies in this incident, suggesting that the Rechabites were critical of the temple, its priests, and its operations.

This supports some, but certainly not all, Ebionite beliefs. Nomads would have typically been livestock herders and definitely not vegetarian, and if the example of Jonadab is typical, not pacifists either. This form of hostility to the temple cult was not based on respect for animals, but antagonism to the idea of worshiping God in a fixed place generally. However, it certainly indicates that some ideas of the northern prophets still survived in the south after the fall of the northern kingdom—and thus, could have survived the second exile as well.

The Location of the Jewish Christians near Galilee

Not only is Jesus tied to Galilee in the New Testament, but the later Ebionites also appear in the same general area (see chapter 19, "The Origin and Geography of the Ebionites"). In the New Testament, Peter's Galilean accent is obvious enough so that he is accused of being a follower of Jesus after Jesus' trial: "certainly you are also one of them, for your accent betrays you" (Matthew 26:73).

What might we conclude about Jewish Christianity based on its Galilean origins? Galilee is the last place you would associate with hyper-orthodox legalism, or where you would expect to find a Galilean preacher or his disciples advocating strict temple observance. The Talmud cites a saying of Johanan ben Zakkai, a notable sage who lived in Galilee at about the same time as Jesus: "O Galilee, Galilee, you have hated the Torah. You will end up working for tax farmers" (P. Shabbat 16.8).

The Talmud makes fun of Galilee, picturing it as an ignorant rural area, an area which knows little about the temple offerings (B. Nedarim 18b). It also ridicules their distinctive accent, connecting their sloppy way of talking with their sloppy way of thinking (B. Erubin 53a, 53b). Geza Vermes concludes that according to the Talmud, with respect to Torah observance and temple offerings, "Galileans were presumed to be ignoramuses" (Vermes, 2003, p. 228).

The character of Galilee renders implausible a number of New Testament details designed to show how Torah-observant Jesus and his family were. How plausible is it that *any* Galilean Jewish sage (whether Jesus or anyone else) would command a penitent leper to make an animal sacrifice several days' journey away (Mark 1:44)? How likely is it that Jesus' family, or *any* Galilean family, would offer animal sacrifices at the time of his birth in the temple (Luke 2:24)? It is possible, in fact, that Galilee, or some in Galilee, were not just "ignorant" of animal sacrifices, but actually *hostile* to them. The Galilean followers of Jesus who objected to animal sacrifice may have been typical of Galilee rather than the exception. Johanan ben Zakkai's comment that Galilee hated the Torah, mentioned above, implies just this sort of thing.

When Galilean teachers of the time are honored, it is for their piety, not for their knowledge. Hanina ben Dosa was known for his saintliness but not for his teachings ("Hanina b. Dosa," in *The Jewish Encyclopedia*). One of his few known sayings emphasizes the unimportance of learning: "Whosoever's fear of sin precedes his learning, his learning will endure; but where learning precedes fear of sin, learning will not endure." This, in fact, seems to be the flip side of the Talmudic comment on the inexactness of the Galilean's learning: fear of sin is more basic than learning.

Nearly a century before Jesus, another famous Galilean, Honi the Circle Drawer, also emphasized piety over learning. He is called the "circle drawer" because on one occasion, praying to God, he drew a circle and declared that he would not step out of it until God sent rain—an almost child-like, pouting approach to the divine power. Josephus relates that Honi became a martyr because of his prayers. Urged to pray for one side during a civil war, he refused to do so, instead offering a prayer urging God to listen to neither side, after which he was stoned to death (*Antiquities of the Jews* 14.2.1). In these stories we see Honi's piety and righteousness, but not his scholarship or knowledge.

Judaism was very diverse in the centuries leading up to Jesus. The period leading up to and including the time of Jesus incorporated personalities and sects such as the ultra-conservative Qumran group, the priests and Sadducees, the iconoclastic John the Baptist, the solitary Essenes, Pharisees such as Hillel and Shammai, and Galileans such as Honi the Circle Drawer. All of these are *Jewish*, but all of these saw Jewish identity in very different ways. They saw the temple (Sadducees), the nation (Zealots), or righteous behavior (Honi, Hanina ben Dosa) as the most critical aspect of their religion. This idea that it is the *law* which is the essence of the religion really only gets the upper hand after the destruction of the nation and the temple in the revolts against Rome, and the rise of the Pharisees.

Conclusions

Opposition to animal sacrifice, ethical concern for animals, and a universal religion were strongly enough supported in ancient Judaism so that they became an established part of the scriptures.

Hostility to the scripture, sacrifices, and the temple all predates Jesus by nearly a millennium. Galilee was an area that was historically less connected with the oral and written traditions or the temple than were other major sects of Judaism at the time (either the Pharisees or the Sadducees, for example). The Jewish Christian hostility to the temple did *not* suddenly break into the world with the coming of Jesus or the Ebionites. This hostility is almost as old as the animal sacrifice business itself. Jewish Christianity simply expressed these ancient grievances.

5. Ebionite Mythology

How did the Ebionites themselves see their own movement before Jesus?

The *Recognitions* and *Homilies* don't add that much to our knowledge of ancient history. But they do add to our knowledge of the Ebionite *view* of ancient history. This is mostly mythological material going back to Adam and Noah, in which the Ebionites have rewritten the accounts in Genesis, but stop (for the most part) when they get beyond David and Solomon.

A key problem is the Ebionite attitude towards the prophets. Epiphanius says that the Ebionites "blasphemed" the prophets, and Irenaeus implies that the Ebionite view of the prophets was "somewhat singular." What's going on here? We might expect the Ebionites to quote the prophetic writings in *support* of their position; but we have to consider the possibility that they held significant *negative* views about the prophets.

The Ebionites, like other followers of Jesus, did not think of their own group as having a beginning as a sect; they thought of themselves as identical to the early church and continuous with Jesus. What really separates the Ebionites from other Christian groups is that they also see their own group as continuous with *Judaism*. While there is very little of what we would call "historical material" concerning their group before Jesus, the Jewish Christians are *unique* in thinking that they were a sect still within Judaism.

History of the World in the *Recognitions*
The Ebionites' own account of their origins, found in the *Recognitions* and *Homilies*, is mostly mythological: it deals with such subjects as Adam and Eve, Abraham, and Moses. At least Abraham and Moses were (possibly!) historical figures, but the Ebionite understanding of

them is mostly drawn from the Old Testament, with a few historical twists.

Both *Recognitions* 1 and *Homilies* 8 give accounts of the origins of Judaism, from their own point of view. *Recognitions* 1.27–38 takes us from the creation of the world to the time when Israel went from judges to kings (starting with Saul). This was when things started going downhill, from the Ebionite point of view.

God's message was that he did not want sacrifices, and in order to convey this to the people, the temple "was often plundered by enemies and burnt with fire, and the people carried into captivity among foreign nations, and then brought back when they betook themselves to the mercy of God" (*Recognitions* 1.37). But the people did not learn this.

After the time of the judges the people "sought for themselves tyrants rather than kings" (which seems to refer to the monarchy of Saul, David, and Solomon), and then erected "a temple in the place appointed to them for prayer" (*Recognitions* 1.38). This seems to refer to the first temple (Solomon's temple). The narrative moves instantly across nearly a millennium to the time of John the Baptist—though interestingly, John is not mentioned—so that "when the time began to draw near" for the true prophet (Jesus), the institution of baptism by water was instituted by God, so that "they might be absolved from all their sins . . . being purified not by the blood of beasts, but by the purification of the Wisdom of God" (*Recognitions* 1.39).

The *Recognitions* bends over backward to exonerate Moses from complicity in the institution of animal sacrifice, even though conceding that Moses did make some commands about animal sacrifice. (This is significantly different from the history presented in the *Homilies* as we will see shortly.) Baptism was specifically instituted to replace animal sacrifice, thus, it occupies the same ritual role that animal sacrifice did.

Recognitions 8.59 implies that the message is universal—the true prophet can speak to anyone with an open heart.

> For He [the true prophet] is within the mind of every
> one of us, but in those who have no desire of the
> knowledge of God and His righteousness, He is

inoperative . . . but He is soon found by those who diligently seek Him through love of the truth, and whose souls are not taken possession of by wickedness.

History of the World in the *Homilies*

The *Homilies* tell much the same story, but with one significant addition: the theory of false texts inserted into the scriptures.

According to the *Homilies*, their community originated with, well, God himself, who gave the law at the creation (*Homilies* 8.10). Humans turned away from God because they had no experience of evil and therefore no sense of gratitude towards their creator. Angels volunteered to help out, and this works well at first. But some of the angels started cohabiting with women, from which came the giants, whose desires were much greater than the earth could fulfill, so that they start eating meat (8.15), and there is even cannibalism (8.16). In response, God finally sends a flood and decides to, in effect, start over. After the flood, God gives a law that allows giants (who seem to have undergone a metamorphosis into demons) to bother only those who practice some abomination such as eating meat, shedding blood, or sharing the same table with demons.

Homilies 8 gives us no further details, but *Homilies* 2 and 3 discuss further the Ebionite history of Judaism. Christ, the true prophet, has appeared countless times throughout history, starting with Adam—who after all was made by the very hands of God, so could not lack having the spirit of the Christ. Christ "has changed his forms and his names from the beginning of the world, and so reappeared again and again in the world" (3.20), a universalist type of message which appears to encompass many different forms of religion. Moses delivered the law, but no sooner had it been written down, than it was tampered with.

> For the Scriptures have had joined to them many falsehoods against God on this account. The prophet Moses having by the order of God delivered the law . . . after a little the written law had added to it certain falsehoods contrary to the law of God. (*Homilies* 2.38)

This is the source of the Ebionite theory of false texts: not everything in the scripture is true, the scribes have falsified it, just as Jeremiah protested: "How can you say, 'We are wise, we have the law of the Lord,' when the scribes with their lying pens have falsified it?" (8:8, NEB). Later, the *Homilies* modifies even this minor concession to the written law, saying that "the law of God was given by Moses, *without writing,* to seventy wise men . . . it was written by some one, but not by Moses" (*Homilies* 3.47, emphasis added).

Homilies 3.47 gives an approximate time of 1000 years between Moses and time of Nebuchadnezzar. It also points out an obvious problem with describing the law as the "books of Moses": Deuteronomy 34:5-6 describes the death of Moses. How could Moses write that Moses died?

It appears that there was quite a bit of discussion of the historical basis of the Jewish scriptures among the Ebionites. Most scholars today don't think that Moses wrote down the law, at least not in anything resembling the Pentateuch we have today. The Ebionites were far ahead of their time by asking these kinds of historical questions.

The Ebionite attention to this issue indicates that there was awareness of this problem *in ancient times*, and annoyance with the results. Peter complains that Simon Magus, whom the *Homilies* present as the great antagonist of Peter and the Christians, is going to cite these false texts in his arguments. "We do not wish to say in public that these chapters are added to the Bible," says Peter, "since we should thereby perplex the unlearned multitudes, and so accomplish the purpose of this wicked Simon" (*Homilies* 2.39). Peter then uses this as a path towards blanket condemnation (in private) of "difficult" passages in the scripture; how can we believe that God lies, changes his mind, hardens hearts, is unjust, desires sacrifices, and makes war (*Homilies* 2.43–44)?

Later, in debating Simon in public, Peter argues that—even after accepting these "false chapters" in the scriptures—God condemns animal sacrifices (among many other things). Peter cites the incident of the quail in the desert, a story also often cited by modern religious vegetarians. After the exodus, when the children of Israel were wandering in the desert, they complained about their steady diet of manna, saying, "Oh that we had meat to eat!" (Numbers 11:4). God does send them quail to eat, but many of them die of a great plague as a consequence—perhaps an ancient case of food poisoning. Therefore, Peter concludes, "He then who at the first was displeased with the slaughtering of animals, *not wishing them to be slain*, did not ordain sacrifices as desiring them" (*Homilies* 3.45, emphasis added).

The Ebionite Jesus and the Law

The Ebionite Jesus, in the *Homilies*, was by no means uncritical of the written law; *Homilies* 3.50 and 3.51 go through an inventory of sayings of Jesus implying a historical criticism of the scriptures (two of these sayings are duplicated at *Homilies* 2.51):

1. Jesus says to the Sadducees, in a dispute over the resurrection: "You are wrong, because you know neither the *true things of the* scriptures nor the power of God" (emphasis added). This is a version of Matthew 22:29 (which in the canonical version omits the qualification "true things"), which the *Homilies* argue shows that Jesus distinguished between true and false things. (This verse is also cited, with the same revision, at *Homilies* 2.51).
2. Jesus said, "Be experienced money-changers" (*Homilies* 2.51, 3.50, 18.20), that is, able to tell the spurious coins from the genuine, which implies that discrimination should be applied to the scriptures. This verse does not appear in the Bible, but is cited by other ancient writers such as Clement of Alexandria (*Stromata* 1.28).
3. Jesus said, "Think not that I have come to destroy the law" and "till heaven and earth pass away, not an iota or a dot will pass from the law," (Matthew 5:17–20) which implies that those things which *have* passed away or which Jesus seemed to be destroying (e. g. the animal sacrifices) in fact did not belong to the law (*Homilies* 3.51 and 3.52).

The Ebionites implied that Jesus shared their view of the corruption of the scripture by appealing to some of his well-known sayings. The prophets were by no means uniform in support of this anti-cultic ideology, but it is definitely present in Hosea, Isaiah, and Jeremiah, and to a lesser extent Amos and Ezekiel. The Ebionite Jesus is continuing a tradition which in their view was already declared by these prophets.

Ebionite Concept of Prophecy

According to Epiphanius, the Ebionites acknowledged Abraham, Isaac, Jacob, and Moses, but "made fun" of David and Solomon, and disregarded Isaiah, Jeremiah, Daniel, Ezekiel, Elijah, and Elisha, and "blasphemed" their prophecies (*Panarion* 30.18.4). Shouldn't the Ebionites be quoting Isaiah to back up their point of view on (say) animal sacrifice, instead of blaspheming him? Irenaeus, in the second century, had said that the Ebionites "endeavor to expound [the prophetical writings] in a somewhat singular manner" (*Against Heresies* 1.26.2).

Did the Ebionites really blaspheme the prophets? Untangling the Ebionite view of prophecy is a tricky business. When we look closer at the *Recognitions* and *Homilies*, we can see that Epiphanius' view of the Ebionites has to be substantially modified.

There are several places where the *Recognitions* and *Homilies* do quote or refer to the prophets, although they are not frequent (see Table 5–1). These citations seem to show that the Ebionites did cite the prophets with approval when they supported their point of view. *Recognitions* 1.37 and *Homilies* 3.56 both cite "I require mercy, not sacrifice"; and *Recognitions* 1.64 refers to Daniel's prophecy about the "abomination of desolation."

On the other hand, they also sometimes expressed unease about prophecy. Even the ungodly can receive prophecies (*Homilies* 17.17), and the ungodly also sometimes *quote* prophecy (*Homilies* 16.6). At *Homilies* 16.14, Peter specifically argues that the one called "Emmanuel" (Isaiah 7:14) is not "the Mighty God" (Isaiah 9:6) in a literal sense, as angels and other beings less than the supreme God are sometimes referred to as gods in the scriptures.

Since a pet project of the orthodox is using just these prophecies in Isaiah to promote the idea of the divinity of Jesus, it would be easy for us to imagine Epiphanius becoming indignant over this interpretation and describing it as "blasphemous." The Ebionites preferred to understand Deuteronomy 18:15–18, rather than anything in Isaiah, as a prophecy about Jesus. What Epiphanius considers to be "blasphemous" reflects his own sectarian interpretations rather than representing a denigration of the prophets by the Ebionites. Epiphanius and orthodox thinkers generally wanted to use the prophets to justify their own views about Jesus; the Ebionites used the prophets to justify their views on animal sacrifice.

The term "prophet" has a technical meaning as well as an honorific meaning, even when it is not qualified with the adjective "false." It means a kind of religious guru. These prophets are sometimes wrong (Hosea 4:5, Jeremiah 14:14). Amos specifically disavows the term: "I am no prophet, nor a prophet's son" (Amos 7:14). And then there are prophets such as Haggai, Zechariah, and Malachi who specifically promote the idea of the temple, whom the Ebionites very well might have regarded as false prophets (although there are no Ebionite references to them).

"Blaspheming the prophets" may not necessarily mean that the Ebionites rejected all the prophetic literature. Rather, they used the prophets selectively and interpreted them in a way appropriate to the context. There is a further mention of prophecy in the discussion of "female prophecies," which appears to be a neo-Pythagorean categorization. In terms of what the Ebionites actually thought about the prophets, it doesn't add much, so we'll discuss this in the next chapter on Pythagoras.

Conclusions

The Jewish Christians thought of themselves as the original Jews, going back to the time of Moses to find objections to animal sacrifice. Moreover, this concept had a sound basis: there *were* Jews in ancient times who objected to the practice of animal sacrifice and looked askance at the development of a written tradition which institutionalized the very tendencies they opposed.

We cannot prove that there was a continuous movement objecting to animal sacrifice from Hosea down to the Ebionites. The Rechabites, who evidently still existed at the time of Jesus and James, would be the closest thing to such a movement (see chapter 4). What we can say, though, is that it is likely that hostility to both the scripture and the temple sacrifices predates Jesus by centuries. The Ebionites cite the prophets and the law carefully, with quite a bit of attention to detail (more attention, perhaps, than many modern scholars). We suspect that the Ebionite view of history, regardless of when it reached written form, was something that already existed in rough form well before Jesus.

Ebionite reference	Scriptural reference	Explanation
Hom. 3.56	Hosea 6:6	"I require mercy, not sacrifice" (also Matthew 9:13, 12:7)
Hom. 3.56	Isaiah 66:1	"Heaven is my throne, and earth my footstool" (also Matthew 5:34–35)
Hom. 16.6	Jeremiah 10:11	Simon quotes Jeremiah to imply polytheism
Hom. 16.7	Isaiah 44:6, 45:21, 49:18 (combined and quoted freely)	Affirming monotheism
Hom. 16.14	Isaiah 9:6	The phrase "the mighty God" does not imply that the predicted prophet will be the same as God
Hom. 17.17	Dan. 2:26–45, Dan. 3:25	Nebuchadnezzar's dream and vision: the impious can receive prophecies
Hom. 18.18	Isaiah 1:3	People were ignorant of the just character of the known God—not the character of an unknown God.
Rec. 1.37	Hosea 6:6	"I require mercy, not sacrifice" (also Matthew 9:13, 12:7)
Rec. 1.64	Daniel 9:27, 11:31, 12:11	The "abomination of desolation"; the temple to be destroyed (see also Matthew 24:15)
Rec. 5.12	Isaiah 45:4–6	Call of the gentiles, who did not know God
Rec. 8.48	Ezekiel 2:6	Allusion to "living with serpents (scorpions)," analogous to living with the wicked
Rec. 10.49	Ezekiel 18:32	Conversion of a sinner preferable to the sinner's death.

Table 5–1. References to the prophets in the *Recognitions* and *Homilies*

6. The Pythagoreans

It was not just the ancient prophets such as Hosea and Amos who inspired Jewish Christianity, but also Greek philosophy and religion, specifically that of Pythagoras and Plato.

Jewish Christianity resembled the Pythagorean movement in several distinctive ways. Besides vegetarianism and rejection of animal sacrifice, both movements opposed divorce, making oaths, war, wine, and sometimes the wearing of wool; both movements practiced, or at least honored, the communal ideal of sharing equally their possessions. Table 6–1 summarizes the comparisons between the Pythagoreans, the Jewish Christians, and New Testament references.

But tracing the exact connection is difficult. Did the Ebionites or their predecessors actually come into contact with Pythagorean groups or explicitly adopt their program? And when did this influence come to bear? Some of these Pythagorean influences turn up in the New Testament, which suggests that the "transmission" of Pythagorean thought occurred fairly early on.

The Pythagorean Movement
Who were the Pythagoreans? At the outset we have a problem. Pythagoras was a historical figure who lived in the 6th century BCE; but the movement which followed him lasted for hundreds of years and changed substantially over time in some respects. If the Pythagoreans impacted Jewish Christianity, they may have done so many centuries after Pythagoras was gone.

Our single most convenient ancient source for the life of Pythagoras and his followers is Iamblichus' *On the Pythagorean Way of Life*. Iamblichus died probably sometime around 320 CE, so this book was written about 800 years after Pythagoras and 300 years after Jesus. He is using a lot of much older material, and at least some of the features we are interested in clearly go back at least to the first century BCE, so his book fairly accurately reflects the state of neo-Pythagoreanism at about the time of Jesus. We'd need a more detailed scholarly analysis to prove which particular features of Pythagoreanism in Table 6–1 could be dated prior to Jesus, but there is likely to be a relationship of influence somewhere.

Pythagoras of Samos began his own mission at about the same time that the exiles were returning from Babylonia (538 BCE). He eventually found disciples for a program which in several ways anticipates that of the Ebionites: monotheistic, vegetarian, and objecting to animal sacrifices. According to Iamblichus, the Pythagoreans formed their own community, the closest disciples of which shared all their possessions in common and were strict vegetarians.

Pythagoras also had a wide range of political, mathematical, religious, musical, and scientific ideas. He is said to have coined the word "philosophy," and is also credited with (but probably was not the first to discover) the so-called "Pythagorean theorem" of geometry. A believer in reincarnation, he once famously claimed to have heard the voice of a friend in a dog's barking.

Pythagoras objected to animal sacrifice, so he would only sacrifice to gods that allowed plant sacrifices (such as Apollo). All the gods were ultimately absolutely subject to the highest God. These religious views put the Pythagoreans in significant tension with the existing pagan order; they undercut piety towards the gods.

The Pythagoreans held women to be equal to men. One of the most famous Pythagorean martyrs was a woman, Hypatia of Alexandria, who made substantial developments in mathematics, and was murdered by a Christian mob in an act of religious violence in 415 CE. The Pythagoreans also objected to divorce, forbidding men to divorce their wives, which in ancient times in Greek, Roman, and Jewish law could be done at the whim of the man. Further, the Pythagoreans refused to make oaths, something echoed in the New Testament.

In the very beginning the Pythagorean movement was highly political. The Pythagorean community came to power in Croton in Italy, where Pythagoras had migrated after travels to Egypt and elsewhere. Under his leadership, Croton grew powerful, defeating its rival Sybaris. But some in the upper class became resentful, and eventually Pythagoras and his followers were driven from power.

Pythagoras had a tremendous influence in the intellectual climate of ancient Greece, most conspicuously manifested in Socrates and Plato. Philosophers debate the exact relationship between Pythagoras, Socrates, and Plato, but it is clear that in many significant respects Plato is simply a good student of Pythagoras. The "ideal state" in Plato's *Republic* looks a lot like what Pythagoras was trying to do in Croton, and "myth of Er" in Book 10 of the *Republic* replicates Pythagoras' views on reincarnation and divine justice.

In the beginning, there were Pythagorean groups, but around the time of Plato, parts of Pythagoreanism were absorbed into Plato's Academy, while other elements were taken up by the Cynics. (John Dominic Crossan, whom we will discuss below, argued that Jesus might have been a peasant Jewish Cynic.)

Later Pythagoreans dropped the political aspect of Pythagoreanism altogether. We can see this transition in Plato, who was so deeply influenced by Pythagoras and was already wrestling with this issue. Plato takes a pessimistic view of the ideal state in the *Republic*. He concludes that even if such a state could be realized, it would inevitably decline. This may reflect his own failed experiments in politics as detailed in *Letter VII*, and probably also reflects the failures of Pythagoras to influence politics with his high ideals.

Around the first century BCE, there was a neo-Pythagorean revival. By this time, followers of Pythagoras had dropped their political goals. Neo-Pythagorean philosophies emerged and some intellectual circles throughout the Greek and Roman world starting discussing Pythagoras and his ideas. However, it is not clear to scholars, or anyone else, what "neo-Pythagoreanism" or the "revival" means here. Were there actual neo-Pythagorean communities who shared their possessions and tried to organize their lives around Pythagorean principles? Indeed, were the early Christians just such a group?

In the late 19th and early 20th century writers such as Eduard Zeller and Isidore Lévy suggested that there was an influence of Pythagoreanism on Jewish thought and especially on the Essenes. The Essenes are a complicated case which we'll consider in the next chapter. Without getting too far ahead of our story, we can say that there is a good case for such influence.

References to Pythagoras and Plato in Early Christian Literature

The *Recognitions* and *Homilies* both quote Plato in their support. Niceta, Clement's brother, quotes Plato in support of monotheism (*Recognitions* 8.20, citing Plato, *Timaeus* 28c). *Homilies* 8.10 also alludes to this intuitive understanding of God in speaking of the law of God which "can be read by all."

At *Homilies* 15.8 Clement's (and Niceta's) father quotes Plato's *Republic* 617e as saying that God is blameless for the choices the soul makes in choosing its destiny. This is a reference to the "myth of Er" which Plato relates in Book 10, outlining Plato's ideas on reincarnation. *Recognitions* 8.15 briefly refers to the Pythagoreans as saying that numbers are the elements of the beginnings of the world. So Jewish Christianity was aware of both Pythagoras and Plato and felt that they contributed support to their overall point of view.

The Ebionite idea of the "eternal Christ" (*Recognitions* 1.43) who was in Adam, appeared to the patriarchs, manifested in Jesus, and is present in all believers, is an echo of the mystical Platonic ideas of the ideal manifest in the material world.

Other early Christian writers also spoke favorably of Pythagoras and Plato because of their monotheism. Arnobius refers to "divine Plato" (*Against the Heathen* 2.36), and Origen (*Contra Celsus* 1.15) and Hippolytus (*Refutation of All Heresies* 9.22) even suggest that Pythagoras picked up monotheism from the Jews. Plato refers to God as "Father," just as Jesus does in the New Testament.

Sometimes, the church fathers see Pythagoras and Plato associated with heretical Christian doctrines. Hippolytus accuses Valentinus, for example, of getting his ideas from Pythagoras and Plato, rather than from the gospels (*Refutation of All Heresies* 6.24). Hippolytus makes a similar accusation against Monoimus, a second century Arab gnostic (8.8).

Hippolytus also says that the Elkasaites (either a Jewish Christian group or closely related to Jewish Christianity, whom we will discuss much later) had views similar to those of Pythagoras. Hippolytus is evidently speaking of the idea of transmigration of souls, which he had outlined previously in reference to Pythagoras (*Refutation of All Heresies* 1.2), and which he describes in connection with Elxai: Christ had been reincarnated many times. This idea of Christ being reincarnated is very similar to the Ebionite idea that the true prophet appeared throughout history. It is not clear whether this is a general theory of reincarnation or whether it is, so to speak, only the most holy people (e. g. Jesus) who are miraculously reincarnated. However, the *Recognitions*, *Homilies*, and other Christian literature indicate both awareness of and support for many of the key ideas of Pythagoras and Plato.

Pythagorean Lifestyle and Ebionite Ideals

Ebionite ideals include a number of "Pythagorean" practices, most obviously vegetarianism, rejection of animal sacrifice, and rejection of wine. But there are some other items also deserving attention here.

1. *James, the brother of Jesus.* Eusebius' description of James, the brother of Jesus, shows several such similarities (*Ecclesiastical History* 2.23.5–6). In addition to not eating meat or drinking wine, James also does not wear wool—something shared with the Pythagoreans, but nowhere else attributed to Jewish Christianity.

James also does not use the public baths or cut his hair. These may also be Pythagorean influences. Iamblichus reports as one of the oral sayings of Pythagoras that one should avoid the baths (*On the Pythagorean Way of Life* 83). James also does not cut his hair, and Pythagoras did not cut his hair during festivals (154) and was referred to as the "long-haired Samian" (11). James did not just have the ideas, but the "look" of a Pythagorean.

2. *Nonviolence.* Plato and the later neo-Pythagoreans express nonviolent sentiments. So does early Christianity, as reflected in well-known gospel sayings such as "love your enemies" and "do not go into battle against one who is evil."

But the Pythagorean interest in nonviolence evolved in a different direction than that of Christianity. Christianity began as a pacifist sect and evolved into a church endorsing "just war." With the Pythagoreans, the evolution seems to have been in the opposite direction. The *historical* Pythagoras, at least during some of his career, appears to endorse military force. In fact, there was a military victory of Croton over one of its rivals under Pythagoras' leadership (Kahn, p. 6–7).

However, when Pythagoras' involvement in politics ended badly some years later, Pythagorean ideas began to evolve. By the time of Plato (fourth century BCE), nonviolence has been turned into a principle. In Plato's *Crito* 49c, Socrates makes statements which anticipate the Sermon on the Mount: "one ought not to return a wrong or an injury to any person, whatever the provocation is."

Did Plato intend this to mean pacifism? Plato is not entirely consistent himself here. Socrates as a young man served in the military. *Laws* 955b–c seems to give sanction to war. Nevertheless, a case for Platonic and Pythagorean pacifism can clearly be made. It appears that Plato's ideas evolved, and they seem to have evolved in the direction of pacifism, pushed along not only by what happened to Pythagoras, but reflecting Plato's own experience in Syracuse.

3. *Communalism.* Both the Pythagoreans and the Ebionites admired the ideal of communalism. Plato refers several times to the saying "friends have everything in common," evidently a Pythagorean maxim (*Phaedrus* 279c, *Republic* 449c, *Lysis* 207c). Iamblichus also quotes this saying, and portrays the Pythagorean community as one that shares all its possessions (see Table 6–1). The Ebionites derived their name (*ebionim* = "the poor" in Hebrew) from the time when the early Christians were sharing all their possessions (Acts 4:32–35), and as they gave everything to the apostles, they were known as "the poor".

There is one possible significant difference in Christian and Pythagorean communalism. Pythagorean communalism, at least at the time of Pythagoras, was a communalism of the philosophical elite. The general impression that Acts leaves is that the Christians were less "particular" about their membership than the original Pythagoreans.

4. *Divorce.* The Pythagorean connection to the Jesus of the gospels on the question of divorce seems stronger than the Pythagorean connection to the Ebionites. The Pythagoreans forbade divorce, and the New Testament takes an unusually strong position (Matthew 19:9, Mark 10:11–12, Luke 16:18).

The Ebionite position on divorce, though, is harder to discern. According to Epiphanius, the Ebionites allowed divorce up to seven times (*Panarion* 30.18.3). However, the *Homilies* cite with evident approval Jesus' words on divorce:

> [Jesus], knowing the true things of the law, said to the Sadducees, asking on what account Moses permitted to marry seven, "Moses gave you commandments according to your hard-heartedness; for from the beginning it was not so: for He who created man at first, made him male and female." (*Homilies* 3.54).

Jesus' saying in the *Homilies* doesn't exactly match *any* of the synoptic gospel accounts of Jesus talking about divorce, though it seems to parallel Matthew most closely. First, there is no concluding statement about divorce in the *Homilies*. The synoptic gospels all have different concluding statements: Matthew allows divorce for unchastity, Mark prohibits all divorce for men, Luke prohibits divorce for both men and women. But in the *Homilies*, there is no conclusion about divorce at all, just the assertion that "from the beginning it was not so."

Second, in the gospels Jesus' statement follows an incident in which the Pharisees ask Jesus directly about divorce. But in the *Homilies* it follows a different incident in which the Sadducees asked Jesus about remarriage and resurrection, concerning a man who marries seven wives consecutively (Matthew 22:23–33 and parallels).

Epiphanius' statement that the Ebionites allowed divorce up to seven times may indicate that he, like the writer of the *Homilies*, has two stories confused—one story in which Jesus talks to the Pharisees about divorce, and another story in which Jesus talks to the Sadducees about remarriage and resurrection. Epiphanius may have further confused the Ebionite position with that of the Sadducees in the second story. Perhaps both Epiphanius and the *Homilies* were using an original confused source, leading to both of them being confused in somewhat the same way (and us as well). Given the rest of the evidence about the Ebionites and the strong gospel opposition to divorce, it seems likely the Ebionites were concerned about divorce and wanted to restrict it in some way, but how is not clear.

Overall, the ethical teachings of Pythagoras seems to have had a striking influence on Jewish Christianity at a rather early stage. All of these teachings go back at least as far as the first century.

The Ebionite Doctrine of Opposites

Pythagorean philosophy also evidently left an imprint on the Ebionites in the form of the Ebionite doctrine of opposites.

The Ebionite doctrine of opposites is an attempt to understand the problem of evil and conflict in the world. Peter announces that God has "distinguished all principles into pairs and opposites" (*Homilies* 2.15). He then sets out these pairs as heaven and earth, sun and moon, day and night, and so forth (2.15, 2.33). In the *Recognitions*, Peter asserts the same idea, but the pairs of opposites listed are quite different; they turn out to be historical or mythical figures and groups, such as Pharaoh and Abraham, Philistines and Isaac, Antichrist and Christ (*Recognitions* 3.61).

This is remarkably similar to the much older Pythagorean doctrine of opposites (see Table 6–2). The Pythagoreans thought of the "One" in the same way as Christian theology thought of God. This supreme One produced all being, including pairs of opposites. The "One" generates a Monad and a Dyad. This dualism of the Monad and Dyad then created opposites—good things under the Monad, and bad things under the Dyad (Kahn, p. 97). These pairs included such items as light and dark, odd and even, straight and curved.

What is distinctive about both the Pythagorean and Ebionite doctrine of opposites is not that there is a dualism of good and evil—this is something found in countless religions and philosophies. Rather, it lies in the idea that *this dualism is part of the divine plan*.

This is very different from the *primordial* dualism of the Manichaeans, in which two co-equal forces of good and evil exist as original principles from the beginning. It is also different from the opposition of good and evil in conventional Christian theology, in which rebellious spirits reject the divine order. The Ebionite and Pythagorean doctrine of opposites is a dualism deliberately set up and controlled by God.

While the basic schema is the same, the actual pairs of opposites are rather different (Table 6–2). In fact, there is more than one

Pythagorean set of opposites, and more than one Ebionite set as well. But we are left with a lot of questions which cannot be quickly answered. Does this doctrine of opposites mean that God is the source of evil? Or does it mean that evil is an illusion? And some of the pairs provoke further questions. In the pair "odd and even," what is so good about "odd" and what is so bad about "even"? And what is the explanation of the "male" and "female" dichotomy, in which "male" is good and "female" is bad? This sounds like patriarchal nonsense.

The "Female Prophecies"
One of these Pythagorean pairs, the "male and female," sheds some further light on the Ebionite view of prophecy. The Ebionite doctrine of opposites led some Ebionites into one of the more obscure points of Ebionite theology. The *Homilies* (but not the *Recognitions*) have a dichotomization of prophecy into "male" and "female" prophecies. This categorization is hopelessly patriarchal; the female prophecies are the inferior, defective, or actually evil prophecies (2.15, 3.22–27).

It is not clear what is "male" and "female" about the male and female prophecies, but it does not appear to have anything to do with the actual gender of the person making the prophecy. The female prophecies (not the female prophets) are those linked to sacrifices, bloodshed, libations, altars, and wars. The male prophecies, associated with Adam (the father of Cain and Abel), hate all of this and are associated with justice, marriage, temperance, and so on.

Elsewhere, the *Recognitions* and *Homilies* take a more gender-neutral stance. Every person is a bride when they receive the true prophet's whole word of truth and is enlightened (*Homilies* 3.27). The female part of love is compassion, which is essential to salvation (*Homilies* 12.32). Males and females differ only in their reproductive organs (*Recognitions* 8.32).

Crossan's Comparison of Jesus to the Cynics
Can we identify any particular Pythagorean group which encountered Jewish Christianity? Two prominently mentioned possibilities, not necessarily incompatible, are the Essenes and the Cynics. If either of these groups are connected with any early Christian groups, it could mean that the Pythagorean influence was very early indeed.

The first-century writers Josephus and Philo discuss the Essenes in terms which suggest that the Essenes were either a neo-Pythagorean sect or heavily influenced by them. But this issue is complicated by the discovery of the Dead Sea Scrolls at Qumran, which seem quite alien to Pythagoreanism. These questions are sufficiently important to justify devoting a separate chapter to the Essenes, which we will do in the next chapter.

What about the Cynics? Many modern scholars have made the argument that Jesus was connected to the Cynics (an ancient Greek philosophical school). Of these scholars, John Dominic Crossan is the most prominent. Crossan argues that both Jesus and the Cynics were ascetic and egalitarian both in their words and their deeds, were populists, were lifestyle preachers, and use dress and equipment to symbolize their message (Crossan 1994, p. 114–122). Crossan concludes: "Maybe Jesus is what peasant *Jewish* Cynicism looked like" (p. 122).

Crossan doesn't go into Pythagoreanism, but limits his discussion to the Cynics. The Pythagoreans were the spiritual ancestors of the Cynics, and all of the similarities with early Christianity which Crossan applies to the Cynics, also apply to the Pythagoreans. The Pythagoreans were *also* lifestyle preachers who advocated their position by word and deed, and dressed distinctively. According to Iamblichus, Pythagoras and his followers dressed in white clothes (*On the Pythagorean Way of Life* 100, 149), reminiscent of the transfiguration (Matthew 17:2) and the young man at Jesus' tomb on Easter morning (Mark 16:5).

Vegetarianism and simple living are key features of the lifestyle of many famous Cynics. Diogenes the Cynic was likely vegetarian. While washing some vegetables, he advised Aristippus that "if you had learnt to make these your diet, you would not have paid court to kings" (Diogenes Laertius, *Lives of the Eminent Philosophers* 2.68). Diogenes the Cynic also sought to get by on as little as possible. He sees a child drinking out of his hands, and throws away his cup, saying "A child has beaten me in plainness of living" (*Lives* 6.37). Interestingly, the Muslim medieval writer Al-Ghazali tells a very similar story about Jesus: Jesus sees a man drinking with his hands, and throws away his cup; he sees a man running his hands through his beard, and throws away his comb (*The Precious Pearl*, p. 77).

Crates, a follower of Diogenes, wrote a poem (which Diogenes Laertius quotes) describing a utopian land which has thyme, garlic, figs and loaves in abundance, and where there is no gluttony or war (*Lives* 6.85). Diodorus of Aspendus (fourth century BCE) was a Pythagorean who could be considered a forerunner of the Cynics: he was a strict vegetarian who had a shabby cloak, rucksack, walking stick, beard, long hair, and bare feet (Riedweg, p. 113).

To be fair, Crossan also notes some differences between Jesus and the Cynics. The Cynics are urban, Jesus is rural; the Cynics are individualistic, Jesus organized a communal movement; the Cynics emphasized a knapsack and a staff, while Jesus (at Mark 6:8) counseled no knapsack and no staff (Crossan, p. 118). But both the earliest Pythagoreans and later neo-Pythagoreans such as the Essenes were communal, just like the Jesus movement; and at least some of the Essenes lived in rural isolation. The connection of Jesus with the Pythagoreans in some respects is actually *stronger* than the connection with the Cynics.

When we think about how Greek philosophy might have influenced early Christianity, we are tempted to think of the influence of Greek philosophy on Christianity in the second, third, and fourth centuries. Crossan reminds us that the Pythagoreans probably had an influence on Jewish Christianity at a much earlier stage.

Conclusions

Pythagoreanism was one of the key movements influencing Jewish Christianity. We don't know the exact time and place that this influence came to bear. The references to Plato and Pythagoras in the *Recognitions* and *Homilies* do not necessarily imply a date earlier than the third century CE. But we also find mention of many key Pythagorean features in first-century Christianity. Paul talks about vegetarianism and animal sacrifice; and pacifism, communalism, rejection of divorce, and rejection of oaths are in the synoptic gospels, Acts, or both.

This evidence adds up to credible testimony that Jewish Christianity, even if it was not an outright Pythagorean group, was influenced by Pythagoreanism and Platonism. In fact, as we shall see in the next chapter, there was likely a specific Pythagorean group in direct contact with early Jewish Christianity: the Essenes.

Table 6–1. Parallels between the Pythagorean movement, Jewish Christianity, and the New Testament.

Issue	Pythagoras / Plato	Jewish Christianity	New Testament Parallels
Oaths	Oaths avoided, OPWL 144, DL 8.22	But to those who think, as the Scriptures teach, that God swears, He said, "Let your yea be yea, and nay, nay; for what is more than these is of the evil one." (*Homilies* 3.55)	"But I say to you, do not swear at all. . . ." (Matthew 5:34)
Nonviolence	Plato, *Crito* 49c: don't return a wrong to anyone; OPWL 155: More holy to be wronged than to kill	Followers of Jesus reject violence: *Recognitions* 1.71, 2.25, 2.27, 2.30, 2.36, 3.42, 4.31; *Homilies* 2.44, 3.19, 3.62, 4.20–22, 9.2, 11.19, 12.26	"Do not resist one who is evil" (Matthew 5:39). "Love your enemies" (Matthew 5:44).
Animal Sacrifice	Pythagoras would not make animal sacrifices: OPWL 35, 54, 107, 108; DL 8.22.	*Panarion* 30.16.5, the Ebionite gospel says Jesus came to destroy the sacrifices *Recognitions* 1.54, "the rising of Christ for the abolition of sacrifices"	"I require mercy, not sacrifice" (Matthew 9:13, 12:7). Also, incident in the temple (Matthew 21:12–13 and parallels) and Speech of Stephen (Acts 7).
Vegetarianism	OPWL 13, 54, 68, 107, 108, 168; DL 8.13, 8.23; Plato, *Republic* 372b-d, vegetarian diet is the ideal	*Panarion* 30.15.3, Ebionites abstain from meats; 30.22.5, Jesus refused the Passover meat; see also *Homilies* 3.45, 7.4, 7.8	No clear parallel except in Paul's opponents: Romans 14:21, meat and wine cause brother to stumble.

continued . . .

Table 6–1 (continued).

Issue	Pythagoras / Plato	Jewish Christianity	New Testament Parallels
Avoid Wine	Pythagoras' followers avoided wine (OPWL 13, 69, 107, 188).	*Panarion* 30.16.1, they take the Eucharist with water only; *Homilies* 11.15	John the Baptist refused strong drink (Luke 1:15). Also, Paul's opponents: Romans 14:21.
Monad, Dyad	DL 8.25 Kahn, p. 98, quoting Eudorus: Pythagoreans believe in the One (the first principle), which brings forth the Monad and Dyad	*Panarion* 30.16.2, Jesus and Satan both request this world be given to the devil *Homilies* 19.12, God produced the evil one	The "prince of this world" (John 12:31)?
Doctrine of Opposites	DL 8.25 Kahn, p. 98, quoting Eudorus: the first principle brings out opposites such as even / odd, male / female, etc.	God has established opposites and we must learn to distinguish between them (*Recognitions* 3.58–59, 3.75; *Homilies* 2.15, 2.33).	No parallel.
Did not wear wool	Pythagoras or followers did not wear sheepskin: OPWL, 100, 149	Eusebius, *Ecclesiastical History* 2.23.5–6: James did not use wool, but wore only linen garments	No parallel.

continued . . .

Table 6-1 (continued).

Issue	Pythagoras / Plato	Jewish Christianity	New Testament Parallels
Communalism	Pythagoreans held their possessions in common: OPWL 72, 74, 81; DL 8.10. Friends share everything, OPWL 32, 92–93; Plato, *Phaedrus* 279c, *Republic* 449c, *Lysis* 207c. See also Hippolytus, *Refutation of All Heresies* 1.2	*Panarion* 30.17.2, they called themselves "poor." *Homilies* 15.9: "Possessions are sins." See also *Recognitions* 2.29, 5.9, 7.6; *Homilies* 3.69, 12.6. Share with others, *Homilies* 7.4, 11.4.	Acts 2:44, 4:32–35, the early church shared everything in common
Divorce	One ought not to drive out one's wife: OPWL 84. Give up concubines, OPWL 132	*Homilies* 3.54, cites Jesus' words on divorce.	Jesus did not permit divorce (Mark 10:2–12 and parallels)

KEY: OPWL = *On the Pythagorean Way of Life*, Iamblichus; DL = "Pythagoras," by Diogenes Laertius, in *Lives of Eminent Philosophers*, vol. 2, pages 320–367 (numbers represent sections within book 8).

Table 6–2. The Doctrine of Opposites in the Pythagoreans and in Jewish Christianity.

"Pythagoreans" (Aristotle)	Neo-Pythagorean Eudorus	Homilies 2.15, 2.33	Recognitions 3.61
[The One Monad / Dyad]	The One Monad / Dyad	[God Jesus / Satan]	[God Satan / Jesus]
Limit / Unlimited	Definite / Indefinite	Heaven / Earth	Cain / Abel
Light / Darkness	Light / Darkness	Day / Night	Giants / Noah
Odd / Even	Odd / Even	Light / Fire	Pharaoh / Abraham
Square / Oblong	Known / Unknown	Sun / Moon	Philistines / Isaac
One / Plurality	Ordered / Disordered	Life / Death	Esau / Jacob
Male / Female	Male / Female	Eternity / World	Magicians / Moses
Resting / Moving	Right / Left	Knowledge / Ignorance	Tempter / Son of Man
Straight / Curved		Male / Female	Nations / Messenger to nations
Good / Bad		Healing / Disease (2.33)	Simon Magus / Peter
Right / Left			Antichrist / Christ

SOURCES: Opposites for the "Pythagoreans" described by Aristotle (*Metaphysics*, Book I, part 5), for the neo-Pythagorean Eudorus (Kahn, p. 98), for *Recognitions* 3.61, and *Homilies* 2.15 and 2.33. Note that the order of each pair varies in the *Recognitions* and *Homilies*; frequently the "lesser" of each pair is listed first.

7. The Essenes

The Essenes have been a popular topic in dialogues on early Christianity. Some think that Jesus was an Essene or born into an Essene family. Others have argued that the Essenes were a neo-Pythagorean group, thus providing a link between the Pythagoreans and early Christianity. But who were the Essenes? And were any of the early disciples of Jesus, or Jesus himself, Essenes?

Much of our information about the Essenes comes from two first-century Jews, Josephus and Philo. Josephus was a Jewish historian who participated in and then wrote extensively about the first great Jewish revolt against Rome (66–74); Philo was a Hellenistic Jewish philosopher who lived in Alexandria and was a contemporary of Jesus. Philo discusses the Essenes in terms which strongly suggest that the Essenes were either a neo-Pythagorean sect or heavily influenced by them; Josephus explicitly states that the Essenes followed a Pythagorean lifestyle.

But this issue is complicated both by divergent accounts of the Essenes and most especially by the discovery of the Dead Sea Scrolls. The discovery of the Dead Sea Scrolls near Qumran and the Dead Sea in 1947—even though the term "Essene" is nowhere found in them—has prompted many scholars to identify the Dead Sea Scrolls as Essene documents. The Dead Sea Scrolls describe a group which existed at roughly the same time as John the Baptist and Jesus, and like them, had apocalyptic expectations and baptized their own followers. Could the Dead Sea Scrolls be Essene documents?

To answer this question, we need to look not just at Josephus and Philo, but also the ancient authors Hippolytus and Epiphanius, and finally the Dead Sea Scrolls themselves. The problem is that while there are some similarities, the Essenes as described in the "classical sources" (Josephus, Philo, and other ancient authors) are very different from the group described by the Dead Sea Scrolls, and quite alien to Pythagoreanism. The Dead Sea Scrolls group accepts war, slavery, meat-eating, and animal sacrifice.

The Essenes according to Josephus and Philo

If you were limited just to the classical sources, and disregarded the Dead Sea Scrolls, you would probably conclude that the Essenes were a Pythagorean sect which resembled early Christianity. Josephus and Philo were both first-century Jewish authors who wrote about events that were contemporaneous with them, so they must be considered excellent sources, and their testimony is hard to overlook.

Before the discovery of the Dead Sea Scrolls, many scholars and philosophers concluded that Jesus was an Essene, such as Martin Buber, the famous Jewish philosopher of religion, and Heinrich Clementz, the German translator of the works of Josephus (Skriver, p. 115, 116). Ernest Renan, the great nineteenth century author of *The Life of Jesus*, concluded that "infant Christianity . . . only followed in the footsteps of the Essenes, or Therapeutae, and of the Jewish sects founded on the monastic life" (Renan, p. 144), and that Jesus sought "the abolition of the sacrifices which had caused him so much disgust" (Renan, p. 173).

A look at the classical sources provides plenty of support. Josephus explicitly states that the Essenes "live the same kind of life as do those whom the Greeks call Pythagoreans" (*Antiquities* 15.10.4). Philo (*Every Good Man is Free* 75, 84, 77, 85–86, 79) and Josephus (*Antiquities* 18.1.5, *Wars* 2.8.3, 2.8.6) agree that the Essenes rejected animal sacrifices, refused to take oaths, lived in voluntary poverty, lived communally, and did not own slaves. Josephus adds that they bathe daily in cold water for "purification" (*Wars* 2.8.5); this could be a daily baptism ritual, similar to that of the Ebionites.

Philo adds in eloquent terms that they were pacifists who rejected slavery.

> Among those men you will find no makers of arrows, or javelins, or swords, or helmets, or breastplates, or shields; no makers of arms or of military engines; *no one, in short, attending to any employment whatever connected with war.* . . . and there is not a single slave

among them, but they are all free . . . and they
condemn masters . . . (*Every Good Man is Free*, 78, 79,
emphasis added)

This description calls to mind such gospel passages as "do not resist
evil" and "call no man master."

Philo describes a second group, the Therapeutae, in another work,
On the Contemplative Life. The group of "Therapeutae" which he
describes there seems to be a communalistic Jewish group in Egypt
similar to the Essenes. They do not have slaves, feeling that "the
ownership of servants is entirely against nature" (*On the Contemplative
Life* 70); they do not drink wine, and their table "is kept pure from the
flesh of animals" (*On the Contemplative Life* 73).

Were the Essenes, as well as the Therapeutae, vegetarian? Neither
Josephus nor Philo give an explicit answer, but Josephus gives some
hints. In addition to saying that the Essenes had a "Pythagorean"
lifestyle, Josephus says that the Essenes were long-lived because of the
"simplicity of their diet" (*Wars* 2.8.10). Since a rather spare vegan diet
was normal for all except the upper class at this time, this implies
vegetarianism or something very close to it.

Porphyry, a pagan author writing in the third century, cites
Josephus and says that the Essenes eat "pure and holy food" (*On
Abstinence from Killing Animals* 4.12.3), by which he evidently means
food not taken from "slaughtering sentient animals" (4.20.1). Jerome,
a Christian author from the fifth century, also refers to Josephus as
saying that the Essenes "practised perpetual abstinence from wives,
wine, and flesh" (*Against Jovinianus* 2.14).

We do not find any such texts in current versions of Josephus. It's
possible that Porphyry and Jerome are just making the same inference
that we are, that a simple diet and Pythagorean lifestyle implies
vegetarianism. But it's also possible that they had an earlier and more
accurate copy of Josephus; Origen and Eusebius both quote Josephus
as saying things that we do not find in our present-day texts of
Josephus (see chapter 18). In any event, it seems that the Essenes were
probably vegetarian.

These descriptions of the Essenes are similar to the ideals or
practices of the early Christians, the Ebionites, and the Pythagoreans.
Before we rush to identify any early Christians as Essenes, there are

a few references to the Essenes in ancient sources which contradict this connection with the Ebionites or other groups of early Christians. Josephus does not entirely confirm the pacifist element of Essene philosophy; he briefly refers to "John the Essene" (*Wars* 2.20.4), one of the Jewish generals in the revolt against Rome.

Philo describes a reclusive, introspective group. Pliny the Elder says that "the solitary tribe of the Essenes . . . has only palm-trees for company" (*Natural History* 5.15.73). This doesn't seem to match the missionary zeal of the Ebionites or of other early Christians. On the other hand, Pliny's statement contrasts with Josephus' assertion that the Essenes "have no certain city but many of them dwell in every city" (*Wars* 2.8.4).

We could still imagine some early Christians as deciding that this message was too important to hide within a contemplative community. In fact, perhaps Matthew 5:15, "nor do men light a lamp and put it under a bushel, but on a stand, and it gives light to the whole house," was a saying directed at the excessively quiet Essenes.

Hippolytus on the Essenes

Hippolytus, a third-century Christian writer, also describes the Essenes at some length, and further complicates our picture of the Essenes. In *Refutation of All Heresies* 9.14–20 he gives an account of the Essenes that, at first, sounds as if he is copying from (or confirming) Josephus and Philo. The Essenes share everything in common, do not make oaths, pray over their very simple food, wear white clothes (all just like the Pythagoreans), do not injure any one, and observe the Sabbath.

But then, disturbingly, he contradicts this picture of peace-loving Essenes with his description of some of them as Zealots! The Essenes, he says, "have been split up into four parties" (*Refutation* 9.21). One kind of Essene will, if they observe a non-circumcised person talking about the law, confront them and force them to convert to Judaism and be circumcised—and will kill them if they refuse! These are called the "Sicarii" or the "Zealots."

He also describes other various characteristics of the Essenes. One kind refuses to carry coins with images on them. Another refuses to address anyone as "Lord" except God himself. Another is very long-lived, attributing this to their very simple food and lack of anger. They refuse to make sacrifices to idols, and will refuse even under torture to do so. Another type of Essene is similar to the others but, unlike the others, will marry.

Hippolytus is unclear; it's not obvious which of the above characteristics he mentions belongs to which of the four different sects. But there are two things that leap out here: (1) it seems that the group which forces people to convert to Judaism is a *very* different group from the one which professes to have rejected anger, eats simple food, and refuses to offer sacrifices to idols even under torture, and (2) the statement that the Essenes have been split into four parties is the earliest *direct* indication that there may be different kinds of Essenes, other than Josephus' suggestion that there was a group of Essenes who, unlike the others, would marry (*Wars* 2.8.13).

Hippolytus is writing several centuries after Josephus and Philo, so our first inclination might be to dismiss those details which Hippolytus provides which are not consonant with Josephus and Philo. Perhaps Hippolytus was just reading too much Josephus that day and got the Essenes and the Zealots mixed up. But perhaps these particular "Zealots" were the authors of the Dead Sea Scrolls. If there were rival groups of Essenes with very different views, this would provide a way to reconcile Philo's pacifist Essenes with Josephus' comment about the Jewish military man "John the Essene."

Epiphanius on the "Ossaeans"

Epiphanius describes two groups that might be Essenes. One is a group labeled "Essenes," the other is called "Ossaeans."

Epiphanius' description of "Essenes" is not very enlightening (*Panarion* 10). According to Epiphanius, the Essenes were a Samaritan group, engaged in some obscure dispute about festivals with other Samaritan groups. Nothing in this description sounds like *anything* in Josephus, Philo, or the Dead Sea Scrolls, either, for that matter.

On the other hand, Epiphanius also discusses a group known as the "Ossaeans" (*Panarion* 19), who merged with the Elkasaites. If in fact the Ossaeans were a different name for Essenes, then Epiphanius may indeed give us some interesting information indeed about the Essenes. He is silent on whether the Ossaeans were pacifists. However, he does give some information about their diet and—most interestingly—directly connects them with Jewish Christianity.

The Ossaeans (or Elkasaites) sound very much like the Ebionites: they are vegetarian, reject animal sacrifices, object to "false texts" in the scripture, and believe that Christ has appeared throughout history, among other things. If "Ossaeans" is a different spelling for "Essenes," that would squarely identify the Essenes as people who were very similar to the Jewish Christian Ebionites. (We will discuss the Elkasaites and Ossaeans in more depth in chapter 24, "The Revelation of Elxai.")

But why would we suppose that the "Ossaeans" were really "Essenes"? After all, Epiphanius clearly distinguishes between Ossaeans and Essenes. Why should we take his descriptions of "Ossaeans" as actually about "Essenes," and then reject his description of "Essenes" as inaccurate?

The Ossaean-Essene identification isn't quite as far-fetched as it might seem. In fact, Hans-Joachim Schoeps makes this equation (Schoeps, p. 29, 118–121). Schoeps identifies the Ossaeans (and the Elkasaites) as Essenes, trying to lump the Dead Sea Scrolls together with the classical sources to provide a unified picture.

Epiphanius in one other situation distinguished between conflicting evidence about the same group name, by attributing each set of contradictory attributes to different groups with slightly different names. As we will see in the next chapter, Epiphanius distinguishes between "Nazoraeans" and "Nasaraeans," even though in fact these are likely the same group, because he has contradictory evidence about them. If he did this with the "Nazoraeans" and "Nasaraeans," maybe he did the same thing with the "Essenes" and the "Ossaeans." Perhaps Epiphanius knew of two different factions of the Essenes, and in order to reconcile the contradictory evidence he had, called one "Essenes" and the other "Ossaeans."

Hippolytus believes there are multiple and widely divergent groups of Essenes. If the Ossaeans were actually a different group of Essenes, this would be consonant with Hippolytus' comment about Essene factionalism, explain Epiphanius' perception that there were groups with very different ideas with names similar to "Essene," and the fact that no ancient writer other than Epiphanius ever refers to the "Ossaeans." While we can't be certain, it seems more likely than not that the Ossaeans were in fact Essenes, and this is new and interesting information about the Essenes.

Enter the Dead Sea Scrolls

However, the whole question of who the Essenes were was turned upside down by the discovery of the Dead Sea Scrolls, uncovered in the middle of the twentieth century near Qumran near the Dead Sea, and gradually published during the ensuing decades.

The Dead Sea Scrolls describe a baptizing, apocalyptic, messianic, and possibly communalistic sect, which existed at about the same time as Jesus and John the Baptist. This suggests obvious similarities to John the Baptist, Jesus, and Jewish Christianity—also baptizing, apocalyptic, messianic, and communalistic.

Jewish Christianity was probably apocalyptic in outlook during at least part of its history. The evidence for an apocalyptic outlook is actually rather thin if you just look at Epiphanius, the *Recognitions*, and the *Homilies*; one gets the impression that there will be an apocalypse, some day, but it might not be for a long time. But because both Paul and some gospel passages indicate an expectation of an imminent end to the world, and because Paul doesn't seem to regard this as a controversial point, we can grant that it is probable that Jewish Christianity was apocalyptic at some stage of its existence.

But the Dead Sea Scrolls are puzzling documents if your expectations of the Essenes are based on Josephus and Philo. The Dead Sea Scrolls endorse slavery, war, and animal sacrifice. It sounds like a very violent group. What's going on here? Are we talking about the same group? Let's enumerate the problems.

1. Philo says that the Essenes refused any activity whatsoever connected to war. But the Dead Sea Scrolls clearly sanction warfare. *The War Scroll* 1–2 contains references to "battle and terrible carnage," "the remaining thirty-three years of the war," and "warriors from all the tribes of Israel." *The Temple Scroll* 61–62 talks about going into battle, killing all the men, and taking the women and children into slavery.

2. Josephus and Philo say that the Essenes did not own slaves, yet the Dead Sea Scrolls presuppose slavery. "He shall not sell them [the Gentiles] his manservant or maidservant" (*Damascus Document* 12.10) presupposes that some of them owned slaves.

3. Josephus and Philo say that the Essenes did not make oaths, with the possible exception of an initiation oath, but *Temple Scroll* 53

contains the statement, "when a man makes a vow to me or swears an oath to take upon himself a binding obligation, he must not break his word."

4. Josephus and Philo say that the Essenes did not offer animal sacrifices; and Josephus implies they are vegetarian. Yet the Dead Sea Scrolls clearly sanction animal sacrifice in principle. *The Temple Scroll* 52–53 contains references to making animal sacrifices and eating meat. *Damascus Document* 12.10–15 contains the statement, "They shall eat no fish unless split alive and their blood poured out," which obviously sanctions killing fish.

5. Josephus and Philo say that the Essenes despised wealth and lived communally. The Dead Sea Scrolls community *might* have lived communally, based on vague statements that everyone devoted to God's truth is to bring all their "knowledge, powers, and possessions" into the community (*Community Rule* 1). But this is immediately followed up by the statement that they will order their possessions "according to His righteous counsel," which suggests that wealth which is still privately owned, but wisely used, fulfills this criterion.

   It seems unlikely that the Qumran group truly owned everything in common. *Damascus Document* 14 contains the statement, "They shall place the earnings of at least two days out of every month into the hands of the Guardian and the Judges," which clearly presupposes the existence of private property; and ownership of slaves also implies private property.

6. The classical Essenes, differing both from Jewish Christianity and the Dead Sea Scrolls, give no indication of being apocalyptic. There is no suggestion from Josephus or Philo of an impending cataclysm, revelation to the world, coming Messiah, or end of the age. One gets the impression of a retiring, stoic, meditative sect.

Scholars are endlessly curious, and they have brought forward countless minor similarities between the Dead Sea Scrolls community and the classical Essenes: injunctions against spitting, rigorous initiation rites, communal meals, and so forth. The problem is that these are either widely shared by many different utopian groups of their day, or turn out actually to be rather different when examined closely, or are swamped by an equal or greater number of minor dissimilarities (Mason, 2008).

There *are* some similarities between Jewish Christianity and the Dead Sea Scrolls. Interestingly, though, they tend to be *different* similarities than those between Jewish Christianity and the classical Essenes. With the Dead Sea Scrolls, Jewish Christianity shares baptism and apocalyptic expectation, but not their vegetarianism, rejection of animal sacrifice, and pacifism. With the classical Essenes, they share vegetarianism, rejection of animal sacrifice, and pacifism, but not apocalyptic expectation.

In Jewish Christianity, baptism is intended to *replace* animal sacrifice. In the Dead Sea Scrolls, there is nothing wrong with animal sacrifice in principle; baptism is an *adjunct* to animal sacrifice. The Dead Sea Scrolls also had apocalyptic expectations, but wasn't there an explosion of Jewish apocalyptic expectation among all sorts of people during this time? How significant is this similarity?

Some modern Christian fundamentalists expect the imminent end of the world through divine intervention. Some modern environmentalists (e. g., James Hansen) expect an apocalypse for completely different reasons; all life on earth could be destroyed through human-caused climate change. Modern apocalyptic expectations, in many diverse sectors of our society, are symptomatic of the times we live in, as our society comes under increasing stress. But we wouldn't conclude that these modern environmentalists are therefore fundamentalist Christians. We shouldn't make a similar mistake about the Jewish Christianity and the Dead Sea Scrolls, either.

Ways of Resolving These Problems

Given these fairly serious problems, and the lack of consensus among scholars, what alternatives do we have? Broadly speaking, there are several choices.

1. The default position of some scholars seems to be that the doctrines of the Dead Sea Scrolls can be harmonized with the ancient references to the Essenes. Geza Vermes concedes that there are "noticeable differences," but says that "it would be

unreasonable to expect complete accord between two such sets of documents" (Vermes (2003), p. 119–120).

But then we would need to ask, what is the core of common belief shared by the group? There is fundamental opposition on numerous central points: pacifism versus militarism, rejection versus acceptance of oaths, rejection versus acceptance of animal sacrifices, rejection versus acceptance of slavery. And the Essene position on each of these issues are among the views which Philo thinks are *most* characteristic of the Essenes. What points of view *cannot* be reconciled, in this view? These must be two groups which are opposed to each other.

2.   Perhaps Philo and Josephus are just wrong? Perhaps Philo imagined that the Essenes were similar to his own philosophy, which was neo-Platonic, so he made them into a neo-Platonic group. Josephus then copied from Philo uncritically. This hypothesis is not absolutely impossible, but is certainly very unlikely. It doesn't sound like Josephus is obviously copying from Philo. In his youth Josephus studied an ascetic lifestyle with Banus, who sounds like he was either Essene or influenced by them. Josephus *does* seem to have had some contact with these types of systems. Why would Josephus, a very literate contemporary of the Essenes, have been so completely careless about one of the central divisions (according to him) of ancient Judaism? The reverse type argument is also possible—that the Dead Sea Scrolls are not Essene documents at all, but just come from some unrelated sect. This would explain why the Dead Sea Scrolls never use the term "Essene" and sound so totally different from the descriptions of Essenes by contemporaries.

It's also possible that the Qumran group was an Essene settlement, but the Dead Sea Scrolls were not *written* by them. In some ancient Jewish traditions, any document which contained the name of God could not simply be destroyed. Instead, they had to be placed in a *genizah*, a depository for worn-out manuscripts containing the name of God, in lieu of (or until) a proper cemetery burial. The Essenes may have come into possession of these manuscripts, and finding the name of God, they placed them in a genizah, where they stayed for nearly 2000 years; but they do not represent Essene views.

3.   The final possibility is the one already mentioned by Hippolytus: there were different types of "Essenes." The Dead Sea Scrolls are documents of one type of Essenes; Josephus and Philo describe a different group. This would allow us to reconcile all the contradictory evidence we have about the "Essenes." Indeed, the term "Essene" might not be the name of a particular sect at all; it might be a generic term (like "prophet," "guru," or "monk"). The term Essene might just refer to "holy people in the desert," regardless of their views.

Conclusions

There is too much information supporting a pacifist communal group opposed to animal sacrifice to simply dismiss their existence or lump them in the same category as the Dead Sea Scrolls community, whatever we call them. For want of better terms, we could refer to "Philo's Essenes" and the "Qumran Essenes." The most likely hypothesis is that Philo's Essenes were a neo-Pythagorean group and were the spiritual ancestors, siblings, or cousins of Jewish Christianity.

The Dead Sea Scrolls, though, describe a very different group, and tell us nothing *directly* about either the classical Essenes or Jewish Christianity. The Dead Sea Scrolls are important documents, no doubt about it, and tell us a great deal about the *milieu* in which the Essenes and Jewish Christianity both developed. But until and unless someone can come up with a really convincing explanation of the serious discrepancies between the Dead Sea Scrolls and the classical descriptions of the Essenes, I am inclined to regard the Dead Sea Scrolls as a gigantic red herring so far as the classical Essenes or any sort of early Christianity is concerned. The classical references to the Essenes do confirm that Jewish Christians were not the only people in ancient Palestine with Pythagorean ideas.

Part III:
The Coming of the Christ

8. The Nazoraeans

The name "Nazoraean" is the earliest and most tantalizing name for Christians, not only because it is a name which evidently preceded Jesus, but also is directly connected both to Jesus himself ("Jesus the Nazoraean") and to heretical Jewish Christianity ("the Nazoraeans"). It is used in both positive and negative ways—to designate Christians generally, and to designate a particular heretical sect. To add to the confusion, there a number of quite different spellings: Nazarenes, Nazoraeans, Nasaraeans, Nasoraeans, and *Notsrim*.

One obvious possibility is that these are just different ways of spelling "Nazarene," meaning "resident of Nazareth." The usage and spelling of the term seems to preclude this possibility, though, as it appears that even in the New Testament the spelling of the name (and often the usage) designating "resident of Nazareth" has been *deliberately* avoided, as I will argue below.

We have several sources of information about this name and the group which it describes: the New Testament, Jewish prayers against the *notsrim*, Latin writers such as Tertullian and Jerome, the ever-helpful Epiphanius, and finally the Mandaeans (a non-Christian group; see chapter 25). We know considerably less about the "Nazoraeans" (in any spelling) than we know about the Ebionites. Both the meaning and even the exact spelling of the name "Nazoraean" remains a mystery to this day.

The New Testament Use of "Nazoraean"
Standard translations of the New Testament frequently refer to Jesus as a "Nazarene," meaning "resident of Nazareth." But the original Greek of this word comes in two different spellings:

1. The normal form we would expect to refer to a "resident of
    Nazareth": the Greek word *Nazarenos* and its related forms
    Nazarene, Nazarenou, or *Nazarenon,* which I will render in English
    as "Nazarene."
2. A second similar, but deviant, form: *Nazoraios, Nazoraiou,* or
    Nazoraion, which I will render in English as "Nazoraean." The
    deviant spelling "Nazoraean" is *also* used by Epiphanius to refer
    to a heretical Jewish Christian sect, the "Nazoraeans," whom he
    talks about in *Panarion* 29.

But there is a serious problem: the New Testament overwhelmingly
favors the *deviant* spelling, using the term which denotes the heretical
Jewish Christian group! "Nazarene" or "Nazoraean" is used 18 times
in the New Testament; the "deviant" usage of *Nazoraios* is used 12
times, the standard term *Nazarenos* is used only 4 times, and twice the
manuscript evidence is ambiguous (see Table 8–1). Taken literally,
Matthew 2:23 ("He [Jesus] shall be called a Nazoraean") would mean
that there was a prophecy that Jesus would be a member of a heretical
Jewish Christian sect!

Nazoraios ("Nazoraean") or variants	*Nazarenos* ("Nazarene") or variants	Ambiguous
Matthew 2:23, 26:71; Luke 18:37; John 18:5, 18:7; Acts 2:22, 3:6, 4:10, 6:14, 22:8, 24:5, 26:9.	Mark 1:24, 14:67, 16:6; Luke 4:34.	Mark 10:47, Luke 24:19

**Table 8–1. Greek spelling of words translated as "Nazarene" or
"of Nazareth" in the New Testament.**

All of this is lost in the standard English translations of the New
Testament. Whether the term is *Nazarenos* or *Nazoraios,* it usually
comes out as designating a resident of Nazareth. On top of that, there
are various different spellings of the town of Nazareth itself. In Greek
it is spelled *Nazaret* or *Nazareth,* but it is sometimes spelled *Nazara* (e.
g. Matthew 4:13, Luke 4:16).

There is a lively debate, also, about whether the town of Nazareth even existed at the time of Jesus (Salm, 2008). There is no unequivocal evidence that Nazareth existed before the destruction of the temple in 70 CE. The town is not mentioned by Josephus nor is it in the Old Testament, and the archeological evidence is heavily disputed. It sounds as if this is a case of the tradition trying to harmonize an earlier spelling and usage (*Nazaraios*) with a later place name (*Nazareth*) in order to avoid the implication that Jesus was part of a heretical sect.

These different spellings may not matter. It may be that these are all variant spellings of "Nazarene," meaning "resident of Nazareth," and that the deviant spelling is just a scribal spelling error of some sort (Shires, 1947). But it is the deviant spelling which predominates. It stretches the limits of credulity that the writers of Matthew, Mark, Luke, John, *and* Acts would all *independently* make the *same* spelling mistake. In fact, we have to suspect that even the four "standard" references to "Nazarene" are editorial attempts to smooth over an obvious problem after the fact.

Did these authors come to the deviant spelling of *Nazoraios* independently, or is scribal copying from an original error possible? *None* of the passages cited above occur in any of the standard lists of verses included in the "Q" source (a hypothetical but strongly attested source preceding the gospels). In fact, there are only three cases in the synoptic passages cited above where copying of the term "Nazarene" might have occurred at all: Mark 1:24 and Luke 4:34 (Jesus rebukes the demon), Mark 10:47 and Luke 18:37 (Jesus heals the blind man at Jericho), and Mark 14:67 and Matthew 26:71 (Peter's denials of Jesus). But in each case, the copying theory would at best only explain why the *standard* spelling spread, not why the deviant spelling spread. It is in Mark, supposedly the gospel from which Matthew and Luke copied, in which we see most of the "standard" uses of the term "Nazarene."

Two usages of *Nazoraios* are especially intriguing: Matthew 2:23 and Acts 24:5. Acts 24:5 refers to accusations against Paul that he is a "ringleader of the sect of the Nazoraeans," describing the Nazoraeans as a specific Jewish group. Matthew 2:23, in the Revised Standard Version, says that Jesus "dwelt in a city called Nazareth, that what was spoken by the prophets might be fulfilled, 'He shall be called a Nazarene.'" But the term translated as "Nazarene" is *Nazoraios*, not *Nazarenos*—it should be translated, "He shall be called a Nazoraean." It is as if the redactor of Matthew saw that there was a problem with the term *Nazoraios*, because it implies that "Nazoraeans" were a group that existed before Jesus, and added the explanatory apology about where Jesus lived—but without correcting the spelling.

Jewish References to Jewish Christianity and the *Birkat ha-minim*

There is also Jewish testimony about the name of the Jewish Christians. Tertullian says that the Jews call the Christians "Nazarenes" ("Nazaraeos"—*Against Marcion* 4.8). The Christians which non-Christian Jews would be most familiar with, obviously, would be the Jewish Christians, so these Jews were likely referring to a Jewish Christian group. Tertullian is writing in Latin, not Greek, and gives contradictory information about the "correct" Greek spelling of the term. He refers to "Nazirites" (quoting from the Septuagint translation of Lamentations 4:7), to the town of Nazareth, and to Matthew 2:23 which refers to "Nazoraean," so he evidently doesn't know the exact spelling and is just throwing out suggestions.

The most important Jewish reference to Jewish Christians, though, is found in the *birkat ha-minim*, which means literally a "blessing of the heretics"—but it is actually a curse or malediction against the heretics. It is number twelve out of eighteen benedictions to be recited in the Jewish synagogues. It consists of a few short sentences:

> For the apostates let there be no hope. And let the arrogant government be speedily uprooted in our days. Let the *notsrim* and the *minim* be destroyed in a moment. And let them be blotted out of the Book of Life and not be inscribed together with the righteous. Blessed art thou, O Lord, who humblest the arrogant. (Van der Horst, 1994)

The reference is generally unhelpful, except in one respect: it shows that Jews were aware of this name and that it likely meant something other than "resident of Nazareth." It could be, in fact, the Hebrew form of the name "Nazoraean," referring to *Jewish* Christians and not Christians generically.

Minim is a term which refers to Jewish heretics generally. The *notsrim* would be a particular group of heretics, generally thought to be Jewish Christians—Nazoraeans, Nasaraeans, Nazarenes, or something else. Other church fathers refer to the Jews cursing the Christians in their prayers. But for it to be a curse against *heretics* (that is, *Jewish* heretics), it could not be a curse against Christians generally—who were mostly gentile and had never been Jewish—but against those heretical Jews who had become followers of Jesus.

Epiphanius and Jerome both mention this curse or condemnation, and believed that it was directed specifically at Jewish Christians. Epiphanius says that the Jews curse the Nazoraeans three times a day (*Panarion* 29.9.2). Jerome, writing in Latin, says that the *Ebionites* are the ones who are being cursed by the Jews in their synagogues:

> Why do I speak of the Ebionites, who make pretensions to the name of Christian? In our own day there exists a sect among the Jews throughout all the synagogues of the East, which is called the sect of the Minei [Latin: "Minaeorum"], and is even now condemned by the Pharisees. The adherents to this sect are known commonly as Nazarenes [Latin: "Nazaraeos"] . . . But while they desire to be both Jews and Christians, they are neither the one nor the other. (Jerome, "Letter 112")

Jerome is probably referring to the *birkat ha-minim*. The "Minaeorum" are probably the *minim* , and the "Nazaraeos" are probably the *notsrim*. Jerome talks as though the Ebionites, the "Minaeorum" (*minim*), and the "Nazaraeos" (*notsrim*), are all one and the same heretical group. The terms clearly refer to a heretical group, not to residents of Nazareth.

What does the *birkat ha-minim* prove? Scholars have given a lot of attention to the *birkat ha-minim* because such a "blessing" (a curse, actually) might have been used to exclude Jewish Christians from the synagogue, and thus help us date the "the break between Judaism and

Christianity." However, whether the *birkat ha-minim* helps us do this is a very murky issue, because there are so many unknowns (Kimelman, 1981; Katz, 1984; Van der Horst, 1994). For us, the *birkat ha-minim* is evidence that the Jews knew the Jewish Christians as *notsrim*. This would imply that *notsrim* and its Greek cognate (likely either "Nazoraean" or "Nasaraean") is not a distinct group from the Ebionites, but is rather another name for the Ebionites. It has nothing to do with residents of Nazareth. It was the name of the Jewish heretics who followed Jesus.

Epiphanius on the Nasaraeans / Nazoraeans

All of this gives us some evidence that there was a Jewish Christian group known as the "Nazoraeans" (in some spelling), and indeed that it preceded Jesus, but doesn't tell us that much directly about their beliefs or history. Now we come to Epiphanius, who *does* attempt to describe the beliefs and history of the Nazoraeans. But Epiphanius' help comes with significant complications. He not only describes the Nazoraeans, but another group with a remarkably similar name—the Nasaraeans. Because none of our sources seems to be terribly precise about the exact name of these groups, we need to look at the Nazoraeans and the Nasaraeans in tandem.

The Nasaraeans have views *very* similar to the Ebionites: they are vegetarian, they reject animal sacrifices, and they reject the "false texts" in the scripture which refer to animal sacrifices. The Nasaraeans are a *Jewish* group, not a Jewish Christian group, and existed *before* Jesus (*Panarion* 29.6.1). They accepted the patriarchs through Moses and Joshua, and they accept the law according to Moses—but deny that the Old Testament contains that law. They also refused to make animal sacrifices or eat meat, considering it contrary to the law of God ("unlawful," 18.1.4). After a "brief period of celebrity" following the fall of Jerusalem, shared with various other groups such as the Ossaeans, the Nasaraeans were "dispersed and dissolved"—and thus, evidently, did not exist in Epiphanius' time (19.5.7).

Epiphanius tells us quite a bit about the Nasaraeans' views, but where did the Nasaraeans get their name? Epiphanius is silent, though he does say that the Nasaraeans, Nazoraeans, and Ebionites were all allies. When Epiphanius turns to the Nazoraeans, by contrast, we get the very opposite treatment: a *lengthy* discussion of the meaning of the name, and *almost nothing* about their views.

Epiphanius is acutely aware of the New Testament spelling of "Nazoraean," the appropriation of this name by the heretics, and the prophecy of Matthew 2:23, "he shall be called a Nazoraean." Obviously he does not want to make Jesus a member of this heretical Jewish Christian group! He seeks to head this objection off by explaining that *all* Christians were known as "Nazoraeans" at one point, but that when the rest of the church changed, the heretical Nazoraeans remained the same (*Panarion* 29.1.2–3, 29.7.1).

Church fathers who described heresies typically tried to point out that the heresies came later, and then deviated from an earlier (orthodox) group by following a heretical leader of some sort. Epiphanius deviates from this pattern. He dates the break between the heretical Nazoraeans and the church not only to the first century, but to apostolic times—Epiphanius points out that the followers of Jesus were first called Christians at Antioch (Acts 11:26). Secondly, he labels the orthodox name as a later deviation, *and the heretical name as the earlier tradition*. It would be unlikely that Epiphanius would make this admission unless he had evidence that it was true.

While Epiphanius thinks he knows a great deal about the *name* "Nazoraean," Epiphanius knows remarkably little about their *views*. He says that the Nazoraeans followed Jesus and followed the entire Jewish law—thus they do not reject "false texts" in the Old Testament but accept it in its entirety. But that's about all. He does not say whether or not they were vegetarians or whether they rejected animal sacrifice. He does not even know if they reject the virgin birth, the very first heretical doctrine which he attributes to the Ebionites.

We might think that accepting the whole law, and not rejecting false texts, would imply acceptance of animal sacrifice, at least during the time when the temple still stood. But *Recognitions* 1.36 implies that Moses *did* give the sacrificial commands, wisely seeing the futility of abolishing sacrifice in his time, and leaving the task of abolishing sacrifice to Jesus. So the Nazoraeans may well have "accepted the whole law" and still rejected animal sacrifice, and this in fact may be where the idea put forward at *Recognitions* 1.36 comes from.

Epiphanius sees the Nazoraeans and Nasaraeans as very similar. "Ebion," he says, had views like those of the Nasaraeans, Nazoraeans, and Ossaeans (*Panarion* 30.1.3). Both the Nazoraeans and the Ebionites accepted the Gospel of Matthew in Hebrew—a version of Matthew which Epiphanius attacks because it presents John the Baptist as a vegetarian (*Panarion* 30.13.4–5) and contains the celebrated text "I have come to destroy the sacrifices" (*Panarion* 30.16.5). The Nazoraeans must have had a gospel with some strongly pro-vegetarian passages. Epiphanius also locates both groups in the same general geographic area east of the Jordan (see chapter 19).

Surely two groups with names so similar and so highly charged with Christian meaning, described as friends and allies, and accepting the same gospel, could not have been placed in almost the same location in first century Palestine by *complete* coincidence. Even the differences between the two groups show a suspicious mirror-image relationship. Epiphanius says a lot about the name "Nazoraean": he says nothing about the name "Nasaraean." He has information about the ideas of the "Nasaraeans": he knows almost nothing about the ideas of the "Nazoraeans." The history of the Nasaraeans ends just as the history of the Nazoraeans begins, right after the fall of Jerusalem (Nasaraeans, *Panarion* 19.5.7; Nazoraeans, *Panarion* 29.7.8).

Epiphanius' Distinction Between These Groups

It is quite likely that the Nasaraeans and the Nazoraeans are the same group, described from different points of view or at different points in time. So why does Epiphanius describe two groups instead of one?

Epiphanius is careless and uncritical with his sources, but he does not appear to make things up. Epiphanius is very likely getting his information from the book of Acts. Epihanius' information on the views of the "Nazoraeans" dovetails almost exactly with Acts' description of Jewish Christian legalists. In Acts, Epiphanius finds references to Jewish Christian "Pharisees" who strictly adhere to the law, will not even associate with non-Jews, and insist that male converts be circumcised. But except for the fact that they "follow the whole law," Acts says nothing about them. Since all Christians were known as "Nazoraeans" at that time (Acts 24:5), Epiphanius reasons that the Jewish Christian legalists of Acts were also known as "Nazoraeans" at the time and just never changed their name.

On the other hand, Epiphanius also knows of a similarly-named group which was *not* legalistic—they attacked the sacrifices and the false texts in the law. A group which keeps "the whole law" is surely very different, Epiphanius may have said to himself, from a group which attacks the sacrifices and the false texts. To reconcile this information, he postulates two groups, not one—the first group conforming to Acts, the second conforming to the independent information he has. Epiphanius likely confronted a similar situation with respect to the "Essenes" and the "Ossaeans": he had conflicting information about the characteristics of the "Essenes," and so created a spelling for the two groups that was slightly different.

Some scholars have assumed that Epiphanius' description of the Nazoraeans vindicates Acts' description of a legalistic Jewish Christian group, which continued to exist in Epiphanius' day (Pritz, 1988 and Pines, 1966). But this is likely circular, since Epiphanius is probably basing his extremely vague descriptions of the Nazoraeans precisely on the book of Acts.

We, of course, know that Acts is inaccurate, and therefore are not forced into convoluted explanations that there "must be" two different groups. Jerome states casually in "Letter 112" that the Ebionites are commonly known as Nazarenes. The most likely explanation is that the "Nasaraeans," "Nazoraeans," and *"Notsrim"* are all the same group known by three different names, similar or identical with the Ebionites.

Origin of the Term "Nazoraean"

So, where did the name "Nazoraean" come from and what does it mean, if it does not mean "resident of Nazareth"? At least three possibilities have been suggested:

1. *Nazoraios* could be a reference to the Nazirites, described in Numbers 6:1–20, and mentioned by Tertullian. If it is, it would seem to mesh well with the Ebionite abstinence from alcohol, but not with their vegetarianism or objection to animal sacrifice. The Nazirites are required to abstain from alcohol, but are *not* required to be vegetarian; in fact, they are supposed to offer an animal sacrifice upon the completion of their vow. Thus, it's unlikely that *Nazoraios* refers to Nazirites.

2. Hans-Joachim Schoeps said that it could be related to *nosri*, which means "to keep" or "to observe," and concluded that "those who bear the name are to be thought of as 'observers of secret traditions'" (*Jewish Christianity*, p. 11). He and others derive the word from the Hebrew root NSR, and thus the most likely original spelling would be "Nasaraean" rather than "Nazoraean." *Homilies* 19.20 quotes Jesus as saying, "Keep the mysteries for me and the sons of my house." For the Mandaeans, their "Nasoraeans" really are expected to keep the secrets (see chapter 25, on the Mandaeans), and this meaning fits quite well. The Elkasaites (a group related to Jewish Christianity to be discussed later) are not known to have used the term "Nasaraean," but Hippolytus says their book was a bit secretive, saying "do not recite this account to all men" (*Refutation of All Heresies* 9.12). *The Gospel of Philip* says that "'The Nazarene' is he who reveals what is hidden," and "'Nazara' is 'the Truth'" (Robinson, p. 144, 147). *Gospel of Thomas* 1 describes itself as the "hidden sayings that the living Jesus spoke." Finally, *nosri* would seem to be a close linguistic match to the *notsrim* in the Jewish benediction against the heretics.

3. Matthew 2:23, "He shall be called a Nazoraean," might provide a clue. No such prophecy about a "Nazoraean," a "Nazarene," or "Nazareth" appears in the Old Testament or anywhere else, as far as anyone knows. Jerome proposed (Letter 57.7) that "Nazoraean" was a reference to Isaiah 11:1 which states, "There shall come forth a shoot from the stump of Jesse, and a *branch* shall grow out of his roots." The Hebrew word for "branch" (*nezer* in Hebrew) contains the consonants NZR, which suggests *Nazoraios*. The "Nazoraeans" could, therefore, base their name on the root NZR rather than NSR, and have derived their name from Isaiah 11:1: they saw themselves as the *nezer* or branch of the stump of Jesse.

It is impossible to decide between the second and third suggestions. Jerome's suggestion is plausible—that "Nazoraean" is derived from the *nezer* of Isaiah 11:1, with some of the vowels being added or changed in the transition from the Hebrew to the Greek. Matthew 2:23 refers to a *prophecy*, not a secret; and Isaiah 11 contains the famous prophecy of the peaceable kingdom, with the wolf, lamb, cow, bear, and little child all living together in peace (Isaiah 11:6–9). John the Baptist and Jesus seem more likely to fit the role of missionaries than leaders of a secret society. This prophecy would have been most useful to Jewish Christian apologists, and even to gentile Christian apologists—Irenaeus mentions this prophecy (*Against Heresies* 5.33.4) as descriptive of the world which Jesus foresaw.

On the other hand, the theme of hidden knowledge also reflects themes in early Jewish Christianity. The Pythagoreans, who seem to have had some influence on Jewish Christianity, were said to have tried to keep some of their ideas secret. In later chapters we will discuss in more detail the Elkasaites, the Mandaeans, and the gnostics, all of whom tend to support the idea of secretiveness as a positive virtue in this wicked world. If the preservation and revelation of secrets was a key problem for Jewish Christianity, their name may have been based on *nosri*, as Schoeps maintains, and there may have been an element of "mysteries" in Jewish Christianity.

Conclusions

The most obvious explanation for the various bits of evidence about "Nazoraeans" and "Nasaraeans" is that there was a first-century Jewish group already in existence before Jesus that rejected animal sacrifice, rejected the "false texts" in the Old Testament, was vegetarian, and was a spiritual ancestor of the later Ebionites. Acts 24:5 (Paul is "a ringleader of the sect of the Nazoraeans") clearly refers to a group by this name, and the prophecy quoted in Matthew 2:23 ("He *shall be called* a Nazoraean," italics added) implies that this group already existed at the time of Jesus.

Later we will encounter more evidence pointing to such a group, in the history of the Elkasaites, the Mandaeans, and the Dositheans. These groups resemble the Ebionites in interesting ways, but did not seem to split away from Ebionism or any other Christian group in any dramatic schism; the most likely explanation is that they, too, were spiritual descendants of a group that existed *before* Jesus. Most likely, this group existed *before* Jesus, was *already* vegetarian and rejected animal sacrifice, and Jesus was not its founder, *but simply its most famous leader.*

9. John the Baptist

With John the Baptist and his followers, we have a concrete and universally acknowledged example of a movement that bears some *strong* resemblances to Jewish Christianity before Jesus. What did Jesus bring that was new, that John had not already said? Or were Jesus and John really both part of a single movement?

John's Mission

John the Baptist's mission resembles the Ebionite mission in several obvious ways. Moreover, several of the things that John and the Ebionites agree on, tend to contradict later orthodoxy.

John practiced baptism, an alternative ritual to animal sacrifice for purification and forgiveness. For Jewish Christianity, baptism replaced animal sacrifice—purification by water instead of by killing an animal. In the *Recognitions*, baptism was directly instituted to replace animal sacrifice, although John is not mentioned by name at this point (*Recognitions* 1.39). During the debate in the temple in *Recognitions* 1, the high priest astutely observes, with some annoyance, that the rite of baptism has been brought in recently in opposition to the animal sacrifices (*Recognitions* 1.55).

John was "a voice in the wilderness" (Matthew 3:3). Living in the wilderness is sometimes connected with rejection of a central place of worship and rejection of the temple. The prophets who denigrated the temple cult sometimes saw the wilderness as a holy or special place (e. g. Isaiah 40:3 and 43:19, Jeremiah 31:2, and Hosea 2:14). The speech of Stephen in Acts favorably contrasts the tent of witness in the wilderness to Solomon's temple. The nomadic (wilderness-dwelling) Rechabites were allies of the Ebionites and protested against the killing of James, the brother of Jesus (see chapter 4).

John's food was simple and his life was simple. For the Ebionites, John was a strict vegetarian (see discussion below), but all of the accounts of John agree on the simplicity of his lifestyle. Luke 1:15 said of John that "he shall drink no wine nor strong drink," agreeing with the Ebionite rejection of alcohol. Interestingly, Matthew 11:18–19 and Luke 7:33–34 imply that Jesus drank wine. But if John and Jesus do disagree over wine, then it would mean that the connection of Jewish Christianity with John is stronger than its connection to Jesus.

John and Jesus also have similar views on divorce. Both the New Testament and Josephus agree that John was killed by Herod because John repeatedly and forthrightly condemned Herod's arbitrary divorce of his wife as immoral. John's opposition to divorce literally cost him his life, just as Jesus' opposition to animal sacrifice cost him his. In the gospels, Jesus forbids or severely restricts divorce (Mark 10:2–12 and parallels). The Ebionite position on divorce is actually less clear than the gospel position, although on balance it seems that they wanted to restrict divorce (*Homilies* 3.54; see discussion of divorce in chapter 6).

The New Testament says that John and Jesus are relatives. Luke 1:36 has the angel tell Mary the mother of Jesus that her "kinswoman Elizabeth" has conceived in her old age.

We don't have to get into detailed discussions of the "historical Jesus" and "historical John" to reach a basic conclusion. Taking any of a wide variety of sources, it still appears that John, Jesus, and Jewish Christianity all have a great deal in common, in terms of the emphasis on key issues such as simple living, opposition to divorce, practice of baptism, and at least passive hostility to the temple.

John's Baptism of Jesus

John's baptism of Jesus is a well-known difficulty for Christianity. It is reported in the gospels, and is almost certainly an historical event. But John's baptism creates huge complications for later Christian doctrines, because John's baptism of Jesus shows Jesus subservient to John.

In terms of later Christian theology, baptism has two functions, neither of which should seem to apply to Jesus: that of joining a Christian community, and that of forgiveness or purification from sin. Presumably, Jesus doesn't need to join a community he founded, and being free from sin, doesn't need forgiveness. If Jesus' baptism indicates any kind of support for a community, it must be John's community—an already existing group.

This is so obviously embarrassing for the gospel writers that they immediately insert language to soften the effect which all of this has on John's status in relation to Jesus, language which is almost certainly not historical. In Matthew, when Jesus asks to be baptized, John immediately defers to Jesus, saying he should really be baptized by Jesus. John only consents to baptize Jesus when Jesus insists.

It was not just Jesus' actions, but also his words, which indicate support for John and his mission. These words are reported both in the Jewish Christian literature and the New Testament. *Recognitions* 1.60 has one of the followers of John quoting Jesus in support of the claim that John himself is the Christ, since "Jesus Himself declared that John was greater than all men and all prophets." This statement is also found at Matthew 11:11, but the gospel writer once again feels constrained to have Jesus add the qualification, "yet he who is least in the kingdom of heaven is greater than [John]." In *Recognitions* 1.60, Simon the Canaanite (speaking on behalf of the Jesus movement, and responding to the followers of John) doesn't use this denigration. Rather, he simply observes that while John is indeed greater than all the prophets, he is still less than the "Son of man" and the Christ.

John's baptism of Jesus also raises problems because, for orthodox Christianity, baptism was *exclusively* a one-time initiation and symbolized one's entry into the Christian community. The Nicene Creed, as revised in 381, states that "we acknowledge *one baptism* for the remission of sins" (emphasis added). This creates problems on both counts. If John's baptism is initiation into a community (which is not implied in the gospel accounts), it would be John's community.

If on the other hand baptism is for remission of sins, repeated baptism would be the most natural way of implementing this rite. For the Ebionites, baptism was a daily ritual, not just a one-time initiation. Epiphanius says, "They [the Ebionites] lied about Peter, saying that he was purified by baptism daily, just as they are" (*Panarion* 30.15.3).

The two possible functions of baptism (remission of sins or initiation into a group) are not absolutely incompatible, but operate in completely different ways. The transition of this rite to a one-time initiation creates a well-known conundrum: since baptism is supposed to cleanse from sin, should one be baptized right away, or wait until one is further along in life?

Either way carries risk for your soul. If you are baptized right away, then you may live a long time, and may commit further sins which you will not be able to cleanse with the one-time initiation of baptism. On the other hand, if you wait until you are older, you may die unexpectedly without ever being baptized. The emperor Constantine is supposed to have delayed his baptism until his death bed just because of such considerations.

John on Vegetarianism and Animal Sacrifice

What did John think about vegetarianism and animal sacrifice? There is a significant contrast between the orthodox and the Ebionite picture of John on these points.

Orthodox Christianity obviously had no place for animal sacrifice; but it conceded a certain legitimacy to the practice of animal sacrifice by depicting Jesus' own death as the successor to the practice of animal sacrifice. "Christ died for our sins, in accordance with the scriptures," says Paul (I Corinthians 15:3). Jesus' death is also pictured as a redemption at Ephesians 1:7: "In [Jesus] we have redemption through his blood."

This would obviously be offensive to the Ebionites. For the Ebionites, animal sacrifice was to be abolished, not somehow mysteriously fulfilled by Jesus. Moreover, the Ebionite idea of baptism clearly contradicts the idea of Jesus' death as redemption; the path to redemption from sin already existed, *even before Jesus' death*, in John's baptism. There was no need to replace the system of animal sacrifice with Jesus' death, because it was *already* replaced with baptism (*Recognitions* 1.39).

There clearly is a hard-fought debate over whether John was a vegetarian. Epiphanius quotes from the Ebionite gospel account of John the Baptist, largely parallel to that in the New Testament, but notes (with considerable indignation) that the Ebionites changed the part about John eating "locusts and wild honey" to "wild honey . . . as a cake made with oil" (*Panarion* 30.13.4). The Ebionites did not think that John ate insects!

The idea of a vegetarian John the Baptist turns up in numerous places outside the New Testament. In the first place, John may have eaten insects, but even Epiphanius concedes that he did not eat any *other* animal flesh, or any alcoholic beverages: "John did not partake of flesh and wine, but partook only of locusts and honey, and certainly also of water" (*Panarion* 30.19.3; cf. Luke 1:15).

Eating insects was not unheard of in ancient Near East, and in fact insects were seen by some as a delicacy and a food for the wealthy (Kelhoffer, p. 46–48). There is another, simpler explanation possible, though, that the reference is to "locust beans," namely the seed of the carob tree. The Oxford English Dictionary (for the term "locust") notes that "the Greek name *akris* [locust], properly denoting the insect, is applied in the Levant to the carob-pod, from some resemblance in form; and from very early times it has been believed by many that the 'locusts' eaten by John the Baptist were these pods." In Greek the word *akrodrua* (tree fruits) is very close to *akrides* (locusts, plural of *akris*). The Greek church maintained that John didn't eat insects, saying that the text actually referred to "shoots" of various plants (Eisler, p. 236–237). There is an etymological connection as well: the carob tree today is commonly known as "St. John's bread."

It's likely that the Ebionites are right about John the Baptist. Locusts were sometimes considered a delicacy and *might* have provided adequate nutrition if John could have managed to catch enough insects, which is far from clear. Carob, by contrast, was widely grown in the Middle East and was very commonly used as a food by the poor at the time. Hanina ben Dosa, who lived at the same time as Jesus and John and was very poor, was said to live on nothing but carob pods from Sabbath to Sabbath ("Hanina b. Dosa"). The "pods" which the prodigal son fed to the pigs (Luke 15:16), but was tempted to eat himself, were likely carob pods.

Interestingly, Josephus also says in *The Wars of the Jews* that John the Baptist was a vegetarian. This is not in the standard text of Josephus, but the "Slavonic" edition, an ancient translation of a presumably different original version of this book. In this edition, Josephus describes a "wild man" who seems to match well-known characteristics of John the Baptist, though this man is not explicitly named. This man baptizes people in the Jordan, denounces Herod, and is killed by Herod, a description which pretty much could only be matched by John the Baptist. This man does not eat any animal food (thus, a vegan diet) and does not drink wine. His diet is "bulrushes, roots, and wood-shavings," a distinctly unappealing though vegan diet (Eisler, note 2, p. 224–225).

Finally, and most interestingly, this idea also turns up in early Chinese Christianity. Seventh-century Chinese manuscripts describe a person who, like John the Baptist in the Slavonic Josephus, is unnamed but clearly can only be John the Baptist, and is vegetarian (Palmer, p. 166). Because this is evidence of an Ebionite influence in China, we will discuss this further in chapter 26.

Conflict Between the Jesus Movement and John's Followers
Jesus' honoring of John was not just embarrassing for orthodox Christianity; it was embarrassing for Jewish Christianity as well. Interestingly, the Ebionite treatment of John the Baptist is just a bit cool, and this is evidently because the Jesus movement did not sweep up all of John's followers.

The New Testament subtly indicates that there were differences between the followers of John and Jesus even during Jesus' lifetime: "Then come to him the disciples of John, saying, Why do we and the Pharisees fast oft, but your disciples do not fast?" (Matthew 9:14). Jesus deflects this issue by saying that while he is alive, there is no need to fast.

When *Recognitions* 1.39 announces that God instituted baptism as a substitute for animal sacrifice, there is no mention of John at all, although this would be the place in the narrative to mention it. *Recognitions* 1 also indicates conflict between some of the followers of John and Jesus at several other points. The movement seems to have been divided since John: "For the people were now divided into many parties, *ever since the days of John the Baptist*" (*Recognitions* 1.53, emphasis added). Some followers of John asserted that John, not Jesus, was the expected Messiah (*Recognitions* 1.54, 1.60).

Worse yet, *Recognitions* 2.8–12 and *Homilies* 2.23–24 both make Simon Magus, the arch-nemesis of the Ebionites, a follower of John the Baptist. After the death of John the Baptist, Dositheus succeeded to the leadership of John the Baptist's group, and then Simon Magus followed after Dositheus. This implies that there was a split among the followers of John the Baptist—some following Jesus, some following Dositheus. In the *Recognitions* and *Homilies*, the Jewish

Christians regarded these other followers of John the Baptist as their greatest enemies!

The conflict between the followers of Jesus and the followers of John looks very much like an internal turf dispute within an existing community over "who is the greatest," not a dispute between two opposing communities with some sort of ideological differences. In fact, it may even be (literally) a family dispute, since the mothers of John and Jesus (according to Luke 1:36) were related. Because there is such a close connection between the family of Jesus and the Ebionites (as we will see later), this would imply that the family of Jesus was already advancing new religious ideas even before Jesus began his ministry.

Conclusions

The Ebionites, like the orthodox, view John the Baptist with caution. They are alarmed because not all of his followers are also their followers, despite the fact that there are no real ideological issues and despite the fact that they are evidently related to each other. But John the Baptist is also their hero, second only to Jesus himself. Not only did the community which Jesus led already exist, but Jesus—or the reaction to Jesus—precipitated a split within that community.

10. Jesus

Who was the historical Jesus? How did he influence Jewish Christianity, and how did Jewish Christianity influence him? Countless books have been written on Jesus, including my own, *The Lost Religion of Jesus*. Jesus is not our primary topic, but obviously he is a pivotal figure in Jewish Christianity.

Much of the evidence for Jesus' relationship to Jewish Christianity is contained in later chapters about the time following Jesus (especially the chapters on Paul). We can't fully go into this evidence now without repeating everything which is said there. So first the verdict and then the evidence. Those who want the evidence before the verdict should skip this chapter, read Part IV (chapters 12–18), and then come back here.

Evidence about Jesus

Jesus was a Jew, his movement remained Jewish for several decades after he left the earth, and it appears that the Ebionites inherited the mantle of the primitive church. On the other hand, the historical Jesus can't be identified with the Ebionite Jesus; the Ebionites undoubtedly distorted and elaborated on their version of Jesus, just as the orthodox did.

We can narrow down the subject by identifying those Jewish Christian ideas which can be found in the first century. We can make a good approximation of this by looking for (a) those views of Paul's Jewish Christian opponents (as described in Paul's letters), and (b) those Ebionite beliefs held by Paul. Every idea that passes either of these two tests was, at the very least, held by *someone* during the apostolic age—decades before the gospels, and before the destruction of the temple, when people were still alive who had known Jesus.

This data set of views very likely represents Jewish Christian views accurately at that time.

By contrast, many scholars start by examining the various gospels, which also give us evidence about the historical Jesus. The "Jesus Seminar" scholars have evaluated the gospel sayings by having scholars vote on each saying by ranking it as "red," "pink," "grey," or "black"—from most probably from Jesus, to least probably from Jesus. There is also much discussion of the Q gospel, the hypothetical (but strongly supported) gospel which underlies much of the common material shared by Matthew, Luke, and the *Gospel of Thomas*. The basic argument for Q (which stands for *Quelle* or "source" in German) is that there are sayings in Matthew, Luke, and Thomas which are very similar—so similar, that these gospel writers must have copied, sometimes in slightly different ways, from an unknown written source which preceded all of them.

Many scholars try to isolate those teachings of Jesus which were "original" with him to insure that we are hearing Jesus and not the tradition which may have distorted or filtered Jesus' teachings. Two widely cited criteria are those of "dissimilarity" and "embarrassment": the saying is dissimilar to the position of the early church, or it is embarrassing to the early church, and is thus likely authentic, as there would be no motive for the church to make up such material.

But isolating Jesus from his movement may also introduce distortion. Suppose Jesus didn't have very much original to say? In this case, insisting on originality could almost completely eliminate Jesus' ideas. There may be things that Jesus said which were *not* original. There may be other things which he clearly believed, but never said, because it didn't seem necessary, since everyone in his movement already believed them. Before we evaluate sayings of Jesus, we have to establish the *context* in which he spoke and acted. That context, I would argue, is "Jewish Christianity."

The gospels were written many decades after Jesus, and evaluating them is an uncertain process. With the letters of Paul, there is much less need for debate. We have a fairly certain date, in the mid-50's CE; and being a contemporary record, there is much less chance to filter out opposing views. There is some possibility that even the authentic letters of Paul have been edited, and this could doubtless be argued at great length. But given the obvious differences between

Paul's letters and the rest of the New Testament, both in style and substance, this seems unlikely. Jewish Christianity, understood in the light of Paul, gives us a lens into early Christianity which is much closer to the ground than anything in the gospels.

What the gospels, Q, and the Jesus Seminar approach all typically leave out is precisely those views which Paul found so contentious, but which (as we will see) were clearly held by the leadership of the early church. Most conspicuously, what it leaves out is the opposition to animal sacrifice and the temple. This opposition was central to the early church and was preserved by the Ebionites. The gospel writers, working after the destruction of the temple when this issue appeared to be moot, saw no reason to revisit the painful and divisive history of this dispute. Moreover, those still trying to make an issue out of the temple seemed to be their sectarian opponents.

Teachings of Jesus

If first-century Jewish Christianity, as seen by Paul, provides the basic context of Jesus' mission, what did the historical Jesus teach? The gospels *do* contain sayings that relate to most of these points, but I introduce them solely as supporting or contrasting evidence, so that we can see what is at stake.

1. The value of voluntary poverty, sharing, or simple living
These ideas are implied by the very name of the Ebionites; *Ebionim* is the Hebrew name for "the poor." The Ebionites traced their name back to the primitive community described in Acts 4:32–35, when "they had everything in common," and were therefore poor (*Panarion* 30.17.2). These ideas are accepted by Paul in his letters (Romans 12:16, 15:26; I Corinthians 16:1–4; II Corinthians 8–9).

They are also, by the way, frequently found in the gospels, in such sayings as "you cannot love both God and money" (Matthew 6:24), "blessed are you poor" (Luke 6:20), "whoever does not renounce all that he has cannot be my disciple" (Luke 14:33), and the story about Jesus advising the rich young man to give everything to the poor and follow him (Luke 18:18–25). There is probably no single doctrine which is better attested in primitive Christianity.

2. *The resurrection as a spiritual phenomenon*

Paul affirms this at I Corinthians 15:50: flesh and blood cannot inherit the kingdom of God. It is also affirmed by the Ebionites at *Recognitions* 3.30 and *Homilies* 17.16. This is one view which in fact the gospels go to some lengths to deny, as the stories about "doubting Thomas" (John 20:24–29) and Jesus eating fish after his resurrection demonstrate (Luke 24:42–43). However, at Matthew 22:30 and parallels, Jesus speaks of our bodies after the resurrection as being like the angels in heaven, suggesting a spiritual version of the resurrection, so gospel evidence can be quoted either way on this issue.

3. *The importance of baptism*

Paul refers repeatedly to baptism in his letters, and the Ebionites thought it was at least very important to salvation, if not essential. In the gospels, there are not a lot of references to baptism, though obviously Jesus is baptized by John.

4. *The value of vegetarianism*

Paul is in conflict with a group of Jewish Christians who are not only vegetarian, but who think that vegetarianism should be required (Romans 14). This group was likely the leadership of the early church (I Corinthians 8–10, Galatians 2). Most traces of vegetarianism have been kept out of the gospels; in fact, the stories about Jesus feeding bread and fish to the multitudes, and eating fish after the resurrection, contradict vegetarianism. On the other hand, there are several gospel sayings which hint at vegetarianism, such as Jesus' kind words for animals (Matthew 6:26, Matthew 12:10–12, Luke 12:6–7, Luke 13:15–16, Luke 14:5; cf. *The Lost Religion of Jesus*, chapter 9).

5. *Opposition to animal sacrifice*

This is a key Ebionite belief, and is incorporated into the Ebionite version of the apostolic decree (Acts 15:29). Paul, as we shall see, opposes this decree (I Corinthians 8–10). Jesus briefly alludes to opposition to animal sacrifice when he quotes Hosea 6:6 ("I require mercy, not sacrifice", at Matthew 9:13 and 12:7). The incident in the temple, about which more below, expresses this opposition in more spectacular fashion.

Is there any reason to suppose that Jesus himself was against blood sacrifices? Here are a few quick reasons: (1) he went into the temple just before his death and disrupted the animal sacrifice business there; (2) his followers, the Ebionites, opposed sacrifices, and described Jesus as coming for the abolition of sacrifices; (3) the movement that he took over, the Nazoraeans or Nasaraeans, opposed sacrifices; (4) vegetarianism was widespread throughout many different factions in the early church. There is contrary evidence, but it is all coming from the opponents of the Ebionites, and there was a huge controversy over this which split the church a few decades after Jesus' departure.

6. Loyalty to the Jewish law
Paul tries to come to grips with the role of the Jewish law repeatedly throughout Romans, so it is evident that a group in the early church held that the Jewish law was still valid. Paul is confused, though, because this group probably did not think of the "law" as being the written texts of the Pentateuch or any other writings in the "Old Testament."

7. Nonviolence towards human beings
Paul quotes almost exactly Jesus' words in the Sermon on the Mount, "bless those who persecute you" (Romans 12:14, Matthew 5:44), and "repay no one evil for evil" (Romans 12:17, Matthew 5:39). These views are also found in the Ebionites' writings.

8. Rejection of the written code
Paul says "we live not under the old written code" (Romans 7:6), and the Ebionites agreed, although for different reasons than Paul. For Paul, the written code is the law which has been superseded by Christ; for the Ebionites, the written code was invalid to begin with because it was filled with falsehoods.

There are several gospel references which probably refer obliquely to the idea of false texts (*The Lost Religion of Jesus*, chapter 6). Jesus rejects the Mosaic idea of divorce (Matthew 19:3–9). Jesus says "for the sake of your tradition [the written law?] you have made void the [true] law of God" (Matthew 15:6). Jesus also says "every plant which my Father has not planted will be rooted up" (Matthew 15:13), quoted with some relish at *Homilies* 3.52, indicating that the Jewish Christians used this text as evidence that Jesus held their views on false texts.

Jesus' Life

What does Jewish Christianity contribute to our understanding of Jesus' life? Two fragments which Epiphanius quotes from the Ebionite gospel, understood in the light of first century Jewish Christianity, are of relevance.

1. *John's baptism of Jesus.* When John baptizes Jesus, in the Ebionite gospel a voice from heaven says "you are my son, today I have begotten you" (*Panarion* 30.13.7). This is very similar to the accounts in the synoptic gospels (Matthew 3:13–17 and parallels), except for the key phrase "today I have begotten you"—a phrase which implies that Jesus received the holy spirit at the time of his baptism, an implicit denial of the intrinsic divinity of Jesus.

This in turn sheds light on the earliest Christian ideas about Jesus' mission. It's highly likely that the Ebionite version, emphasizing that Jesus received a divine mandate as a result of John's baptism, was the earliest understanding, indeed possibly the understanding which Jesus himself had. The phrase "today I have begotten you" is a quote from Psalm 2:7, and Matthew especially is fond of quoting from the Old Testament to make a point. Moreover, Justin Martyr in the second century twice relates the story of Jesus' baptism, *also* quoting from Psalm 2:7 and thus agreeing with the Ebionite version (*Dialogue with Trypho* 88.8, 103.6).

2. *The statement "I have come to abolish the sacrifices."* The Ebionite Jesus says, "I came to abolish the sacrifices, and if you cease not from sacrificing, my anger will not cease from you" (*Panarion* 30.16.5). The hostility towards animal sacrifice is a prominent theme of the Ebionites; here it is actually put into Jesus' mouth.

This saying is not an exact prediction of the destruction of the temple; it does *not* say, that is, "if you cease not from sacrificing, this temple will be destroyed," which would be so easy for an Ebionite to say after the year 70. Indeed, *Recognitions* 1.64 describes Peter as making just such a prediction. Just for this reason, this saying is likely to be rather early, prior to the destruction of the temple, and thus predating all the canonical gospels. If the Jesus Seminar were to "rate" this saying, it should be "pink" or "red" (that is, Jesus is very likely to have said this or something like it).

Jesus manifested his mission not only in accepting John's mission through his baptism, but in the way he died. Jesus' disruption of the animal sacrifice business in the temple (Matthew 21:12-13), one of the few events of Jesus' life which is in all four gospels, led immediately to his death. Most scholars believe that these accounts reflect an historical event in the life of Jesus. The saying "I have come to abolish the sacrifices" establishes both the motive for the Romans to have Jesus crucified (he is a threat to public order) but also for Jesus to carry out this action against the temple business anyway.

This incident is usually known to Christians as the cleansing of the temple, or "Jesus overturns the tables of the dishonest moneychangers." But in the gospels Jesus' wrath is directed primarily toward those who are buying and selling animals—the animals to be offered in sacrifice. In none of the gospels are the money-changers at the top of the list of those towards whom Jesus is angry, and in Luke they are not even mentioned.

Jesus' opposition to animal sacrifice explains a lot which otherwise becomes mysterious. It explains the generations-long conflict between the priests in the temple and the Jesus movement. First the priests want Jesus out of the way, and then Stephen is killed, and then James the brother of Jesus, so these bitter feelings lasted decades. It also explains the split between Jewish Christianity and Paul. It explains the later history of the Ebionites, as otherwise their opposition to animal sacrifice—long after the practice had disappeared—becomes an incomprehensible quirk. This means that essential facts about Jesus *known to us today are not found clearly in the gospels*.

Jesus as Leader of the Primitive Community
Jesus was the leader of a sizable and already existing community. What was the relationship of Jesus to his movement? Most contemporary scholarship assumes that Jesus was the founder or initiator of the Jesus movement: before Jesus, there was no Jesus movement. This issue is seldom argued; it's a traditional Christian

view. But Jesus could have been very, *very* important and still not be the originator of the primitive community, as we saw from the hypothetical example given earlier of future historians trying to understand the "historical George Washington" (see the Introduction).

What exactly did Jesus *add* to John's mission and message? We could easily put almost any of the teachings of Jesus into John's mouth without causing offense or coming up with something obviously implausible— voluntary poverty, nonviolence, not taking oaths, vegetarianism, opposition to divorce and animal sacrifice, and so forth.

There are some elements of the Jewish Christian message which are not clearly found in John. Jesus *may* have brought these new beliefs to the movement—perhaps it was his pacifism, his rejection of oaths, or his rejection of "false texts." But the perennial difficult of scholars in coming to any agreement on the words of the "historical Jesus" may have a fairly straightforward explanation: it is difficult or impossible to separate Jesus' ideas from those of the movement which he led.

Conclusions

Jesus took up the vegetarianism, pacifism, and simple living of the movement which he led. Paul, James, and John may not have referenced the "sayings of Jesus" because such sayings were at that point not seen as authoritative, separate from the movement of which Jesus had been the leader. Jesus may have presented some unique ideas which gained acceptance through the force of his own personality and ideas. But the views which he *shared* with his movement were likely more crucial than any views which were distinct from it.

The very idea of Jesus as saying something different from what his own movement believed probably originated at the time of, and largely through, the gospel writers themselves. The gospel writers often refer to sayings of Jesus which the disciples did not understand, or represent the disciples as misunderstanding basic teachings (see chapter 12). That is, they put forward the idea of a Jesus who was *independent* of his own tradition—who said and did things which his own first followers did not agree with or did not understand. Where did this idea come from? It first arose when later Christians found the tradition of these disciples, handed down through the Jerusalem church, to be disagreeable and sought to modify them.

Understanding Jewish Christianity is both more humble and more fundamental than determining the words of the historical Jesus. It is more humble because determining the exact words of Jesus is completely beyond our scope. But it is more fundamental, because it establishes the basic context within which we must evaluate the historical Jesus. And if we do not understand the basic context, how can we hope to understand the exact words?

11. Pentecost

Jesus' earthly ministry came to a sudden close after a confrontation in the temple in Jerusalem. After disrupting the temple business of sacrificing animals during the Passover season, he was quickly arrested and executed by crucifixion on the Roman governor Pilate's orders. But then his followers became convinced that he had been resurrected by God, and his ministry continued to spread. How did Jewish Christianity view these events? And what does their viewpoint contribute to our knowledge of early Christianity?

Resurrection

The Ebionites believed that Jesus had risen from the dead. We don't know precisely how the Ebionites saw this event. The *Recognitions* and *Homilies* aren't clear, and Epiphanius complains: "For a while now, however, various of [the Ebionites] have been giving conflicting accounts of Christ" (*Panarion* 30.3.1).

There is a brief mention of Jesus' resurrection at *Recognitions* 1.42. They felt that the true prophet had repeatedly appeared in history (*Recognitions* 1.33, 1.34, 1.52, 2.22, 2.48, 8.59–62; *Homilies* 3.20). If you count these appearances as *physical* appearances of Jesus (cf. *Panarion* 30.3.5), the Ebionites didn't think of resurrection as something new for Jesus. If these appearances were "rebirths," they would have a reincarnation theory of bodily resurrection.

They also believed in a final *spiritual* resurrection:

> God is seen by the mind, not by the body; by the spirit, not by the flesh. Whence also angels, who are spirits, see God; and therefore men, as long as they are men, cannot see Him. But after the resurrection of the dead, when they shall have been made like the angels,

they shall be able to see God. (*Recognitions* 3.30; compare *Homilies* 17.16)

Recognitions 1.52 seems to express a contrary view, that the righteous will recover their own bodies before entering paradise, or in the case of the very righteous (such as Enoch, Genesis 5:24) God will directly "translate" them bodily into the kingdom. Which view did the Ebionites hold—physical resurrection, or spiritual resurrection?

The Ebionites might have reconciled the two views, arguing that our resurrected bodies will be "spiritual bodies" rather than bodies of flesh and blood, as Paul in fact does (I Corinthians 15:44). In this case, "bodily" resurrection does not imply "physical" resurrection. Or, this passage might be the insertion of an orthodox editor. Or perhaps this was one issue which the Ebionites, whose ideas sometimes had critical ambiguities, hadn't fully worked out (see chapter 21). Most likely, their original view in the first century was in a *spiritual* resurrection, because this made the most sense out of Jesus' appearance to them.

Pentecost

What propelled the movement forward after Jesus' death? Most likely it was not an Easter experience, but a *Pentecost* experience.

In the gospels and in Acts, Jesus rises from the dead, appears to his disciples, and ascends into heaven. As the disciples gather in the upper room at Pentecost to pray, there was a miraculous event: tongues of fire appeared to rest on each of the participants in the upper room experience, and people began speaking in different languages. In Acts, it was the *Pentecost* event which impelled the disciples to take the message out to the world, not Easter. By understanding why Pentecost was pivotal, we can gain a better understanding of how the disciples understood the resurrection.

Pentecost is clearly a historical problem for the standard accounts of Easter. If the disciples truly thought that Jesus had risen from the dead, why did they not immediately go out and begin preaching? Any self-respecting disciple who had *witnessed* their master rising from the dead and ascending into heaven would surely not need much urging to go forth and witness. In fact, in Mark (contradicting Acts), this is *exactly* what the disciples do. It takes just one verse after Jesus ascends into heaven before "they went forth and preached everywhere" (16:20).

Why did Pentecost need to happen first? Acts sees that this is a problem, and explains this paradox away with the excuse that they had a specific command from the risen Jesus (Acts 1:4–5). But the necessary answer is that Pentecost was persuasive in a way that Easter was not.

In the New Testament, many of the resurrection experiences were visions, rather than experiences of a physical Jesus. Paul gives the earliest testimony we have of the resurrection (I Corinthians 15:5–8). He puts his own vision of Jesus, well after the Pentecost, as roughly equivalent with the disciples' experiences: "at last he appeared even to me." Paul never claims to have seen the physical body of Jesus, and implies that the risen Jesus is not physical: "flesh and blood cannot inherit the kingdom of God, nor does the perishable inherit the imperishable" (I Corinthians 15:50).

Even in the gospels a number of resurrection experiences are rather ephemeral. There are visions of angels (Mark 16:5–8, Luke 24:4–9, John 20:12); Jesus is not recognized by the disciples, and the instant he is finally recognized, he vanishes (Luke 24:13–31); Jesus is recognized by Mary, but warns her "not to hold me" (John 20:17).

Contrast this to Jesus' eating fish to demonstrate he was a physical body (Luke 24:42–43), or his invitation to "doubting Thomas" to examine the nail holes and the wound in his side from his crucifixion (John 20:24–29). These latter stories specifically describe *physical* appearances, and set the standard for Christian dogma; Jesus appeared physically after his resurrection. But they were almost certainly added much later.

Pentecost suggests that the disciples' own experience of Jesus was more like a vision. This doesn't mean that the disciples didn't believe in the resurrection of Jesus. On the contrary, to the disciples Pentecost *was* an experience of the risen Jesus. Historically, when Paul refers to Jesus appearing to more than five hundred at one time (I Corinthians 15:6), he is probably talking about Pentecost, even though Acts does not mention Jesus in its Pentecost description, just the "spirit" (Acts 2:17).

None of the resurrection appearances in the gospels feature an appearance to more than about a dozen people. An appearance to just a few people, or to just one, is not going to be nearly as convincing as an appearance to five hundred. Different disciples likely had different experiences at different times; not everyone had such experiences at all, and the disciples were understandably perplexed by this. Mary Magdalene appears in the gospels as the first believer in Jesus' presence, and the other disciples are initially skeptical. Pentecost was more convincing than the earlier appearances of Jesus to various disciples, which evidently failed to galvanize the movement into action.

However, the Pentecost experience, while witnessed by a large number of people, was not specific enough to be considered a "physical" experience. The believers are convinced that the spirit of Christ has touched them, but not that Jesus has appeared bodily. Later gospel writers, seeking to validate the resurrection experiences, turned these stories into tales of Jesus as a *physical* presence, eating fish and inviting "doubting Thomas" to examine his hands and his side.

Regardless of what happened to Mary Magdalene or other disciples, Pentecost was the decisive event in the life of the new community without Jesus. Mary by herself, even Mary with James and Peter by themselves, could not propel the community forward. "Easter" itself was insufficient, and did not convince the church to move forward. Pentecost did.

Practical Issues Posed by Pentecost

The accounts of Pentecost posed a practical doctrinal problem relating to whether Jesus' appearances were physical. Allowing a mere vision of Jesus to convey his message is much too broad. It would allow anyone to take over the movement on Jesus' authority, claiming a vision of Jesus. Since Jesus could appear anywhere at any time, how would we know who was speaking the truth?

In fact, this was *exactly* the concern which Jewish Christianity had concerning Paul, who in their eyes had hijacked the movement under just this pretext. Paul was a follower of Jesus who had his own vision of Jesus and then proceeded to proclaim a message rather different from that of the early church leaders (Galatians 1:1). *Homilies* 17:13–19 stresses that a vision of the risen Jesus is not as persuasive or important as an acquaintance with the earthly Jesus—an attack which belittles Paul's experience of Jesus.

The gospels and Acts suggested the same general type of solution. They describe at least some of the resurrection appearances in the forty days after Easter as physical appearances, and in theory publicly verifiable, before Jesus ascended into heaven. This is very different from Paul's vision, from Pentecost, or from visions which you or I might have today. These accounts suggest that only his appearances during this forty day "window" conveyed any kind of authority.

In the telling of the tale, Pentecost fell outside this "window" of time. We don't know exactly why this happened, or why the period before Jesus' ascension wasn't fifty-five or sixty days. It may have been that there were too many witnesses to Pentecost and the experiences were not specific enough to be categorized as physical appearances of Jesus. At Pentecost Jesus either did not manifest himself physically (I Corinthians 15:6), or at all (Acts 2). So the decisive experience propelling the primitive church outward was, as the story was told, demoted in importance, while the gospel writers elaborated on the earlier stories at length.

The "Jesus Family Tomb" at Talpiot
What if we were to discover the tomb of Jesus? What would this do to Christian faith? Actually, we may have discovered this tomb, so this question takes on a fresh urgency.

In 1980, a tomb was discovered in Talpiot, near Jerusalem, during the construction of some new apartments. It contained 10 ossuaries, six of which were inscribed with names: Jesus son of Joseph, Jose, Matthew, Mary, Mariamne, and Judah son of Jesus. Shortly after the 1980 discovery, one of the ossuaries then went missing.

An ossuary is a bone box for the deceased, not a coffin. The practice of using ossuaries for burial in ancient Palestine stopped in the year 70 CE after the destruction of Jerusalem, so any ossuary found in an archeological excavation can be fairly precisely dated. We don't know why the practice of using ossuaries went out of style among Jews after the destruction of the temple, but they did. The "Jesus Family Tomb" was investigated further in 2005 by Simcha Jacobovici and his co-workers, and was the subject of a documentary and a book (Jacobovici and Pellegrino, 2007).

In 2002, another ossuary, marked "James, son of Joseph, brother of Jesus," was publicized in *Biblical Archeology Review*. This was probably not the "missing" ossuary from the "Jesus Family Tomb," as a photograph of the James ossuary predates 1980. The antiquities dealer who found the "James" ossuary was put on trial for forgery, though the case had heavy political overtones and he was ultimately acquitted.

There is evidence that this ossuary could have originally been from the same tomb, based on the patina from this ossuary and soil samples. Samples from the soil in the "Jesus tomb" and from the patina of the other ossuaries match each other as well as that on the James ossuary; they do not match that from other tombs in the region (Tabor and Jacobovici, 2012).

There was fragmentary DNA evidence from the Jesus ossuary which indicates that Jesus and Mariamne did not have the same mother—implying that Mariamne must have been included in the tomb because of marriage, not because of being related as a sister to Jesus.

Could this be the tomb of the historical Jesus? This is at least a strong possibility. A surprising cluster of these six names is found in the New Testament: Jesus son of Joseph, two Marys, and Jose, and Matthew. Matthew is a name known in the New Testament not only because Matthew was a disciple, but also is a name found in the biblical "genealogies" of Jesus in Matthew and Luke. "Judah son of Jesus" (another of the inscriptions) is not known in any early texts. The New Testament reports that "Joses" is one of the brothers of Jesus ("Yose" in Hebrew).

The possibility of modern fraud seems to be virtually non-existent. The Israeli Antiquities Authority was involved in the initial discovery of the tomb, and they actively discouraged the idea that this was the tomb of "the" Jesus, making fraud extremely remote. The James ossuary is more problematic, as fraud was alleged, but the evidence seems to support the authenticity of this inscription as well, and to locate the ossuary in the same tomb with Jesus and the others.

It is true that the names Jesus, Joseph, and Mary were very common, and occur on many other ossuaries. But the chance of such a *cluster* of such names occurring together randomly, especially taken in conjunction with Jose (a very rare nickname) and James, is quite remote.

Other objections are commonly made: any tomb of Jesus should have been in Nazareth, his hometown; there was no tradition of veneration by pilgrims; there is no inscription of "the Messiah" on the tomb. But these are mostly trivial and in any event trumped by the presence of physical evidence.

Implications of a Jesus Tomb

Assuming that this really is the tomb of Jesus—or that it is not, but there is a similar future discovery of the tomb of Jesus—what are the implications of this for our knowledge of Jesus and his first followers? By and large, the major implication is just to confirm what we already knew: there was a historical Jesus, there was a family of Jesus, and this family was the core of his early disciples.

There are a few sensational details, though. The most startling for modern sensibilities is that Jesus and Mariamne (who is possibly Mary Magdalene) may have been married and had a son, Judah, who was buried in the tomb as well. This shatters the traditional view of Jesus as celibate, elevates the status of Mariamne, and forces us to re-examine other references to Mariamne or Mary Magdalene in ancient gospels.

The most important implication for traditional Christian doctrine is the light it sheds on how the first followers of Jesus viewed the idea of the resurrection. Paul and the Ebionites had a view of a spiritual resurrection: Jesus still lives, but not in a physical body, rather as some sort of angelic presence. The later church viewed this as a heresy; there must have been a physical body. "Doubting Thomas" is invited to inspect the nail holes in Jesus' hands (John 20:27); Jesus says to the amazed disciples, "a spirit does not have flesh and bones as you see that I have" (Luke 24:40).

Now there is no *logical* reason why a physical tomb for Jesus could not co-exist with the idea of a physical resurrection. Even if we insist on a first-century resurrection of Jesus, Jesus could have acquired an entirely new body created from scratch, and it would be logically possible for Jesus (in his new body) to see his own former body laying dead on the ground.

However, this is not how the early church framed this issue. The empty tomb *signaled* the resurrection: "He has risen, he is not here; see the place where they laid him" (Mark 16:6 and parallels). The whole point of Pilate having the tomb guarded (Matthew 27:64) was so that the disciples would not steal the body away and claim that Jesus had risen from the dead. The presence of a dead body, that is, would have demonstrated that Jesus was not physically resurrected. Somehow, the idea arose that if Jesus *was* resurrected physically, then it would be using the material from his old body.

A tomb for Jesus, lovingly cared for by his family, supports the idea that *historically* the first followers of Jesus did not believe in or accept this idea of a physical resurrection, as expressed in the gospels. It is another link between the Ebionites and the first followers of Jesus.

The final implication is for the status of Matthew. To be buried in the Jesus family tomb, Matthew would presumably be a relative of Jesus as well. The Ebionites used the gospel of Matthew only (Irenaeus, *Against Heresies* 1.26.2). Is the Matthew in the tomb the author of the original gospel of Matthew before various editors set upon it? If this is so, it would tie the Ebionites to this gospel in a more dramatic way. It certainly gives a boost to anything we can find in Matthew that we can't find elsewhere in the gospels, indicating that information in this gospel may have a special connection to the early Jewish Christians.

Conclusions

The Talpiot tomb, if it turns out to be truly the tomb of Jesus, is a sensational find, no doubt about it. However, even if the claims regarding Talpiot are true, it doesn't add quite as much to our knowledge of early Christianity as we might initially suspect.

Whatever its form, and however Jesus appeared to his followers, Pentecost is what propelled the movement around Jesus forward. Pentecost gave the movement an identity *separate* from the followers of John the Baptist. While the impetus came from Pentecost, those who carried this movement forward were those said to be buried in the Talpiot tomb: the family of Jesus.

Part IV: The Apostolic Age

12. The Family of Jesus

In the aftermath of Jesus' death, Jesus' own family formed the core of the church. We know about Jesus' family both through the New Testament and through writings of the early church fathers about them.

Of all Jesus' relatives, ancient writers give James, the brother of Jesus, the most attention. James was the leader of the early church and the target of an assassination plot on the part of Saul (Paul before his conversion). The history of this plot has an interesting parallel in the story of Stephen, who in Acts is the first Christian martyr after Jesus. Later, James is the key protagonist in the controversy in the church between Paul and the other apostles (see chapters 13–17). But besides James, other relatives get attention as well.

Paradoxically, the New Testament is often *hostile* to Jesus' family. This hostility was likely motivated by the fact that Jesus' relatives were allied with the heretical Ebionites. Finally, there is one set of early relatives who get almost no attention from anyone in the ancient world, Jesus' wife and children—if they existed.

Hostility Towards the Family of Jesus

The New Testament often expresses hostility towards the family of Jesus. This hostility takes several forms: (1) the saying that a prophet is not without honor except among his own, (2) the hostility of John's gospel towards "the Jews," (3) related sayings and stories directed against the disciples and those closest to Jesus, and (4) the doctrine of the virgin birth.

The gospel of Mark states that Jesus spoke of himself as a "prophet without honor" among his own: "A prophet is not without honor, except in his own country, and among his own kin, and in his own house" (Mark 6:4). The other synoptic gospels report slight variations in this saying (Matthew 13:57, Luke 4:24), but all of the sayings implicitly or explicitly say that his own relatives rejected him. In its original historical form, the saying may not have been directed against Jesus' relatives at all, but against those Jews who rejected him. But the *use* to which the saying has been put and the modifications to it, clearly demonstrate hostility towards Jesus' family.

The gospel of John shows similar hostility. "He came to his own home, and his own people received him not" (John 1:11), evidently refers to rejection by his family. John 7:5 says that "even his brothers did not believe in him." John's gospel appears to lump the family of Jesus in with the rest of "the Jews" who are unbelievers. This is part of a general theme pursued in the gospels—especially Mark and Luke—that Jesus was rejected by those closest to him and that his disciples were unable to understand him (Mark 7:17–19, 8:21, 8:31–33, 9:31–32, 10:13–16, and Luke 9:43–46, 22:24).

Another way in which the family of Jesus was attacked was through the doctrine of the virgin birth—something Jewish Christians generally denied, but gentile Christians generally accepted. The Ebionites took the common sense position that Jesus was the son of Joseph and Mary (*Panarion* 30.20.5)—as Matthew and Luke also imply through their genealogies, and as even Paul seems to accept (Romans 1:3).

We might initially guess that the motive behind the notion of the virgin birth would have been Christological. The motive would be to support a particular idea of Jesus and his relationship to God, specifically that Jesus was God, or was at least miraculously and supernaturally exalted even before his birth. But consideration of the strength of Ebionite support among the family of Jesus yields another possible motivation, that of denigrating the Ebionite claims to the family of Jesus.

The doctrine of the virgin birth tremendously lessens the importance of Jesus' relatives. This decrease is much greater still in a patriarchal culture, because it is being related to the patriarch (the father) that counts in a patriarchal culture, not being in the same nuclear family. Since there is no human patriarch in the case of the virgin birth, that means that the claim of anyone to be biologically related to Jesus is greatly deflated. If we say (in accordance with Catholic doctrine) that his mother was not only a virgin, but remained a virgin her whole life and gave birth to only one child, Jesus, then James the brother of Jesus would not be biologically related to Jesus at all.

Jewish Christianity likely saw the fact that Jesus' own relatives were among their number as significant evidence of the truth of their own views, as they kept elaborate genealogies (Eusebius, *Ecclesiastical History* 1.7.14). The gospel-writers' polemic against Jesus' relatives is further, though indirect, confirmation of this claim—the opponents of the Ebionites knew that Jesus' relatives really *were* Ebionites.

The family of Jesus had a powerful organizational hold in primitive Christianity and was the core of later Ebionite Christianity. No one in ancient times challenges the Jewish Christian claim that relatives of Jesus are among their number, and even in their leadership. Instead, we see an attempt to denigrate the family of Jesus, a tacit admission of this fact.

Jesus' Wife and Children

In such books as *Holy Blood, Holy Grail* and the fictional work *The Da Vinci Code*, we have sensationalistic ideas about the family of Jesus—most notably, that Jesus was married to Mary Magdalene, that she later went to France, and that there are descendants of Jesus alive today. Did Jesus marry and have children?

The Talpiot tomb, if we accept it as valid evidence about Jesus, would seem to indicate that the answer to these questions is "yes," but people are still sorting out the evidence with regard to whether this is really the Jesus family tomb. If we put aside the evidence from Talpiot, the arguments both for and against Jesus' marriage to Mary Magdalene (or someone else) seem evenly divided, circumstantial, and inconclusive.

In favor of his marriage is the following: there are gospels, both heretical and orthodox, which describe the close association of Mary with Jesus. In *Gospel of Thomas* 114 the disciples of Jesus are jealous of Mary's status. In the *Gospel of Mary*, Peter says that Jesus told Mary things which he didn't discuss with the other disciples. The *Gospel of Philip* says that Jesus frequently kissed Mary. Even in the canonical gospels Mary is the first witness of Jesus' resurrection. Normal Jewish males would have been expected to marry; there is no sexual ascetic ideal in orthodox Judaism. Peter was evidently married (Matthew

8:14), and Jesus' brother Judas had grandchildren (discussed in chapter 18 below). The wedding at Cana (John 2:1–12) might have been Jesus' own wedding. When Paul argues for the relative merits of celibacy, he conspicuously does not cite the example of Jesus himself, and in fact says "I have no command of the Lord" (I Corinthians 7:25).

Against his marriage is Jesus' commitment to spreading the message and his itinerant life. "Foxes have holes, and the birds of the air have nests, but the Son of Man has nowhere to lay his head" (Matthew 8:20). Marriage was often about property, and Jesus probably did not own property and probably gave it away for his cause if he did. In ancient times, heterosexual sex usually meant babies, and thus sexual relations for anyone aspiring to be responsible for their actions implied some sort of family life. Jesus as a young idealist would probably not have entered into a married family life unless he had been able to provide for his partner and their children. While this might be another expression of hostility to Jesus' family, there are also the gospel references to hating one's family (e. g., Luke 14:26); and church tradition has it, also, that Jesus was not married, and this tradition must have come from somewhere. Some non-orthodox Jewish groups of the time *did* have a sexual ascetic ideal, such as some of the Essenes, who did not marry; and Jesus did not seem to be bound by conventional expectations in other matters.

The weak point in the *Holy Blood, Holy Grail* and *Da Vinci Code* type of theories is not that Jesus could not have married Mary Magdalene or had children, but the idea that Mary and their children then flee to France. In the first place, why do they need to flee? There was persecution, true, but it was relatively mild in the early years of the church. James the brother of Jesus, Peter, and John all survived the first wave of persecution. The family of Jesus survived and continued to lead the churches in Palestine well past Mary's lifetime. Why would Mary have chosen to leave the rest of her relatives behind, since they would surely be the first line of defense for someone in Mary's situation?

Moreover, France is a completely illogical place to go. A long journey to a far distant and unknown land would have been perilous even for the most liberated, young, wealthy, and healthy woman of the first century. More practical would have been a shorter journey to, say, the other side of the Jordan—to the region of Pella—with other members of the church. There are countless legends from ancient times saying that a famous disciple or saint appeared in this or that place, often with the appropriate relics; the legend of Mary's appearance in France was likely a "pious fraud" produced by ancient people living in France.

It is the very strength of the involvement of Jesus' family in subsequent Jewish Christianity which is fatal to *Holy Blood, Holy Grail* and similar theories. If we are looking for descendants of Jesus and Mary Magdalene, or other modern relatives of Jesus, we are more likely to find them in present-day Syria, Jordan, or Iraq, than in Western Europe. Mary's departure for France is a convenient Euro-centric myth.

If the tomb found at Talpiot really is the Jesus family tomb, this would be good evidence that Jesus was married, and in fact to Mariamne, perhaps the woman known to later church tradition as Mary Magdalene, and that they had at least one child. If they had any other children (or if, though this seems doubtful, "Judah son of Jesus" had children), then it is possible that some descendants of Jesus are alive today. It would also be fairly decisive evidence that Mary never went to France—that she died somewhere in or near Jerusalem, sometime before the catastrophe of the year 70 CE, and was buried next to Jesus.

James the Brother of Jesus
After the death of Jesus, his brother James became the leader of the early church.

We have more solid information about James, the brother of Jesus, than about any other member of Jesus' family (besides Jesus himself); entire books have been written about James. The Ebionites had a reverence for James and believed that James was the first leader of the church after Jesus' death (*Recognitions* 1.72, 4.35). Most other early church traditions agree.

1. In Galatians 2:9 Paul mentions that "James and Cephas [Peter] and John, who were reputed to be pillars," extended to Paul "the right hand of fellowship." James is listed as a pillar, and is mentioned first.

2. In Acts 15:13 ff., James at the "apostolic council" speaks last and gives the "judgment," which mentions matters no one has previously discussed, and which is accepted by everyone. In Acts 21:18, Paul in his final visit to Jerusalem goes in to see James when "all the elders were present," indicating that James was the leader.

3. In *Gospel of Thomas* 12, the disciples ask who will be great after Jesus leaves. Jesus replies, "wherever you have come, you will go to James the righteous, for whose sake heaven and earth came into being."

4. Eusebius in *Ecclesiastical History* 2.23.4 straightforwardly quotes Hegesippus as saying that James "succeeded to the government of the church in conjunction with the apostles."

The tradition making Peter the first leader is based on a single verse (Matthew 16:18) which is almost certainly a later convenient insertion. That James was the first leader of the church after Jesus has substantial significance for the history of Jewish Christianity.

1. This supports the Ebionite belief that James, not Peter, was the first leader of the church, and indicates that the Ebionites knew something that the rest of the church either didn't know or (more likely) wasn't willing to admit.

2. This would mean that James' successors (other Palestinians who were also relatives of Jesus) would later be the true leaders of the church, not Peter's successors. In fact, the whole story about Peter's coming to Rome and founding a church there may be a convenient myth. This likely explains why the rest of the church couldn't countenance James as the first leader of the church.

3. James has a character which is very close to the Ebionite ideal, abstaining from meat and wine, and living a simple and righteous life. Eusebius quotes Hegesippus as saying that James was "holy from his mother's womb; and he drank no wine nor strong drink, nor did he eat flesh" *(Ecclesiastical History* 2.23.5–6). This not only makes James a lifelong vegetarian, it also means that he was *raised* as a vegetarian—and thus his lifestyle sprang from a commitment by his entire family. Why would Jesus' family have raised James as a vegetarian, but not Jesus?

The explanation that James was the exception in his family, perhaps dedicated as a "Nazirite," is just another attempt to isolate the church leaders (Jesus and James) from the movement and the family of which they were an integral part. We have to smile at the idea that Mary and Joseph ate meat themselves and gave meat to Jesus to eat, but made sure that James never got any. The natural and obvious explanation, both today and in ancient times, is that anyone *raised* vegetarian lives in a vegetarian family.

Other church traditions support Hegesippus' story; even the cranky nonvegetarian Epiphanius concurs about James' vegetarianism (*Panarion* 78.14.2). Eusebius expands this description of James to paint Jesus and the apostles with the same colors: Jesus rejects animal sacrifice, and all the apostles abstained from wine and meat (*Proof of the Gospel* 3.3, 3.5). Paul's statement, "it is right not to eat meat or drink wine or do anything that makes your brother stumble" (Romans 14:21), seems to be aimed at James, or very important people like him in the early church whom Paul sought to placate and who abstained from meat and wine.

The early Jewish Christians celebrated communion with water instead of wine (Irenaeus, *Against Heresies* 5.1.3), and it is easy to see why; a bread and wine communion would have excluded James, the leader of the church. There were many competitors to the standard bread-and-wine celebration; Andrew McGowan (*Ascetic Eucharists*) examined these alternative versions, and found the bread and water alternative to be especially widespread, and not derivative from the bread and wine Eucharist. According to McGowan, the choice of bread and water was a deliberate rejection of the Greek and Roman sacrificial systems in which meat and wine played a prominent part (McGowan, chapters 4 and 5).

James was not the only relative of Jesus destined to hold authority in the early church. We also have information on Simeon, the successor of James and a cousin (or half-brother) of Jesus, and two grandsons of Judas, another brother of Jesus, whom we will discuss later (see chapter 18, "The Destruction of the Temple").

Julius Africanus locates the relatives of Jesus in Nazareth and Cochaba (quoted in *Ecclesiastical History* 1.7.14). But curiously enough, Epiphanius locates two Jewish Christian groups (the Nazoraeans and the Ebionites) in Cochaba (*Panarion* 29.7.7, 30.2.7–8)—so the relatives of Jesus and the heretical Jewish Christians lived in the same town. It is likely that this is not a coincidence; the relatives of Jesus were heretics.

The Second Incident in the Temple

Recognitions 1 describes a second incident in the temple, after Jesus' confrontation which immediately preceded his death. This time it involved James, the brother of Jesus. This took place seven years after Jesus' death: "a week of years was completed from the passion of the Lord" (*Recognitions* 1.43). Like the first incident which precipitates Jesus' arrest and crucifixion, there is an angry and very physical confrontation. Unlike the first incident, though, there is no overt attempt by James to disrupt the temple business; the Romans are not involved, and those taking action against the Christians are some thugs evidently commissioned by the high priest. And unlike the first incident, the authorities' target (James) survives.

The high priest, evidently unimpressed by Jesus' rising from the dead, had not forgotten the Jesus movement, and considered them seven years later still to be deadly enemies. Now, the followers of Jesus were preaching in the temple to a large crowd, with Peter and James leading the way. Peter's speech had defined the issues as the Ebionites saw them; because of God's displeasure with animal sacrifices, the temple was to be destroyed (*Recognitions* 1.64). Peter's speech creates a tumult, but the meeting is adjourned.

The next day James begins preaching again, and urges (through seven successive days!) that everyone should be baptized. James is on the point of converting everyone to the cause, when he is interrupted by "one of our enemies," who strides into the meeting, starts pushing and shoving, and urges people to kill them all, and sets the example by striking people with a burning brand from the altar. He throws James down from the top of the steps, leaving him for dead. James is seriously injured but does not die, and is carried from the scene by his friends.

This enemy is not explicitly named, but must be Saul (Paul before his conversion). A marginal note in one of the early manuscripts says "Saul," and *Recognitions* 1.71 adds that this enemy was armed with letters from the high priest to arrest all those "who believed in Jesus," and was heading off to Damascus in pursuit of Peter to "wreak havoc" among the faithful in Damascus. This description certainly sounds like Saul, who according to Acts encountered the risen Jesus on the road to Damascus. This is the only time that Saul (Paul) appears in the *Recognitions* and *Homilies*.

Saul's motivations may have not been entirely religious. The Ebionites said that Saul was a convert to Judaism, and had fallen in love with the high priest's daughter (*Panarion* 30.16.8–9), and this may have motivated him to try to ingratiate himself with the high priest.

Saul's targets may have been much broader than the Jesus movement. There is a very revealing passage in *Recognitions* 1.70: as Saul strides into the temple with a few men to help him kill James and disrupt the proceedings, Saul asks in a loud voice, "Why are ye led headlong by most miserable men, who are deceived by Simon, a magician?"

Saul assumes that Simon Magus and the Jesus movement are in the same camp! This out-of-place statement lends some authenticity to this whole story, which is not reported anywhere else in early Christianity, but which does have a significant analogue in the story of Stephen in Acts (about which more in a moment).

Saul has Simon Magus confused with Jesus because both Simon Magus and Jesus are followers of John the Baptist. He naturally assumes that this is all one movement. It also lends support to the idea that John the Baptist, like Jesus, had not been friendly with the priests—all the followers of John the Baptist are on the priests' "black list," adding credibility to the idea that John was just as hostile to the temple as Jesus.

Stephen in Acts

This second of three serious incidents in the temple (the final one, in the year 62, results in the death of James) is not reported anywhere else in early Christianity. There is, however, a significant parallel in Acts: the stoning of Stephen, the first Christian martyr after Jesus. In fact, the parallels are so close that this may be two descriptions of the same event, leaving unresolved the questions as to whether it was Stephen, James, or both who were involved in this event.

In Acts, Stephen gives an incendiary speech condemning animal sacrifice, just as Peter did in *Recognitions* 1. It is the most inflammatory speech in the entire New Testament on the subject, so it is actually just slightly surprising that it has survived the editor's pens. Partially that is because his statements about animal sacrifice are split up by some lengthy parenthetical remarks. A modern reader could read Stephen's whole speech and completely miss the implications.

In Acts, Stephen is accused of altering the law on animal sacrifice:

> This man never ceases to speak words against this holy place [the temple] and the law; for we have heard him say that this Jesus of Nazareth [actually "the Nazoraean"] will destroy this place, and will change the customs [the commands to offer sacrifices] which Moses delivered to us. (Acts 6:13–14).

In reply, Stephen essentially confirms this charge. He first gives a long description of the history of the Jewish world from Abraham down to Moses and Solomon, just as Peter does (in private) at *Recognitions* 1.32–38. Stephen then comes to the point where animal sacrifice enters the picture:

> Our fathers refused to obey him [Moses], but thrust him aside . . . And they made a calf in those days, and offered a sacrifice to the idol and rejoiced in the works of their hands. (Acts 7:39, 41)

Stephen then ties the worship of the golden calf (and accompanying animal sacrifices) to the prophetic utterances against animal sacrifice—he quotes Amos 5:25–27 (from the Septuagint). Stephen then points out it was not until Solomon that a temple was built, which Stephen condemns by saying "the Most High does not dwell in houses made with hands" and quoting Isaiah 66:1–2 in support. Stephen follows this up by saying "as your fathers did, so do you" (Acts 7:51), suggesting that his hearers were just as idolatrous as those who made the golden calf.

There is also a definite hint of the theory of false texts, since Stephen implies that no commands regarding animal sacrifice were actually given. And in both cases, Saul is involved: "And Saul was consenting to [Stephen's] death" (Acts 8:1).

The fact that these accounts are so strongly parallel indicates that there is likely a historical core here; only the personnel involved (James, Stephen) and the outcome (survives, dies) have been slightly altered. In Acts, Stephen is stoned to death by a mob enraged by his denunciation of the temple; in the *Recognitions*, James is badly injured, but is carried away and survives. It's also possible that James and Stephen were both attacked, but only Stephen died. But either way, there was present in apostolic Christianity the most vehement rejection of animal sacrifice possible for a first-century Jew: that it is idolatrous and demon-inspired.

Jewish Christianity survived this attack by Saul, but sometime later Saul converted to Christianity and became Paul. But the new relationship the Nazoraeans had with Paul turned out to be more problematic than anyone thought. A few decades later they had another, almost as traumatic encounter with Paul, which permanently split the church into irreconcilable factions.

13. Paul and the Table of Demons

Paul is a critical figure in the history of Jewish Christianity. In the Ebionite account, we first met Paul seven years after the death of Jesus—before his conversion, still known as "Saul." He tried to ingratiate himself with the high priest by persecuting the followers of John the Baptist. Saul thinks they are followers of Simon Magus—another follower of John the Baptist, but one who, as we shall see later, was actually opposed to the Jesus movement.

But when we meet Paul in his letters, seventeen years have passed (Galatians 1:18, 2:1). So if Jesus died (say) in the year 30, then Saul's attack on James (and Saul's conversion shortly thereafter) would be in 37 ("a week of years" later, *Recognitions* 1.43), and this would put Galatians at the year 54. While we only have fragmentary knowledge of many aspects of Jewish Christianity, we are in luck in one respect. We have *incredibly* detailed information about the early history of Jewish Christianity around the middle of the first century, through the letters of Paul. Paul's direct, eyewitness, first-person accounts of Jewish Christians are unique and invaluable.

By general scholarly consensus, there are seven authentic letters of Paul in the New Testament: Romans, I and II Corinthians, Galatians, Philippians, I Thessalonians, and Philemon. The so-called pastoral epistles (I and II Timothy and Titus) are pious frauds from the second century which have no relationship to Paul. The remaining letters (Ephesians, Colossians, and II Thessalonians) probably were written by some of Paul's followers, and reflect Paul's ideas, but are not from his hand either.

Since we are primarily interested in the historical information from Paul, not his ideas or theology, we will focus on the seven authentic letters attributed to Paul and the information they give about Paul's opponents—specifically, the Jewish Christians.

Paul's Opponents

In his letters, Paul indicates that he has opponents *within* the Christian movement and attempts to answer them. But who are these opponents? Upon reading Paul's letters, it becomes clear that they are in fact Jewish Christians, and this is important information—from a very early source indeed—about Jewish Christianity.

There are five passages which (I will argue) clearly relate to Jewish Christianity:

1. Galatians 1–2: this is an account of Paul's interactions with the Jerusalem church. It is an angry and pointed attack on the leadership of the early church. It is clear that his opponents are Jewish Christian both from his rhetoric and from the fact that he names them. They are the "pillars" of the church, namely James, Peter, and John. The issue which provokes this division is a food issue, the character of which is not clearly defined.
2. Romans 14: this is an attack not on vegetarianism, but on the idea that vegetarianism should be *required*. "The weak man eats only vegetables," says Paul. But Paul also advises the strong (those who understand that we can eat anything), "never to put a stumbling block or hindrance in the way of a brother" (14:13) and "we who are strong should bear with the failings of the weak" (15:1). He does not want to cause conflict: "Everything is indeed clean, but it is wrong for any one to make others fall by what he eats; it is right not to eat meat or drink wine or do anything that makes your brother stumble" (Romans 14:20–21).
3. In I Corinthians 8–10, he addresses concerns about eating meat offered to pagan idols, with some concern to meat consumption in general. Much of the language and the conclusions are shared with Romans 14. Paul advises his readers to "eat anything sold in the meat-market without raising any question on the ground of conscience" (10:25). But care should be taken not to offend the weak consciousness of fellow Christians who do not grasp this point.
4. In II Corinthians 10-13 Paul contends against enemies who are preaching "another Jesus" different from the one Paul preaches (II Corinthians 11:4). He attacks "false apostles" disguising themselves as "apostles of Christ" but who are actually servants

of Satan, disguising themselves as "servants of righteousness" (11:13-15).

5.   Philippians 1:15–17, and 3:2–7, avers that some preach Christ out of love, but others preach Christ out of partisanship .

These five items seem to summarize Paul's complaints about the Jewish Christian leadership of the church. There is also an interesting reference in one non-authentic letter, Colossians 2:16, "let no one pass judgment on you in questions of food and drink or with regard to a festival or a new moon or a sabbath." This seems to be a reinforcement of Romans 14:3, "let not him who eats [meat] despise him who abstains, and let not him who abstains pass judgment on him who eats." Since Colossians was probably not written by Paul, but by some of his followers, we will pass it by, though it does tend to show that "food and drink" was a hot topic in early Christianity—someone evidently *was* taking people to task about food and drink.

Paul's opponents in three of the five sections cited above can be quickly identified. In Galatians, II Corinthians, and Philippians, it is clear that the opponents are Jewish Christian. Galatians makes this clear from the identity of his opponents (James, Peter, John, the leaders of the church). II Corinthians also makes it clear that Jewish Christians are the opponents: "Are they Hebrews? So am I. Are they Israelites? So am I. Are they descendants of Abraham? So am I" (II Corinthians 11:22; see discussions in Tabor (2012), pp. 217-221, and Bütz, pp. 154-161).

Through the references to "circumcision" and "mutilating the flesh," Philippians makes it clear that the opponents are other Jewish Christians: "look out for the dogs, look out for the evil-workers, look out for those who mutilate the flesh. For we are the true circumcision . . ." (3:2–3). If Philippians really was written from his jail cell in Rome (suggested by 1:12–26), and thus after his final visit to Jerusalem, it might have reflected some of the bitterness that Paul still felt towards his Jewish Christian opponents, and indicate that even after this final visit critical issues were left unresolved.

Romans 14 and I Corinthians 8–10

That leaves us with Romans 14 and I Corinthians 8–10. These two sections are by far the most weighty of any of the discussions by Paul of his opponents and therefore the most interesting. But who are these opponents? Are they also Jewish Christian, or is it someone else?

First, it would appear that *whoever* the opponents are in these two sections, they are the *same* opponents, or at least are raising the *same* issues. The arguments are strongly parallel.

— We can eat any meat without being concerned about moral consequences (Romans 14:3, 14:6, 14:20, I Corinthians 10:25).
— God does not judge us on the basis of what we eat (Romans 14:3, I Corinthians 8:8).
— Whichever practice we follow and whatever we eat, we glorify God (Romans 14:6, I Corinthians 10:31).
— We should avoid offending our fellow Christians by not doing things offensive to them (Romans 14:20, I Corinthians 8:9, 10:24).
— If food is the cause of my brother's stumbling, I will never eat meat (Romans 14:21, I Corinthians 8:13).

Second, the opponents in I Corinthians raise the question of Paul's apostleship: "Am I not an apostle? Have I not seen Jesus our Lord? If to others I am not an apostle, at least I am to you," says Paul at 9:1–2. This exactly parallels the attack made on Paul by Paul's Jewish Christian opponents described in II Corinthians 11:5: "I think that I am not in the least inferior to these superlative apostles." It is also echoed by the later challenges which the Ebionites raised concerning Paul's apostleship. The people most likely to raise questions about Paul's legitimacy as an apostle would be the same group: Jewish Christians in the early church. After all, if Paul was in good standing with the Jewish Christian leadership, he could simply appeal to this leadership. But he doesn't—probably because, as is explicit in Galatians, he disagrees with the leadership on critical issues.

Third, who are the opponents in I Corinthians who are "offended" by meat offered to idols? Paul says, counseling diplomacy, "Give no offense to Jews or to Greeks or to the church of God" (I

Corinthians 10:32). This seems to narrow the identity of his opponents down to three groups: Jews, Greeks, and the church. Surely the Greeks wouldn't be offended, since at this time many Greeks offered pagan animal sacrifices all the time. It would be either the Jews or the church of God (at that time dominated by Jewish Christians); both of which imply that Paul sees the other Christians who might potentially be offended as being *Jewish* Christians. Thus, Paul is advising his friends in Corinth not to offend Jewish Christians—so his opponents in I Corinthians 8–10 are likely Jewish Christians.

Fourth, Paul's opponents in I Corinthians 8–10 and Romans 14 have a striking resemblance to the later Ebionites:

(a) They are vegetarian and object to animal sacrifice.

(b) They despise Paul, questioning his right to be called an apostle.

(c) They *linked vegetarianism and rejection of animal sacrifice.*

(d) They believed that vegetarianism should be required of all followers of Jesus.

If Jesus had eaten meat—and there were plenty of people still alive at this time who had known the earthly Jesus—it's hard to understand how this controversy could even have arisen. This controversy only makes sense if we postulate that it concerned whether a practice of Jesus and his religious movement (vegetarianism) was optional, or was required, analogous to similar later discussions as to whether celibacy was optional or required.

The Table of Demons Revisited

The most interesting characteristic of the opponents in I Corinthians 8–10 is the concern which they have regarding the table of demons. Paul's opponents in I Corinthians are raising objections relating to eating at the table of demons—just as the later Ebionites did. Moreover, concerns about the table of demons would explain not only why the opponents in I Corinthians were avoiding meat sacrificed to idols; it also could explain Peter's behavior of not eating with the gentiles, about which Paul is so upset in Galatians 2.

Paul raises the question of food offered to idols, acknowledging that there are disagreements among Christians on this issue. By working through Paul's defense, we can infer the position of Paul's Jewish Christian opponents, namely that eating meat offered to idols, or sold in the meat-market, is eating at the table of demons. Paul's argument is hard to follow for several reasons, mostly because Paul has several different arguments going on at the same time and because he distinguishes between idols and demons (a distinction lost on most modern readers).

Paul agrees that we should avoid idolatry: "Shun the worship of idols" (I Corinthians 10:14). But, an idol doesn't really represent anything. Paul agrees that one should not eat at the table of demons, and that pagans are in fact eating at the table of demons by eating meat sacrificed to idols. "What pagans sacrifice they offer to demons and not to God . . . You cannot partake of the table of the Lord and the table of demons" (I Corinthians 10:20, 21). But a Christian can eat the very same meat, because the Christian does not sacrifice to idols and does not acknowledge the idol. "Eat whatever is sold in the meat market without raising any question on the ground of conscience. For 'the earth is the Lord's, and everything in it'" (10: 25–26).

Paul distinguishes between *idols* and *demons*. There's a big difference: an idol is an object of stone, brass, etc., which is worshiped; any Christian, of ancient or modern times, can see and knows that an idol has no real power. On this point, Jewish Christianity agrees (*Recognitions* 4.20, *Homilies* 10.7). A demon, by contrast, is *real*. And when the pagans sacrifice their animals, they offer them up to *demons*. The pagan may *believe* that he is sacrificing to Zeus or to an idol, but he is actually sacrificing to the demons. That is what makes this idolatry downright dangerous; it is not merely a foolish superstitious gesture, it also gives power to the very real metaphysical forces of darkness.

God is ruler of heaven and earth, and the Christian knows this and acknowledges it. Why should what the pagan does as he sacrifices an animal or eats meat affect a Christian? Thus Paul asks, "Do we not have the right to our food and drink?" (I Corinthians 9:4). Paul's opponents acknowledge the distinction between idols and demons, but take the common-sense position that eating meat sacrificed to demons, is eating at the table of demons.

If you think that demons are real, Paul's argument may sound a little dodgy. In fact, it sounded dodgy to a lot of early Christians, too, so that the so-called "apostolic council" decided that all things sacrificed to idols are forbidden to Christians (Acts 15:29). Everyone is agreed that we should shun idols and not eat at the table of demons. Paul, however, thinks that pagans and Christians could eat the *exact same meat* on the table. The pagan, offering the animal to Zeus or an idol, becomes partners with demons; the Christian, acknowledging that God is Lord of heaven and earth, does not.

The ultimate issue is one of complicity: to what extent are we "partners with demons" by associating with meat sacrificed to demons? We see three possible positions in the letters of Paul and in the Jewish Christian literature:

1. One is complicit based on what one *says, does, or believes*, as one eats (Paul's position in I Corinthians 8–10).
2. One is complicit based on *what one eats* (the stated criteria at *Homilies* 7.4, 7.8).
3. One is complicit based on *who one eats with* (Peter's behavior in the *Homilies*; Peter's behavior in Galatians).

The ambiguity in what "complicity" with demons really amounts to, might also account for Peter's change of heart in Galatians. There was evidently a shift in Peter's behavior: "before certain men came from James, he ate with the gentiles; but when they came he drew back and separated himself, fearing the circumcision party" (Galatians 2:12).

Paul also develops a second, more conciliatory argument. He admits that this is a contentious issue, that many sincere Christians disagree with him, and that he doesn't want to create division in the church. He says that he will never eat meat again, if it causes his "brother" (fellow Christian) to stumble (I Corinthians 8:13). If you are eating with an unbeliever, you can eat whatever they offer you; but if an overly-sensitive vegetarian Christian is present, it would be better to abstain (10:27–28).

Are the Kosher Regulations an Issue?

Many have assumed that Peter's behavior in Galatians is motivated by concern over the gentile observance of the kosher regulations, rather than a concern about demons. Actually, there is a germ of truth in this view, if we go back to the original meaning of "kosher," which is food that is proper. The problem is that what is "proper" for the first followers of Jesus was a *moral* issue, not a ritual issue. What was proper for these disciples is not necessarily what is proper for Jews today, or even Jews in the first century.

Peter in the *Homilies* doesn't think that meat is proper, so he does have "kosher" concerns in some sense. But if we interpret "kosher" concerns as a reference to the *specific* set of Jewish concerns we know today, i. e. not eating pork, not mixing meat and milk at the same meal, and so forth, then this is clearly not the concern of the historical Peter in Galatians.

1. There is no evidence that Paul is talking about kosher laws or any other Jewish beliefs in Galatians. There is no explicit reference of Paul to the kosher laws (as we understand them today) in *any* of his letters. The reference to what is "clean" in Romans 14:20 is followed by the elucidation at 14:21 that it is "meat and wine" which make foods unclean—evidence for a much more restrictive concept of what is kosher.
2. Modern kosher laws would be irrelevant in Romans 14. Peter's idea of what is kosher in the *Homilies* is much more restrictive than the modern Jewish concept of kosher; Peter's involves vegetarianism, the Jewish concept does not.
3. The kosher laws do not require separation from gentiles, even at the table. If the gentile is a guest in your home, you could presumably determine the menu and insure that the food is kosher.
4. Some have argued that kosher meat was not available in Rome and that these "vegetarians" were just Jewish legalists unsure about the source of their meat. But this same discussion about the table of demons was repeated in Corinth and Antioch. This argument distorts the plain meaning of the text in order to conform to the theological picture that Acts draws of legalistic Jewish Christians. Instead, we should regard Paul's words as evidence *against* Acts' views about legalistic Jewish Christians.
5. The leadership of the early church is evidently ready to reach an accommodation on the question of circumcision, another question of Jewish ritual, in Galatians 2:3. Yet they are less willing to reach an accommodation on the question of food, suggesting that something more fundamental is at stake.

What does this tell us about the history of Jewish Christianity in the first century? It tells us this.

1. Some of Paul's opponents were vegetarian, objected to animal sacrifice, and objected to Paul's apostleship (just like the Ebionites).
2. These same opponents also were concerned about demon possession based on what you ate or with whom you associated at the table (just like the Ebionites).

Therefore, the most likely explanation is that Paul faces *the same opponents* in Romans 14, I Corinthians 8–10, and Galatians 2: Jewish Christians, including the Jewish Christian leadership of the church (James, Peter, and John). Other more convoluted and tortuous explanations that would salvage Christian orthodoxy are certainly possible, but this is the simplest and most obvious.

Conclusions

The letters of Paul give us important information about Jewish Christianity. There was a group of Jewish Christians in apostolic times, including the leadership of the church, which had some of the same characteristics as later Ebionite Christianity. This early Jewish Christianity supported vegetarianism, supported the Jewish law (as they understood it), raised questions about Paul's apostleship, objected to animal sacrifice, and objected to sharing the same table with gentile unbelievers.

The disagreement about meat-eating and animal sacrifices continued for decades and centuries, but the Ebionites remembered the dispute in almost the same way that Paul did: as a dispute over the nature of demons and complicity with demons. Both Paul and the Jewish Christians agree that demons are real and that we should not eat at the table of demons.

These facts, taken in combination, add up to a strong argument that not only were there persons in the early church who objected to meat, things sacrificed to idols, and who questioned Paul's apostleship, but also that we know their identity: the Jewish Christian leadership of the early church.

14. Paul and the Poor

Paul attacked the Jewish Christian leadership, saying "I wish those who unsettle you would mutilate themselves!" (Galatians 5:12), and the Ebionites responded to Paul in similar terms, calling him "an apostate from the law" (Irenaeus, *Against Heresies* 1.26.2). These divisions are deep and bitter, and evidently lasted for centuries. In fact, the hostility is so deep that we have to ask, what did these people ever see in each other? How did they ever become part of the same movement?

Modern partisans for or against Paul sometimes get caught up in this debate and make criticisms of either Paul or his Jewish Christian opponents that are probably not historical, or at least not as important to the contemporaries of Paul and James as these partisans think. The Jewish Christians become legalists insisting that followers of Jesus be circumcised and convert to Judaism. Paul becomes a sexist, an apologist for slavery, a homophobe, and a reactionary.

There's an element of truth on both sides here, and there certainly were angry words exchanged between Peter and Paul. But this dispute was based on a broad consensus which existed between these opponents. In some ways, the agreements between Paul and the Ebionites are more interesting than their disagreements, because they show the milieu in which early Christianity developed. In fact, it is highly ironic that in several respects both Paul and Jewish Christianity had more in common with each other than either had with the later orthodox church. The later church rejected the Ebionites; but it also, paradoxically, rejected the historical Paul, renouncing his ideas and revising them *ex post facto* in the book of Acts at the same time that it embraced him as a saint.

This therefore is not a tale of good versus evil. It is neither about the "good" Paul who liberates us from Jewish Christian legalism, nor the "bad" Paul who sells out basic values of early Christianity to make his gospel more appealing to upper-class Romans. It really is a tragedy, because in the resulting chaos Christianity not only lost what they disagreed over, but most of what they agreed on as well.

In describing their agreements, though, we are on far more slippery ground in describing Jewish Christianity. Paul often notes disagreements with his opponents; but Paul does not always ascribe any viewpoint he *agrees* with specifically to Jewish Christians. How can we attribute *any* point of view which Paul defends in his letters to Jewish Christianity?

By and large, we can do that by looking at the ideas of the later Jewish Christian Ebionites, and then comparing these views with those found in Paul's letters. When we find a significant area of agreement, we can say that, prima facie, we have agreement between the *early* Jewish Christians and Paul as well. If Paul held such an idea, then *someone* in early Christianity held it; and if the later Ebionites also agreed with it, most likely this is because they are coming from a common shared point of view in early Christianity. This argument is not foolproof, but in general the existence of agreement between Paul and a later Ebionite position implies that the early Jewish Christians shared that point of view as well.

Sharing, Simplicity, Rejection of Wealth

As a rule, Paul does not explicitly identify Jewish Christian beliefs with which he agrees. But there is an important exception to this rule, and that is the belief in the importance of "remembering the poor." This occurs at Galatians 2:10—"only they [James, Peter, and John] would have us remember the poor, which very thing I was eager to do." Here Paul specifically attributes an idea to the Jewish Christian leadership of the church, that we should all "remember the poor."

Both Paul and Jewish Christianity emphasized the values of sharing, of simplicity of possessions and lifestyle, and rejection of wealth. Paul mentions on several occasions the collection he is taking up for the poor, probably in specific response to James' request at Galatians 2:10 (Romans 15:26, I Corinthians 16:1–4), advises us "be not conformed to this world," (Romans 12:2), tells us to live with the lowly (Romans 12:16), and discusses at length the virtues of giving and sharing (II Corinthians 8–9). We feel quite confident, therefore, that the early Jewish Christians shared Paul's general ideas that the poor (or at least the believing poor) should be helped, and that sharing of one's possessions with those more needy is something which God smiles upon. It is interesting that *Homilies* 7.4 makes the phrase "be of one mind in many bodies" part of the Golden Rule, echoing Paul's celebrated metaphor that Christians are "one body in Christ" (Romans 12:5, I Corinthians 12:12). According to the Ebionites, this title of "the poor" referred to the entire church, based on the primitive church's decision to own everything in common (*Panarion* 30.17.2, Acts 2:44–45, 4:32–35). The rejection of wealth and non-attachment to possessions is also found in abundance in the synoptic gospels. "Sell everything you have, and give it to the poor," Jesus advises the rich young man, and elsewhere he makes comments such as "blessed are the poor," and "how hard it is for the rich to enter the kingdom." There is widespread agreement among scholars that these sayings authentically represent the views of Jesus himself, and it appears that they were part of early Jewish Christianity as well.

Nonviolence

Neither Paul nor the Ebionites make a major theme out of nonviolence towards humans, but they both clearly acknowledge it. *Recognitions* 2.36 explicitly rejects war—"peace is the perfection of the law." When Saul (Paul before his conversion) attacks James and the others in the temple, *Recognitions* 1.71 remarks that they did not fight back, preferring to suffer evil rather than violently to resist evil.

The saying attributed to Jesus in the gospels, "pray for those who persecute you," is quoted almost exactly by Paul (Romans 12:14). Paul adds "repay no one evil for evil" (12:17), and advises his readers not to take vengeance because vengeance is the Lord's (12:19). This clearly establishes a common ground of agreement in the early church. Paul nowhere suggests that this is a bone of contention in the church, as he clearly does over the questions of vegetarianism and meat offered to idols.

We do not find Paul directly attributing these sentiments to Jewish Christians, but it is inescapable that both Paul and early Jewish Christianity accepted the principle of nonviolence.

Adoptionist Christology

The "status" of Jesus, theologically speaking, was probably not a major concern in apostolic times. Paul and early Jewish Christianity existed at the same time, and they have similar views of Jesus' status with respect to God.

Both Paul and early Jewish Christianity had a roughly "adoptionist" Christology. That is, they believed that Jesus was a human who *became* God's son (or the Christ), rather than being the Son of God (or the Christ) intrinsically, by his very nature. This expression "adoptionism" is itself somewhat pejorative, since it implies that to really be God's son one wouldn't be adopted, one would have been *born* God's son.

This "adoption" is described as coming through receiving the Holy Spirit at Jesus' baptism in the Ebionite gospel—which describes a heavenly voice saying "You are my son, this day I have begotten you." This passage suggests that from the time of his *baptism* on, but not before, Jesus had the spirit of God with him (*Panarion* 30.13.7). For Paul, Jesus was designated the Son of God at his *resurrection* (Romans 1:4) rather than at his baptism. But in both cases, Jesus was not a pre-existing supernatural being co-eternal with God, or anything even close. Jesus *became* the Son of God.

The *Recognitions* and *Homilies* exalt Jesus even further. They speak of Jesus as the true prophet or the "eternal Christ" (*Recognitions* 1.43). This true prophet or eternal Christ, though subordinate to God, is and was always present, even before his birth as Jesus, manifesting himself to those who seek out God. If we equate Jesus and Christ, then this is a substantially different idea than that Jesus became God's son as his baptism. It implies a more "Arian" point of view, in which Jesus was God's son at his birth, but is still subordinate to God.

Both Paul and the Ebionites sometimes speak of Christ as separate from Jesus. The Ebionites might reconcile their gospel, where Jesus becomes God's son at his baptism, with their doctrine of the true prophet by considering Christ as *entering* Jesus (see chapter 21, "Ebionite Theology in a Nutshell"). Paul's words in Philippians also suggest something like this; Christ took "the form of a servant" (Philippians 2:7), implying that Christ *entered* Jesus.

Paul and Jewish Christianity also agree on another small but related point: the denial of the virgin birth. In Paul, this occurs very briefly when Paul states that Jesus "was descended from David according to the flesh" (Romans 1:3). The most obvious explanation of Paul's comment is that he thought that Jesus was born of two human parents, and that the Jewish Christians held the same view. At this stage of Christian history, it is highly doubtful that the subject of the virgin birth was even being raised.

Spiritual Resurrection

There was a dispute in early Christianity about the nature of the resurrection, and Jesus' resurrection specifically. The orthodox said that after Jesus' resurrection he had a physical body of flesh and blood, and that this would also obtain for us at the end of time. Others maintained that Jesus *never* had a physical body, but he was a spirit who only seemed to appear physically on earth—the idea of the "docetic Christ." Still others took a middle position; Jesus had a physical body on earth, but that after his resurrection he became a spiritual being, as we would be when we were resurrected.

Interestingly, Paul and the Ebionites agreed with each other on the nature of the resurrection; they take the middle position, that Jesus existed physically on earth, but that the resurrection was spiritual in nature.

"How are the dead raised?" Paul asks (I Corinthians 15:35). Paul explicitly answers the question by declaring that the dead will be raised in spirit. "What is sown is perishable, what is raised is imperishable . . . I tell you this, brethren: flesh and blood cannot inherit the kingdom of God, nor does the perishable inherit the imperishable." (I Corinthians 15:42, 50)

Peter echoes this sentiment both in the *Recognitions* and the *Homilies*.

> For in the resurrection of the dead, when they have been changed, as far as their bodies are concerned, into light, and become like the angels, they shall be able to see Him [God]. (*Homilies* 17.16; compare *Recognitions* 3.30)

The gospels not only do not confirm this idea of a spiritual (rather than physical) resurrection, they in fact take pains to combat this perception. The resurrected Jesus declares that he is no mere ghost and eats fish to prove it (Luke 24:38–43); Jesus invites "doubting Thomas" to inspect Jesus' body, putting his hand in the nail holes and in his wounded side (John 20:27). So it is a matter of some interest to determine whether the *early* Jewish Christians, as well as the later Ebionites, shared this viewpoint of a spiritual resurrection for Jesus.

Does Paul testify that early Jewish Christians accepted his view of the resurrection? There does appear to be a controversy over the resurrection in I Corinthians, which Paul mentions at 15:12 and 15:35. However, this dispute does not seem to affect the Jewish Christians; in fact, it is explicitly implied that the Jewish Christians agree with him that there was a resurrection. Among the people to whom Jesus has appeared, he includes Peter, James, "the twelve," and "all the apostles" (I Corinthians 15:5-8). Paul attributes to Jewish Christians belief in the resurrection based on their own direct experience of it. He does not specifically attribute to Jewish Christians a belief in a *spiritual* resurrection, but it is the most natural assumption, because he mentions the appearance of Jesus to himself (which was a vision of some sort) in the same general way that he mentions the appearance of Jesus to Peter, James, and the others.

Paul's accounts of the resurrection are the earliest records we have of the resurrection. He does not mention the empty tomb or any tomb at all. The early Jewish Christians may have had vague or confused beliefs about the spiritual resurrection, but they likely agreed with Paul on this basic point. The original tradition was probably that of a spiritual resurrection, corresponding to the encounter with Jesus which both Paul and others had.

Subordinate Status of the "Written Code"

Allegiance to the law of Moses seems to be a point of significant disagreement between Paul and the Jewish Christians, but we are in for a surprise. The disagreement is not as great as we might think, and in fact conceals a significant agreement between Paul and the Ebionites, in which both of them not only agree with each other but also disagree with the later position of orthodox Christianity.

"We serve not under the old written code but in the new life of the spirit," says Paul (Romans 7:6). This has an almost Ebionite flavor to it. The Ebionites also condemned certain written texts, specifically the texts supporting war and animal sacrifice. The Ebionites, therefore, *also* did not serve under the "old written code" (the "Old Testament").

Paul and Jewish Christianity have two completely different ideas of what the law is, but there is a substantial area of agreement. For Paul, "the law" is the written text of the first five books of the Old Testament, or possibly the entire Old Testament. It really *is* a written code. It was given at the time of Moses; before Moses, there was no "law" (Galatians 3:17). For the Ebionites, however, "the law" is eternal, was present at the creation, can be read by all (*Homilies* 8.10), and is *not* the same as the text of the Old Testament. Once we get beyond the terminological confusion, we see that neither Paul nor Jewish Christianity followed the Old Testament text. The Ebionites did not do so because it was not the true law; Paul did not do so because it *had been* the true law, but was preceded by faith, and superseded by Christ. Paul does not have a theory of false texts, but the result is roughly the same.

Recognitions 1.32–34, in fact, seems to outdo even Paul's enthusiasm to subordinate the written code to Christ. The "true prophet" appears to Abraham and then to Moses. The true prophet not only trumps the written code (as in Paul, "the law was our custodian until Christ came," Galatians 3:24) but actually *precedes* it. *Recognitions* 1.54 suggests that Christ came to abolish the animal sacrifices, and *Homilies* 3.51 says that those things which Christ appeared to be destroying, did not belong to the true law, both of which echo Paul's statement "Christ is the end of the law" (Romans 10:4). In fact, the idea of an uncorrupted law—the original law "read by all" in *Homilies* 8.10—is also found in Paul, when he says that "the law of the spirit of life in Christ Jesus has set me free from the law of sin and death" (Romans 8:2).

There is a surprising correspondence between Paul and the Ebionites in thinking about the Jewish law. Both Paul and the Jewish Christians in the church were struggling with a common problem: the fact that the written code seems to contradict key parts of the Christian message.

The gospels sometimes seem to imply that Jesus and his disciples accepted the written code. Jesus himself says "not an iota, not a dot, will pass from the law" (Matthew 5:18). "Iotas" and "dots" are characteristics of a *written* law. The gospel writers most likely projected their ideas of late first century and second century Judaism into their accounts of early first-century Christianity. This idea of an early Jewish Christianity meticulously following the written code has numerous problems (as discussed in chapter 2). A simpler explanation is available: early first-century Christianity was not interested in following the written code at all.

The theory of false texts fits hand-in-glove with the rejection of animal sacrifices. Early Jewish Christians clearly rejected animal sacrifices, and there is no way that this can be squared with "the written code." When Paul makes his declaration, "we serve not under the old written code" (Romans 7:6), he does not sound as if it were a matter of debate which he needs to argue for. He speaks as if he is explaining a new theory based on some common ground which is already shared.

Baptism

Jewish Christianity clearly believed in the importance of baptism; Epiphanius says that they baptized daily. The *Recognitions* and *Homilies* indicate that baptism is helpful, if not essential, for salvation, and drives out the demons which have infested a world inured with violence. Most importantly for Jewish Christianity, baptism is a replacement for animal sacrifice.

Baptism is discussed in passing by Paul at Romans 6:3–4, I Corinthians 1:13–17, 10:2, 12:13, 15:29, and Galatians 3:27. Paul accepts baptism, and even names some people he has baptized. He complains in I Corinthians that he is more interested in preaching the gospel than baptizing.

From all this it seems that baptism was a central ritual of early Christianity. Though baptism's precise effect is left rather vague, it seems to be a ritual that confers some sort of benefits, and was quite important to at least some early Christians.

Conclusions

Early Jewish Christianity and Paul shared a number of common assumptions and beliefs, which make it plausible that they could have worked together for years before it became clear that there was a serious problem. These items are:

1. The value of simple living and sharing, rejection of wealth
2. Nonviolence towards other human beings
3. Adoptionist Christology
4. Belief in a spiritual resurrection
5. Rejection of the old written code
6. The importance of baptism

This is an important result. We have a strong prima facie argument, *even before looking at the gospels*, and even before considering the relative merits of the debate between Paul and Jewish Christianity, that this was part of the core of primitive Christianity and gives direct evidence of the teachings of Jesus.

15. Paul's Visits to Jerusalem

What exactly does the New Testament book, the Acts of the Apostles, add to our knowledge of Jewish Christianity?

Acts is the linchpin of both modern and ancient ideas of Jewish Christianity. Here the depiction of a "Jewish" faction in the early church comes out clearly, as well as an account of how Paul came in conflict with this faction. Acts offers a soothing framework (for modern Christian sensibilities, anyway) to answer the problem of how this dispute was handled. While it is clear that many of details provided by Acts are unreliable, the soothing overall picture remains and is dominant even to this day.

In fact, there are so many problems with Acts that one could well ask why we even bother reading it at all. But on analysis, Acts—stripped of its inconsistencies—provides important information about the disputes in the early church. Specifically, it offers a *chronology* of how the dispute unfolded as well as important evidence as to what its *resolution* was. In this chapter, we will focus on the chronology, and in the next chapter, the resolution.

The Chronology of Paul's Disputes with the Jerusalem Church

There is no obvious sequence to Paul's letters; we don't know exactly what order they were written in. What Acts offers is a chronological framework within which we can interpret Paul's letters, so that we can understand what contemporary events Paul is talking about, which isn't always obvious. Acts tells us that Paul visited Jerusalem four times after becoming a Christian. Acts describes an introductory visit by Paul, Paul's bringing the offering for the famine, Paul's visit to discuss the problem of gentile converts, and Paul's final visit. (Some argue that Acts 18:22 briefly refers to a visit by Paul to Jerusalem, which would be a fifth visit, but the Greek text does not refer to Jerusalem.)

150

Paul #1. Initial visit with Peter and James three years after his conversion (Galatians 1:18–20). Paul sees none of the other apostles.	Acts #1. Initial visit after Paul's conversion. Other apostles are initially afraid of him. (Acts 9:26–28).
Paul #2. Meeting with Peter, James, and John, 14 years later. Gentiles in the movement are discussed. No restrictions are placed on gentile converts. Paul is given a mission to the "uncircumcised" gentiles (Galatians 2:1–10).	Acts #2. Paul, accompanied by Barnabas, brings an offering to relieve the world-wide famine (Acts 11:27–30). This just follows Peter's vision and declaration that the movement must be open to gentiles (Acts 11:1–18).
Paul #3. Visit to Jerusalem to bring the offering for the world-wide famine. Only described before the fact as Paul's plans: Romans 15:25–27, I Corinthians 16:1–4, II Corinthians 8–9. After Jerusalem, Paul's next planned visit is to Spain.	Acts #3. Dispute over circumcision. Apostolic council to resolve the problems, presided over by James, with Paul, Peter, and Barnabas present. The resultant "apostolic decree" makes only four demands on gentiles, and circumcision is not one of them. (Acts 15).
	Acts #4. Paul visits Jerusalem a fourth time. Offers to go to the temple to placate Jewish Christians, but is arrested first (Acts 21:15–36). Paul later states (at Acts 24:17) that he brought the offering for the world-wide famine at this time, just like his second visit.

Table 15–1. Paul's visits to Jerusalem in his letters and in Acts.

But here is where it starts getting complex. While Acts describes *four* visits by Paul to Jerusalem, Paul only describes *three*. These trips are described in Table 15–1. Paul describes two of these visits in Galatians 1–2. He describes a third visit only in advance, as a trip he *intends* to take, in Romans and I and II Corinthians.

This third trip (Paul #3) almost certainly follows the trips described in Galatians. Paul's letters describe this upcoming visit as a famine visit; he intends to bring a collection for relief from the world-wide famine to Jerusalem. He talks as if this is his last visit to Jerusalem for a while; he mentions in Romans that after this visit, he will go to Rome and then to Spain. He talks with assurance about issues relating to his mission to the gentiles, a mission which James and Peter gave him during Paul #2. Paul #2 (Galatians 2:1-10) cannot be this famine relief visit, because Paul makes no mention in Galatians of the offering that he has brought—in fact, he even notes that James asked him to "remember the poor," which would have made no sense if Paul had *just* brought a collection for the poor.

On the face of it, the fact that Paul describes three trips and Acts describes four does not seem an insoluble or even terribly difficult problem. Perhaps Acts is making one of the visits up, or has described one of Paul's visits twice; or perhaps Paul forgot to write about one of his visits. We should be able to "compare and contrast" the different accounts and determine any discrepancies and the overall chronology of the dispute.

This is easier said than done. The accounts in Acts and Paul's letters are *so* different, in subtle ways, that it's not clear when (or if) Paul and Acts are even discussing the same events. We can't possibly consider in detail all the competing theories about integrating Paul's letters with the narrative of Acts. We will simply present and briefly defend an overall chronology which seems to make the most sense of Paul's letters in light of the later history of Jewish Christianity. If it seems confusing, it isn't your imagination: a lot of very smart and well-informed scholars have been unable to reach an understanding. The root cause of this confusion is the book of Acts itself.

Acts' Presentation of the Disputes in the Church

There are three key events in the dispute between Paul and the Jerusalem church we'd like to know more about:

1. Paul receives a mission to take the gospel to the gentiles, which is described in Galatians 2:1–10. Acts describes a mission to the gentiles as well, but it is started by *Peter* and Paul is not involved until much later.

2. The apostolic council (Acts 15) sets minimum demands on gentiles. This seemingly resolved disputes over the role of gentiles in the church, specifically whether male gentiles needed to be circumcised before they could be part of the movement. According to this "apostolic decree" (Acts 15:20, 15:29, 21:25), gentile converts need *only* adhere to the "Jewish law" on four points: abstaining from blood, from "what is strangled," from "what has been sacrificed to idols," and from unchastity. Circumcision and Sabbath observance are conspicuously absent among these points.

3. There is a major dispute between Peter and Paul at Antioch. Galatians 2:11–14 relates Paul's first-hand account, and Acts 14:26–15:2 describes this from another perspective.

Where in Paul's letters and in Acts are these events described? And *when* did these events occur?

This is critically important, because a key aim of Acts is to demonstrate that the dispute at Antioch was later settled by the "apostolic council." But Paul seemingly never describes the apostolic council in his letters, and actually attacks one of the key provisions of the apostolic decree, to abstain from food offered to idols (I Corinthians 8-10). Moreover, Acts doesn't even have Peter present in the incident at Antioch. All of this indicates that Acts is covering up the messy details of the angry disputes in the early church.

The Bias of Acts

Many scholars have pointed out that Acts is biased and inaccurate. Acts was likely written *at least* 50 years after the letters of Paul, and there are numerous discrepancies between Paul's letters and Acts. This bias has to be constantly kept in mind in evaluating the different accounts. If there is any contradiction between Paul's letters and the account in Acts, we really have only one choice: to prefer Paul's letters, written by a contemporary and an eye-witness to events, as the more accurate version.

In Galatians, Paul acts with aggressive independence from the church leadership: he is an apostle *"not from men nor through man,* but through Jesus Christ and God the Father" (Galatians 1:1, italics added). Paul is given the mission to the gentiles (Galatians 2:9). Peter appears to vacillate: at first he agrees that there should be no restrictions on gentiles (2:1–10), but then he backtracks, refusing to eat with the gentiles. Paul is outraged, and Paul attacks Peter's hypocrisy to his face (2:11–14). Paul attacks those who "rely" on the Jewish law, saying they are under a curse (3:10). Paul also attacks the idea that Christians must abstain from meat offered to idols (I Corinthians 8–10).

This is in complete and stark contrast to the account in Acts. In Acts, Paul appears as a loyal supporter of the church organization. Paul dutifully goes to Jerusalem *only* after being appointed its representative (15:2). It is *Peter*, not Paul, who initiates the gentile mission (Acts 10–11). There is no confrontation at all between Peter and Paul at Antioch: when the dispute at Antioch comes up, Peter is not even there (14:26), and at the subsequent apostolic council (Acts 15), Peter backs up Paul's position to the hilt. As an act of conciliation towards the "legalistic" Jewish sensibilities, Acts says that Paul even agrees to go to the temple to fulfill a vow and make a sacrifice (21:26). Paul, Peter, and James all agree on principles that *forbid* any Christian from eating meat, or anything else, offered to idols (15:29).

There is a blatant contradiction at almost every critical point in the narrative. What do we make of these contradictions? Joseph Tyson makes a strong case for Acts being written about 110–120 CE, as many passages seem to answer the preaching of the famous heretic Marcion point by point (Tyson, 2005). Acts shows that, contrary to Marcion:

1. Jesus fulfilled the predictions of the Hebrew prophets,
2. Paul was just another apostle who answered to Peter,
3. Peter was not a "false apostle," as Marcion argued, and in fact converts the first gentile (Cornelius in Acts 10),
4. Paul was a Torah-observant Jew,
5. Paul and the apostles agreed some parts of the law should continue to be observed.

Obviously Acts could not be written in response to Marcion unless the author knew of Marcion (who lived approximately 80 to 160 CE). Many of these same points could be raised about parts of Luke and some of the other gospels, so it is likely that editing not only of Acts but of parts of the gospels continued well into the second century. Acts has completely sanitized the conflict; the repeated inconsistencies cumulatively have a chilling effect on its believability.

Paul's First and Last Visits

It is likely that Paul's first and last visits in Acts, are the same as Paul's first and last visits in his letters.

If we look at Paul's very first visit, the account in Acts (Acts #1) and in Galatians (Paul #1) do roughly correspond. Galatians 1:18–20 doesn't exactly match Acts 9:26–28, but they at least sound like two versions of the same event. Both accounts emphasize the hesitation of the other apostles; Paul says he never saw anyone besides Peter and James, where Acts says that at first "they were all afraid of him."

It also appears likely that Paul's last visit to Jerusalem (Paul #3) as described in his letters (Romans 15:25–27, I Corinthians 16:1–4, II Corinthians 8–9) is the same as Paul's last visit to Jerusalem described in Acts (Acts #4). Paul, in Acts 24:17, describes Acts #4 as a famine visit.

Confusingly, though, Acts describes *two* of Paul's visits as "famine" visits, Acts #2 and Acts #4. Acts #2 (Acts 11:27–30) is the first famine visit, in which Paul (still called "Saul") is mentioned only briefly. But later in Acts, Paul describes Acts #4 as his famine visit.

Did Paul really make *two* famine visits? This is hard to believe, just because there is nothing anywhere else to suggest that two separate famines occurred during this historical period. So we can reasonably conclude that there was only one famine visit, which was Paul's last visit to Jerusalem (Paul #3 = Acts #4).

The Mission to the Gentiles Visit = The Apostolic Council?

What about the meeting in which Paul receives his mission to the gentiles (described by Paul), and what about the apostolic council (described by Acts)?

We at once notice two very peculiar things about these two events:

1. Paul clearly describes a meeting in which he receives the mission to the gentiles (Galatians 2:1–10), but in Acts we have no clear

record of such a meeting. In fact, in Acts it is *Peter* (not Paul!) who initiates the mission to the gentiles (Acts 10–11).

2.   Acts clearly describes an apostolic council to deal with the question of the gentiles in the movement (Acts 15); yet in Paul's letters, there is no obvious reference to the apostolic council, even though it seems to back up Paul's point about circumcision.

Many scholars adopt an obvious solution here: these two events are actually one event. Paul's "mission to the gentiles" visit (Galatians 2:1–10) *is* the apostolic council (Acts 15)—Paul #2 = Acts #3.

This idea has quite a bit going for it. In the first place, both accounts describe discussions about circumcision which are resolved in Paul's favor. In neither account is there any need for male converts to be circumcised. The dispute in Acts 15 seems to be occasioned exactly by some men from Judea saying that unless you are circumcised (males, we presume) you cannot be saved; the apostles rule otherwise.

Just as we were about to congratulate ourselves on solving the problem, we discover three absolutely fatal complications: (1) it gets the chronology of the dispute at Antioch backwards; (2) the content and venue of the meetings don't seem to match; (3) we can't explain Paul's stand on meat offered to idols.

1.   *Chronology of incident at Antioch.* Paul #2 is immediately followed by a huge dispute at Antioch, when Paul angrily denounces Peter to his face. This incident obviously *follows*, rather than precedes, Paul #2. After Paul describes glowingly his meeting with James, Peter, and John, where he receives his mission to the gentiles, Paul then describes how he feels betrayed that Peter has gone back on his word by refusing to eat with gentiles, and how he angrily confronts Peter at Antioch.

By contrast, Acts takes pains to locate the conflict at Antioch *preceding* the meeting in Jerusalem (Acts #3)—a meeting intended to *resolve* the problems at Antioch. It locates the dispute at Antioch (Acts 14:26), sets the stage by making circumcision the issue (Acts 15:1–5), and provides the information that Paul and Barnabas had "no small dissension and debate" with the men who "came down from Judea." Then we have Acts 15 and the so-called "apostolic decree," which specifies that circumcision is not a requirement.

The dispute at Antioch doesn't fit the chronology here: Paul #2 precedes this dispute, while Acts #3 follows it. There is a contradiction between Acts and the letters of Paul on this point, and we have only one choice: to prefer the eye-witness testimony of Paul.

2. *Content and venue.* Paul #2 describes a small, private meeting with Paul, James, and Peter; the issue seems to be circumcision; Paul and the apostles reach complete agreement; and there are no restrictions *whatsoever* on the gentiles. Acts #3 (Acts 15) describes a large, semi-public meeting with Paul, Barnabas, Peter, and James all present with all the other apostles; while circumcision is mentioned, the outcome of the meeting (Acts 15:20, 29, the "apostolic decree") mentions food items repeatedly; and there *are* some restrictions, albeit minor, placed on gentile converts.

3. *Meat offered to idols.* But most alarmingly, it is evident from Paul's letters that Paul did *not* agree with at least one point of the apostolic decree, namely, the prohibition on eating meat offered to idols. Paul argues in I Corinthians 8–10 that (at least in private) there is nothing wrong with eating meat offered to idols: "Eat anything sold in the meat-market without raising questions of conscience" (I Corinthians 10:25). Yet this is *exactly* what Acts 15:29 forbids.

The issue of meat offered to idols must have been real. Why would Acts, otherwise so intent on preserving the image of harmony in the early church, have created this issue out of thin air? The writer of Acts conceivably might have *deleted* the reference to meat offered to idols, knowing of Paul's opposition, but it is hard to imagine that Acts would have *manufactured* something so obviously detrimental to Paul's position and to Acts' own predisposition to emphasize the harmony of the early church.

The genial meeting with church leaders which Paul describes in Galatians 2:1–10 could not *possibly* have been the "apostolic council." The apostolic council imposes restrictions on gentiles that Paul is opposed to, and which are nowhere mentioned in Galatians 2:1–10, even though it seems to grant him his point about circumcision. It is also inescapable that there *was* a requirement imposed at some point forbidding meat offered to idols, and this restriction was *not* part of Paul's initial understanding in his meeting with James, Peter, and John.

The Gentile Question Revisited

The situation is confusing because everyone naturally assumed that the apostles would only need one meeting to deal with the gentile question. They would sit down, they would figure it out, and that would be the end of it. When we look at Acts, we see that Acts describes *two* discussions of the status of gentiles.

1. Peter's mission to the gentiles (Acts 10–11). Here there are *no* restrictions on gentile converts.
2. The apostolic council (Acts 15). Here there are *some* restrictions on gentiles, although they are presented as minor, and although Paul's letters offer serious objections to at least one of the restrictions—the prohibition of meat offered to idols.

This sounds like what Paul describes in Galatians: initially, there are no restrictions on gentiles (Galatians 2:1–10) but then "certain men from James" come and suddenly Peter refuses to eat with gentiles, implicitly putting new restrictions on gentiles (Galatians 2:11–14)—behavior which Paul angrily attacks as hypocritical.

Acts appears to have scrambled Paul's appearances in Acts 11:1–18 and Acts 15. Paul is seen as absent in the first case and present at the second; based on Paul's letters, it seems that he was present in the first case and absent at the second. All we have to do is assume that Acts 10–11 describes *Paul's* mission to the gentiles, not Peter's, and the chronology falls into place.

While the events surrounding the gentile mission in Acts 11 are very different from Paul's description of his meeting with James and Peter in Galatians, the *outcome* is remarkably the same: there are no restrictions on gentiles at all. There is *no* discussion of meat offered to idols, of "blood," or even of unchastity.

Acts 10–11 describes Peter's vision in which he sees the unclean animals and hears the voice saying "Rise, Peter, kill and eat." Peter interprets his vision to mean that gentiles must be accepted as well as

Jews, he gets a visit from the gentile Cornelius, and the apostles agree that "to the gentiles also God has granted repentance unto life" (11:18). The story of Peter's vision of the unclean animals, of course, is nowhere found in Paul, but the *outcome* of the meeting is marvelously in harmony with Paul's ideas.

Acts omits Paul from these meetings because it has a bias. Acts wants to minimize the independence of Paul and to focus on the harmony between Peter and Paul. Both of these motives are served by leaving Paul out of the discussion of the gentile mission altogether, and giving *Peter* the credit for starting the mission to the gentiles. On the other hand, the writer of Acts has a vague recollection that Paul was around at the time (Acts #2, Acts 11:27–30). This leaves us with this schema:

> Acts #1 = Paul #1 (initial visit)
> Acts #2 (supposedly Peter's mission to the gentiles)
>   = Paul #2 (Paul's mission to the gentiles)
> Acts #3 (apostolic council)—Paul was not there
> Acts #4 = Paul #3 (the famine visit)

How do we reconcile Paul's acceptance of meat offered to idols in his letters, with the prohibition of meat offered to idols in Acts? Basically, we can't. We might imagine that Paul wrote the letters detailing his objections to this prohibition (I Corinthians 8-10) but later changed his mind. This is possible, but it would be out of character for Paul, who seems to have aggressively declared his independence of the apostles elsewhere (e. g. Galatians 1:1); and there's no evidence to support this idea outside of Acts, which repeatedly contradicts Paul's letters. The most likely scenario is that Paul opposed the apostolic decree.

Conclusions

Having discussed the chronology, we now want to know about the outcome of this dispute. What did the apostolic decree actually mean? There are a lot of competing theories, and again it would be impossible to comprehensively consider them all. We will deal with this question by explaining *how the Ebionites saw the apostolic council,* and what light this sheds on early Christian history.

16. The Apostolic Decree

We have discussed at some length the chronology of events. We now turn to the apostolic decree itself.

Chronology and Content

Why have we gone to so much trouble to re-arrange the events and details in Acts? It's because the *narrative* of the apostolic council resolving the gentile question has such a powerful hold on the imagination both of Christians and scholars. Acts has flipped the sequence of the dispute at Antioch and the apostolic council. Obviously if we think the dispute at Antioch *preceded* the apostolic council, then most likely the council *resolved* the controversies which had come up at Antioch, as Acts implies, and all seems to be well in the church. But if the incident at Antioch *followed* the apostolic council, then most likely the apostolic council *created* the controversies at Antioch with its decision (Achtemeier, 1986).

We can't possibly examine in detail all the competing theories, but (contrary to Acts) this revised sequence seems the most likely:

1. Paul's initial visit.
2. Paul's second visit: gets mission to the gentiles. No restrictions on gentiles.
3. Apostolic decree—some restrictions on "gentiles" imposed, including prohibition on meat offered to idols.
4. Disagreement at Antioch and controversy.
5. Paul's third visit; brings offering.

This revised sequence of events, in which the conflict at Antioch *follows* the apostolic council, makes *perfect* sense of the events described in Paul's letters. It also makes perfect sense of the subsequent history of the Ebionites. Paul is fairly straightforward about the disputes in the early church, but Acts is *not* straightforward. This revised chronology may seem twisted to Christians and scholars raised to believe the book of Acts, but it is actually the book of Acts which is twisted.

Ambiguities in the Decree

The mysterious apostolic decree announced by James at Acts 15:20, and repeated at Acts 15:29 and Acts 21:25, forbids "what has been sacrificed to idols and from blood and from what is strangled and from unchastity." James, in announcing the decree, frames it as the *minimum* requirements for gentiles converting to Christianity, saying that he wishes "to lay upon you no greater burden than these necessary things" (15:28). What does this mean? And why would it ever become so contentious?

The prohibition of "unchastity," at least, is fairly straightforward: it prohibits sexual immorality. But the other three items, "blood," "what is strangled," and "what has been sacrificed to idols," are all a bit ambiguous.

1. "Blood" could mean:
   (a) drinking or eating blood, a reflection of Genesis 9:4;
   (b) *Shedding* blood, either the killing of humans (as in war) or the killing of animals (as in animal sacrifice), or both.
2. "What is strangled" is a really puzzling expression. It could mean:
   (a) Land animals killed by asphyxiation (rather than killed by bleeding to death), a violation of kosher laws. This method of slaughter, except perhaps for animals caught in traps, was not widely practiced in the ancient world.
   (b) *Any* animals, including fish or sea animals, killed by asphyxiation. This would be the literal meaning, although killing fish by asphyxiation—the standard method—is *not* a violation of kosher laws. Interestingly, *Damascus Document* 12.10–15 also prohibits killing fish by asphyxiation.
   (c) Any food, especially meat, cooked in a rich sauce. The Greek term for "things strangled" (*pniktos*) can be a Greek idiomatic expression having just this meaning (Proctor, 1996).

3. Even the prohibition on idolatry, which might seem straightforward, is expressed differently at different places:
    (a) At Acts 15:29 and 21:25, the prohibition is against "what has been sacrificed to idols," which would imply any meat or other item sacrificed to a pagan idol. "What has been sacrificed to idols" would typically be meat; the New English Bible translates this prohibition as "meat that has been offered to idols." OR
    (b) At Acts 15:20 the prohibition is against the "pollutions of idols." Paul believes that one can *eat* things sacrificed to idols without necessarily becoming *polluted* by them (as he argues in I Corinthians 8–10), so the wording in Acts 15:20 would seem to give Paul just a bit of wiggle room to defend his position as consonant with the teaching of the apostles.

So what does this all mean? Ancient writers and modern scholars have had a variety of different opinions. Church councils interpreted the decree as having minimal implications; the Ebionites thought that it had a broad scope.

Is the Apostolic Decree the Noahide Commandments?
One suggestion, made by some scholars, is that the apostolic decree is simply a version of "the Noahide law." If this is the case, we can explain the apostolic decree without recourse to anything the Ebionites said at all.

The "Noahide laws" are those commands listed in the Talmud as the minimum Jewish demands on righteous gentiles, which are much less stringent than the full Jewish law. This sounds like just the sort of compromise that James is looking for: it leaves out all the troublesome Jewish rituals, imposing a simple basic morality. The Noahide laws were the laws given to Noah and are binding on all humanity. There are six prohibitions—of idolatry, sexual promiscuity, murder, blasphemy, theft, and eating parts of a living animal. A seventh positive law is to establish justice. Circumcision is conspicuously omitted from this list, as is Sabbath observance, the kosher laws, and all the familiar Jewish rituals and customs.

The first problem with this interpretation is that it fundamentally reinterprets the whole thrust of the primitive

Christian message. The gospels frequently represent Jesus as intensifying the law and presenting demands which are more sweeping than the conventional morality on matters such as violence, anger, and divorce (e. g., Matthew 5:21–48). Where has the radicalism of the primitive community gone, in this view?

But there are numerous other problems. The apostolic decree doesn't exactly match the Noahide commands, and it is obviously woefully inadequate when understood as any kind of foundation for Christian behavior. We have to understand the apostolic decree as some sort of "minimum requirements," or it does not address the circumcision issue (Acts 15:1); but once we try to see it as a "minimum," it is clear that the decree is completely unsatisfactory.

For example, there are no prohibitions on theft, lying, blasphemy, or murder! One might interpret the prohibition on "blood" as actually prohibiting "bloodshed" and thus murder—in spite of the fact that early church councils interpreted this as a dietary restriction on eating blood (citing Genesis 9:4).

But we cannot have it both ways. If we make this prohibition a dietary restriction, it leaves us without a prohibition on murder! Surely, with the apostolic decree, James did not intend to allow theft, blasphemy, and murder, did he? If he didn't, then how can we interpret the apostolic decree as the *minimum* requirement on gentiles? And if James' decree does not address the question of the *minimum* requirements for gentiles, how can it be construed to address the circumcision issue, which is supposedly the occasion for the conference?

In fact, this was tacitly acknowledged as a problem in some early New Testament manuscripts of Acts. These manuscripts have a variation on the apostolic decree, in which "things strangled" is replaced by the "Golden Rule" in negative form: "Abstain from doing to others what you would not like done to yourselves" (Simon, 1970). That some copyists would feel the need to insert this into the apostolic decree is, in effect, an admission that there is a serious problem here. These copyists saw (correctly!) that the apostolic decree was being advertised in Acts as some sort of foundational principles of behavior; yet the literal text is hopelessly inadequate in that respect. So they attempted to fix the problem by inserting the "Golden Rule" as a sort of catch-all ethical guide.

It's arguable that the apostolic decree is just the Noahide commandments, but one has to stretch the evidence repeatedly. The idea that the apostolic decree was some version of the Noahide laws does have appeal, but the appeal is simply that it supports the viewpoint of the gentile church: this whole controversy was over a trivial issue of Jewish rituals.

The Church's View of the Apostolic Decree

The apostolic decree became something of an embarrassment in the early church. For all practical purposes, this founding resolution of the early Christian church was gradually, but unceremoniously, dropped by almost everyone.

Various church councils and statements from time to time referred to the decree, giving it a very narrow interpretation which would have only minimal (if any) impact on anyone's daily eating habits. The decree only concerned, in the church's view, eating or drinking blood of animals, killing an animal by suffocation, or eating meat sacrificed to idols.

Several official statements of the church refer directly or indirectly to the apostolic decree. The Council of Gangra (mid-fourth century) issued several canons directed against the Manichaeans and ethical vegetarianism. Canon 2 anathematizes anyone "who condemns the eating of flesh, except that of a suffocated animal or that offered to idols" (NPNF–2, vol. 14, p. 92). The practical effect was to condemn those who attacked meat-eating, *unless* they were attacking eating the meat of an animal offered to idols or suffocated—still giving a tip of the hat to the apostolic council. The Council of Trullo (in 692), canon 67, condemned the eating of blood (op. cit., p. 395). As late as 731, Pope Gregory the Third condemned the eating of blood or "things strangled" (op. cit., p. 93).

In all of these various statements, we see no suggestion that anything but a very narrow interpretation of the decree is possible. It refers to land animals killed by suffocation or the drinking or eating of blood. Of course, this makes nonsense of the interpretation of the decree as any kind of minimal requirements on gentiles, since it allows murder, lying, and theft.

Augustine took a simple but logical approach to the apostolic decree. In Augustine's eyes, the apostolic decree was a temporary arrangement due to the fact that for a short time both Jews and gentiles were followers of Jesus. Now that there are no Jews in the movement, Augustine doesn't feel that the apostolic decree should apply to us *at all*, and cites common practice and scripture in support.

> No Christian feels bound to abstain from thrushes or small birds because their blood has not been poured out, or from hares because they are killed by a stroke on the neck without shedding their blood. Any who still are afraid to touch these things are laughed at by the rest: so general is the conviction of the truth, that "not what entereth into the mouth defileth you, but what cometh out of it" [Matthew 15:11]; that evil lies in the commission of sin, and not in the nature of any food in ordinary use. (*Against Faustus* 32.13)

This is important evidence that few people, except perhaps church scholars, were paying any particular attention to the decree at all.

The Ebionite View of the Apostolic Decree

So what is this decree doing in Acts? How did something so contentious and earth-shaking at the time, come to be ignored by Paul, Augustine, and eventually everyone else as well? There's an obvious possible answer to this question: the original meaning of the decree was completely unlike the interpretation suggested by Acts and later endorsed by church councils.

The Ebionites *do* clearly allude to the apostolic decree at *Homilies* 7.4 and 7.8, giving it a very different meaning from that given by the various church councils. The Ebionites took the most literal and radical approach to each of the ambiguous items mentioned above. *Homilies* 7.4 says that we are enjoined to "abstain from the table of devils [table of demons], not to taste dead flesh, not to touch blood." Abstaining from *blood* is linked in the same breath to abstaining from the table of devils and abstaining from dead flesh, thus specifically linking the killing of animals to "blood." *Homilies* 7.8 says that we should "abstain from the table of devils, *that is,* from food offered to idols, from dead carcasses, from animals which have been suffocated or caught by wild beasts, and from blood" (emphasis added).

Here, *all* of the food prohibitions in the apostolic decree (against blood, what has been strangled, and food offered to idols) are specifically linked to the "table of devils." They are understood to prohibit any meat or fish at all. This directly contradicts the interpretations of the decree offered by various church councils and by Augustine.

But the *Recognitions* and *Homilies* go even further: they link their interpretation of the apostolic decree with an implicit defense of Peter's behavior in Galatians 2. They offer "not eating at the table of devils" as the reason for Peter separating himself from unbelievers at mealtime (*Recognitions* 1.19, 2.3, 2.71–72, 7.29, 7.34; *Homilies* 1.22, 13.4). The rationale has nothing to do with Jewish purity; it is about demon possession. When taken in conjunction with *Homilies* 3.45, 7.4, and 7.8, it implies not only abstaining from meat and fish, but also not eating with anyone who does. For the Ebionites, eating is a sacred act and the table at which one eats should not be defiled by the presence of those who have contempt for life. The closest Jewish analogy with the Ebionite interpretation of the decree here is actually with the kosher laws, but not the kosher laws which we associate with ancient or modern Judaism. The Ebionite application of this decree is a new kind of "kosher": it is a radical kosher regulation which *eliminates* meat consumption altogether.

Paul's View of the Apostolic Decree

The views of the later Ebionites, therefore, is that the apostolic decree was intended to prohibit eating at the table of demons—killing animals, or eating their dead flesh. This clarifies the position of the *later* Ebionites, but what about the *early* Jewish Christians, and what about Peter and James?

To decide how the early Jewish Christians interpreted the apostolic decree, we turn to Paul. But Paul discusses *all* of these very items. He discusses "the table of demons (or devils)," the bloodshed of animals, meat offered to idols, and eating with those who believe otherwise (the "gentiles"). Moreover, he discusses them *precisely in the passages we have already examined because they gave evidence of early Jewish Christian belief.*

Paul *does* refer to the apostolic decree, and is arguing *against* it. In Romans 14, I Corinthians 8–10, and Galatians 2, Paul argues against the requirement to abstain from meat, argues against the requirement to abstain from "food offered to idols," and argues against separation from those who are unbelievers at meal time. He agrees that we should avoid the table of demons, but feels that *none* of these behaviors constitutes eating at the table of demons. His only concession is his advice to avoid offending the sensibilities of vegetarians in the early church. The Ebionites and Paul have different views on whether they *like* the decree, but they both seem to agree on its meaning.

Someone was taking these Ebionite positions in the early church, because Paul discusses them or actually attacks them. Indeed, if we look at Galatians, we can identify who these people were: James, Peter, and John, the pillars of the early community.

Now of course, it's possible that the apostolic decree was never intended by the historical apostles to mean that believers should not eat meat with nonbelievers, and that *Homilies* 7.4 and 7.8 is an overly extreme interpretation of the apostolic decree. But two things are apparent: (1) Peter, in Galatians 2, *acts as if* he has been persuaded to this point of view by James, and (2) Paul, in Romans 14, I Corinthians 8–10, and Galatians 2, *argues against* this point of view—at one point naming James and Peter as its proponents. The people who had this "extreme" view of the apostolic decree, therefore, evidently included the apostles themselves.

There are countless possible interpretations of what the apostles "really" meant by the apostolic decree. While many scholars and Christians will be unhappy with this conclusion, the simplest explanation is just that the apostolic decree prohibited meat and things sacrificed to idols, that this came from the very leadership of the church, and that Paul rejected it. In this one case, at least, Acts *does* report something of great historical significance which is not in Paul's letters.

Was Paul at the Apostolic Council?

The apostolic council is probably the most interesting event in Paul's entire life. And this is the *very* visit that Paul doesn't describe. This might be because Paul forgot to write a letter about this council, or that he did write such a letter but it is lost to history. But there's another possibility, which this revised sequence suggests—Paul doesn't describe it because he wasn't there. The apostolic council, far from being a *resolution* of the dispute between Paul and Peter at Antioch, was more than likely what *caused* the dispute (elegantly argued in Achtemeier, 1986). In this light, Paul's intense anger in Galatians becomes quite plausible and the whole history of the early church makes sense.

Most likely, the apostolic council occurred without Paul (or Peter, for that matter) being present. When "certain men from James" came to Antioch (Judas and Silas, according to Acts) what they brought was the apostolic decree, prohibiting "blood" and "what has been sacrificed to idols." In fact, Acts indirectly provides evidence for this, because a close reading of the text indicates that Paul's presence at the apostolic council in Jerusalem was added after the fact:

1. Paul's actual participation in the council is limited to a fragment of a verse (Acts 15:12), which describes his speech in vague terms, while Peter and James get several verses apiece of direct quotations.
2. Most significantly, while Paul and Barnabas are packed off to Antioch with Judas and Silas (Acts 15:22), James' letter to Antioch *only refers to Judas and Silas* (Acts 15:27), and after they finally get to Antioch *only Judas and Silas* exhort the brethren (Acts 15:32). It appears that the participation of Paul and Barnabas in Jerusalem has been inconsistently added to Acts 15 after the fact.
3. Moreover, when James tells Paul about the apostolic decree later (Acts 21:25), during Paul's last visit to Jerusalem, James *seems to be telling Paul about it for the first time*, when by the account in Acts 15 Paul must have actually been at the apostolic council (with James!), concurred in the decision, and carried the news of it to Antioch.
4. Finally, we note the "sharp dissension" between Barnabas and Paul (Acts 15:39), so serious that Barnabas and Paul then go their separate ways. Why would this happen? If we read Galatians 2:13, we find out that after the incident at Antioch, "even Barnabas was carried away" with the Jewish Christians' persuasive views. The writer of Acts seems to have been aware of a serious disagreement between Paul and Barnabas, and it is likely

that this in fact was the consequence of disagreement over the apostolic decree itself.

The evidence from Acts, therefore—when we remove these later insertions referring to Paul—is that there was an "apostolic council" of sorts, but Paul wasn't there.

Conclusions

We are left with the likely chronology of Paul's visits as described in Table 16–1. Acts has incorrectly placed the reports of dissension and debate *before*, rather than *after,* the apostolic decree. However, Acts has correctly placed the split between Paul and Barnabas after the decree (Galatians 2:13).

But while the overall chronology is mostly right, the details—probably set to paper 50 years or more after the letters of Paul—are consistently wrong. They are distorted in the direction of minimizing the conflict between Paul and the rest of the church.

This solves the problem of why Paul never refers to the apostolic decree and the apostolic council, which supposedly healed the split in the early church, in any of his letters. He does not refer to the apostolic council because he wasn't there. *He does refer to the apostolic decree rather extensively*, and disagrees with it. When Paul talks about the actual issues involved in the apostolic decree—blood, and things sacrificed to idols—it's clear that he is not involved in a debate with Jewish legalists who believe in the kosher regulations. He is engaged in a debate with vegetarians who believe in demon possession.

Incident	Paul's Letters	Acts	Description
Paul's first visit	Gal. 1:18–20	Acts 9:26–28	Paul sees Peter, James.
Paul's second visit	Gal. 2:1–10	Acts 11:1–18, 11:27–30	Paul, Peter, and James agree: no restrictions on gentiles. Acts erroneously omits Paul from the discussion and makes his visit at 11:27–30 the one with the offering.
"Apostolic council"	Not discussed	Acts 15:4–29	Some food restrictions on gentiles; neither Peter nor Paul are present, although Acts erroneously places them there.
Incident at Antioch	Gal. 2:11–14	Acts 14:26–15: 2; Acts 15:39–40	Dissension and debate; Acts erroneously places the incident at Antioch before, rather than after, the apostolic decree, except for the split with Barnabas. Acts erroneously fails to place Peter at Antioch.
Paul's arguments against the decree	Romans 14, I Cor. 8–10, Galatians throughout	Not discussed	Paul argues against the decree after the fact.
Paul's third visit	Romans 15:25–27, I Cor. 16:1–4, II Cor. 8–9 (prospective)	Acts 21:15–36; 24:17	Paul's third visit; brings offering.

Table 16–1. Paul's career, synchronized with Acts' descriptions.

17. The Church Divides

The apostolic decree divided the church. This division was never overcome, it simply ended when Jewish Christianity died out. Moreover, it ended in a way that the apostles could scarcely have foreseen, because those that followed the leadership of the Jerusalem church ultimately found themselves on the losing side, condemned as heretics by the successors of the churches to whom Paul preached.

Most modern Christians and modern scholars would think that the idea that early Christians might actually be concerned about animal sacrifice, or consider the slaughter of innocent animals as demon-inspired, is far-fetched. However, this is *precisely* the point of view of the Ebionites and *precisely* the point of view of Paul's opponents. Paul argues so strenuously against the apostolic decree, in all likelihood, because he knows that it will not be well received in the gentile congregations to whom he is preaching. It is easy to see why the fight was so bitter.

This was not the end of vegetarianism in Christianity. Many gentile Christians were also vegetarian, and monastic groups often adopted vegetarianism as part of their discipline. Eusebius reports favorably on one Christian martyr who declares that even the blood of animals is forbidden to Christians (*Ecclesiastical History* 5.1.25). Augustine reports that orthodox Christian vegetarians are "without number" (*Of the Morals of the Catholic Church* 33). But when Paul's letters were incorporated into the scripture, it *did* mean the end of *ethical* vegetarianism. To say that it was ethically wrong to eat meat was, from then on, necessarily a heresy.

The Social Dynamics of Forbidden Foods

What happened, precisely, when the historical Peter at first ate with the gentiles, and why was it objectionable, so that he later withdrew

(Galatians 2:11-14)? The exact events are likely lost to history. Paul doesn't say, and James may have only suspected without really knowing himself. Peter's behavior may have been (1) he was served only plant foods, and ate only plant foods, but with pagan idolaters; (2) he was served a variety of foods, but picked through the meat and ate only vegetables; or (3) he was served meat and ate meat. It's unlikely that this incident would have caused such a fuss with James, or a counter-reaction from Paul, had Peter been served by pagan vegetarians; so it seems fairly likely that the historical Peter was faced with meat, probably meat offered to idols, on the table.

We know quite a bit about the context of this incident just based on what foods were commonly eaten at the time. For most people in the ancient Roman or Jewish worlds, a very spare vegan diet was the norm. Most of their nutritional needs were met by grains, with the welcome addition of "relishes" such as lentils, olives, onions, and salt. Meat and fish were quite rare; fish was sometimes more expensive even than meat (see McGowan, p. 35–45). So when Peter describes his diet as bread, olives, and "pot-herbs" (which were perhaps green leafy vegetables), he is describing what is actually a fairly typical diet (*Recognitions* 7.6, *Homilies* 12.6). "Meat and fish were special-occasion dishes for all but the rich, and meat carried overtones of sacrifice as well as of luxury or even of dissipation" (McGowan, p. 45).

Therefore, those whom Paul is counseling in Romans and I Corinthians are in the upper class. They had ready access to meat: "eat whatever is sold in the meat-market without raising questions of conscience" (I Corinthians 10:25). If an unbeliever invites you to dinner, Paul adds, you should generally feel free to eat whatever they offer: "why should my liberty be determined by another man's scruples?" (I Corinthians 10:29).

It is not impossible that Peter ate meat on this occasion, despite the vegetarianism of James and the early Jesus movement. Perhaps he reasoned that unless he killed the animal himself, he wasn't guilty of anything; or perhaps he just didn't want to offend his host. Alternatively, Peter may have declined to eat meat, risking a "scene" by making an issue out of his host's generosity. In either case, it was likely a new type of situation for the Jesus movement. Before Paul the followers of Jesus had not traveled in social circles which brought them into day-to-day contact with the upper class, and thus had not encountered many meat-eaters at the table.

The social dynamics of food have probably not changed much in two thousand years. If you are a guest at someone's table but have ethical objections to the food served, it is an awkward moment, whether you are a modern vegan, kosher-observant Jew, Buddhist monk, or "halal" observant Muslim. Some who are normally vegetarian or vegan "compromise" just for this reason: strictly observant in their home, they are willing to tolerate honey, dairy products, or even meat when placed in a socially difficult situation. The variations and the issues are endless. The Ebionite rationale removes even the temptation of eating forbidden items for social reasons: you must avoid eating *anything* at the table of demons.

Paul's Accommodation to the Larger Society

Vegetarianism was an embarrassing issue in apostolic times, not just a creation of some later fanatical Ebionites. Paul explicitly refers to those who do not eat meat or drink wine, so we have every reason to believe that there were radical vegetarians during the apostolic age; but it is intuitively likely just on sociological grounds as well.

Paul likely understood that forbidding meat and wine was not going to go well with those in the upper class, and that Christianity would spread if it could reach across class barriers to those who were well off in the ancient world. It is plausible that a movement might *ameliorate* the views of its founders on a lifestyle issue, to accommodate the larger society, despite the radical views of its founders. But the reverse is quite unlikely: a movement would be much less prone to develop more *strict* views than those of its founders, when this also ran against the larger society.

When the then-pagan emperor Constantine co-opted the church at the Council of Nicea, the movement ameliorated its original radical ideas of pacifism in favor of accommodating the larger society. Suddenly it was not only morally acceptable, but even praiseworthy to kill people in battle, provided of course that you were fighting on the right side. The church also found a way to accommodate commercial interests and became wealthy and worldly. Much of the monastic movement began as a protest against this compromise of what many thought was a "sell-out" to the larger society.

This is also what has happened with vegetarianism in the case of two modern Christian groups, the Seventh-day Adventists (Ellen White) and Unity School of Christianity (Charles and Myrtle Fillmore). In both cases, the founders were ethical vegetarians, but in both cases the adherence to vegetarianism was steadily weakened and in the case of Unity seems to have almost completely disappeared. This tendency only rarely works to take groups in a more radical direction, but in the accommodationist direction it is all too common.

What are the Ebionites Hiding?

Acts is hiding some embarrassing features of this dispute in the early church. But the Ebionites as well may have found these events quite embarrassing and preferred to forget them. There are several things which are apparent in Paul's letters and from a close reading of Acts, that the Ebionite picture of events tends to distort or omit, relating to Paul and the apostolic council.

What is the evidence for evasion? Jewish Christian references to Paul often avoid explicitly naming Paul. *Recognitions* 1 tells the story of an unnamed "certain enemy," presumed to be Saul (Paul before his conversion) who attacks James in the temple and nearly kills him. There is a reference to "the man who is my enemy" (probably Paul) in the pseudo-Clementine *Epistle of Peter to James* 2.

Surviving Ebionite details on Paul concentrate on Paul's behavior as Saul, *before* his conversion to Christianity. Saul attacks James in the temple before he sets out to Damascus; Saul was a convert to Judaism rather than born a Jew, and persecuted the Christians because he was in love with the high priest's daughter. But there are no references to things that Paul did after his conversion. Moreover, the whole project of Peter debating Simon Magus in the *Recognitions* and *Homilies* sometimes puts Paul's views in the mouth of Simon Magus, rather than addressing Paul's views by name. If Paul is the great Ebionite nemesis, why are there no more explicit references to Paul, and why this reluctance to name Paul specifically?

Of course, there may be prosaic reasons for this. The Ebionites may have been very specific about Paul in documents now lost to us. Or, the Ebionites may have had other things on their mind besides Paul; they were more concerned with the historical Simon Magus and with Marcion than with Paul. It's also possible that the Ebionites were reluctant to criticize Paul's behavior after his conversion or Paul's letters, because the letters of Paul were very popular among early Christians. Paul may have been a heretic, but he was also a good writer.

But there might also be a darker reason: because they didn't want to draw attention to their treatment of Paul. The Ebionites may have not wanted to raise the subject of their own treatment of Paul during his third visit to Jerusalem—the "famine visit" described in Acts 21. In his letters, Paul seems to want to smooth things over in his third visit to Jerusalem. He is ready to compromise: "I will never eat meat, lest I cause my brother to fall" (I Corinthians 8:13). Acts, likewise, wants to emphasize the harmony of the apostles. So given all this, how do we account for the fact that Acts has no record of Paul's offering ever being accepted during Paul's third visit?

This *could* have been a careless omission on the part of Acts, but perhaps it wasn't. Perhaps Acts left this out because it didn't happen (see Lüdemann, p. 44–49). Perhaps something even more sinister happened: the Jewish Christian leadership either did not help Paul after his arrest, or perhaps even betrayed him to the Romans. Acts contains no reference to the offering being accepted, which is really hard to explain if the writers of Acts knew that it had been accepted. That there is no description of the offering's acceptance *could* mean that James rejected Paul's offering.

The second embarrassing thing, from an Ebionite standpoint, is the fact that they had any dealings with Paul at all. The Jerusalem church evidently had a long relationship to Paul. For someone who was an "apostate from the law," the Jerusalem church seemed to be quite slow to notice this, and operated fairly comfortably with him for a long time. Just as references to Trotsky were purged from the Soviet account of the Russian Revolution, so references to Paul may have been purged as well, and for the same reason; the long period of cooperation with someone later denounced as a traitor is hard to explain.

Thirdly, we have the behavior of Peter and James. Peter doesn't seem to understand critical elements of the Ebionite message, being forced to backtrack on who he's willing to eat with. Even from a vegetarian perspective, it seems that James and the other leaders of the Jerusalem church overplayed their grievance and probably bear some considerable responsibility for the split in the church—and in hindsight, for the subsequent downfall of the Ebionites. The Jewish Christians refused to eat with anyone except other (baptized and vegetarian) believers, a position which most people in the modern world, even many radical vegans, would find strange. Surely some sort of compromise was possible.

This seems to run counter to Jesus' willingness (in the gospels) to eat with anyone. "Why does your teacher eat with tax collectors and sinners?" ask the Pharisees (Matthew 9:10 and parallels). The gospels are orthodox documents, and the writers may have penned this narrative just to combat the Ebionite tendency to be "picky" with their food. The historical Jesus probably did not encounter historical Pharisees in Galilee, but even accepting this text at face value, the Pharisees' question concerns more why Jesus eats with those who are despised rather than why he eats with the upper class. Eating with meat-eaters or with anyone in the upper class at all was a problem which neither the historical Jesus nor the early church may have ever faced for decades, since meat-eating was relatively rare.

The rejection of eating with nonbelievers might not have seemed quite as radical to them as it does to us. Interestingly, this rejection of sharing food with nonbelievers continues today as an orthodox Christian practice. Modern Roman Catholics, the Eastern Orthodox, and some Protestant churches (at least officially) accept only believers, or members of their own churches, at the communion or Eucharist. The difference between this "closed communion" and the Ebionites on this point was just that for the Ebionites, *every* meal was communion.

Room For Compromise?

Was there room for compromise in this dispute? Was there a middle ground between the gentile churches to which Paul preached, and the churches which acknowledged the Jerusalem church? One interesting document suggesting a middle ground is the *Didache*, or the "Teaching of the Twelve Apostles," which some argue is from early in the second century. It nowhere directly mentions Paul or his writings; on the other hand, it also avoids any distinctively Ebionite teachings.

The subject of food comes up: "Concerning food, bear what you can, but carefully keep away from food sacrificed to idols" (*Didache* 6.3). This evasive phrasing suggests that the author is aware of the controversy and seeks to steer a middle path, giving something to both sides. "Bear what you can" suggests that a vegetarian diet might be the highest ethical ideal, but is not to be imposed as a rule on the community.

The *Didache* doesn't refer to all the items in the apostolic decree. It prohibits things sacrificed to idols and unchastity ("adulteries, lusts, fornications"), but the other two prohibitions in the apostolic decree, against "blood" and "things strangled," are not mentioned at all. If the *Didache* really is an early document, it suggests that there was confusion over the issue of food and that some early gentile Christians were not eager to come down heavily on one side or the other. The Jerusalem church and its Ebionite successors were not able to exercise decisive influence at this time; but Paul's teaching was not yet unquestioningly accepted, either.

Conclusions

The one feature of Jewish Christianity about which we know the most is the time when its path irrevocably diverged from that of gentile Christianity. This happened at Antioch, when Paul openly denounces Peter, resulting in a split in the church which was never healed. The letters of Paul, when understood in the light of the *Recognitions* and *Homilies*, demonstrate clearly that the movement which we know as Jewish Christianity first emerged as a distinct group separate from other Christians in the incident at Antioch, and that the apostolic decree became its declaration of principles.

18. The Destruction of the Temple

The destruction of the temple in the year 70 was not the end of the first great Jewish revolt against Rome, but it was the climax. It also signaled the end of the apostolic age. Some of the original apostles may have survived the revolt; John is said to have lived to a ripe old age. But the time when the Jerusalem church could claim to represent the whole church was over.

The Third Incident in the Temple

In the year 62, just four years before the great Jewish revolt against Rome began, a lynch mob organized by the high priest killed James, the brother of Jesus and the leader of the church. In this third violent incident in the temple we once again see evidence, if any more is needed, of the opposition between the Jesus movement and the temple hierarchy.

Our main source of information on this event is Josephus, for whom this is a key event in the years just before the Jewish revolt. If we can credit Josephus, the Jewish community was outraged by this perversion of justice, and the high priest was dismissed shortly thereafter. The enemies of the Jerusalem church were not "the Jews" or the Jewish establishment as a whole, but a specific set of powerful enemies—the priests in the temple.

Who was responsible for killing James? Hegesippus (quoted by Eusebius) blames the "scribes and Pharisees" for killing James, though the Sadducees were clearly present and presumably approved (*Ecclesiastical History* 2.23.8–19). But Josephus gives a much more plausible account (*Antiquities* 20.9.1), which holds the high priest directly responsible.

According to Josephus, Ananus was a Sadducee and also very "insolent." He set up a court and brought James and some of his companions before it, accused them of breaking the law, and then had them stoned to death. But in doing so, Ananus had brushed procedures aside and had quite overreached his authority. People complained both to the Romans and to King Agrippa, and as a result Ananus was quickly dismissed.

The killing of James did *not* have the support of the Jews. In fact (according to Origen and Eusebius), Josephus said that Jerusalem was destroyed as punishment for the murder of James, an innocent man (*Against Celsus* 1.47, *Ecclesiastical History* 2.23.19–20). We do not have this passage in our standard texts of Josephus, so it may have been removed by copyists somewhere down the line. Such a passage would not conform to standard Christian narrative (as Origen himself says), which presented the destruction of Jerusalem as a consequence of the murder of *Jesus*, not of James.

This story illustrates the relative impunity from persecution that the church had experienced for decades previously, despite the long-standing grudge which the Sadducees and the priests held against the Jesus movement for over three decades. They weren't *impervious* to persecution; James lost his life, while Ananus only lost his job. But they were not completely without protection, either.

James' Successors

James' successor in the Palestinian church was Simeon (or "Simon") son of Clophas. Who exactly was Simeon son of Clophas?

According to Hegesippus (Eusebius, *Ecclesiastical History* 3.11, 4.22.4), Simeon was a cousin of Jesus—the son of Clophas, who was a brother of Jesus' father Joseph. But in fact, Simeon *may actually be Jesus' half-brother*. James Tabor (*The Jesus Dynasty,* p. 79–81) makes this argument and points out an interesting reference to Clophas, Simeon's father, in the New Testament at John 19:25.

Tabor's analysis is too long to duplicate here. In outline, he looks at the references to "Mary wife of Clophas" in the New Testament, one of the women standing at the cross when Jesus died, and compares it to "Mary mother of Jesus" (John 19:25, Mark 6:3, 15:40, 15:47, 16:1). If the Clophas of the New Testament was the same Clophas described by Hegesippus as the father of Simeon, then that means that "Mary wife of Clophas" and "Mary mother of Jesus" both had sons named James, Joses, and Simeon (or Simon).

This could be coincidence or confusion on the part of the gospel writers; but it could also mean that the same woman is being referred to. It could mean that Mary the mother of Jesus was at different times married to both Joseph and, after Joseph died, to Clophas; she had several sons, including Jesus, James, Joses, and Simeon, among others. In this account, not only was Mary the mother of Jesus not a virgin, but she had at least two different husbands and was mother to three early leaders of the church—surely a most remarkable woman.

In any event, control of the primitive church remains in the hands of Jesus' family after James. Hegesippus also reports that other relatives of Jesus were active in the church and "ruled the churches" at the time of Domitian—two of the grandsons of Judas, another brother of Jesus (Eusebius, *Ecclesiastical History* 3.20.1–8). Their names were Zoker and James (Bauckham, 1996).

Hegesippus does not name Zoker and James, but says that they were hauled before the Roman Emperor Domitian (reigned 81—96 CE) during a persecution of the church. Domitian feared that, as sons of David, Zoker and James were planning a Jewish revolution of some sort. When Domitian asked them about the kingdom which they expected, they said it was not an earthly kingdom, but a heavenly one which would appear at the end of time. Domitian, seeing they were not wealthy, released them as harmless and stopped the persecution of the church.

Julius Africanus tells us that the *desposynoi* ("those who belong to the master," a euphemism for the family of Jesus) had genealogies they had carefully kept for many years. These relatives lived both in Nazareth (in Galilee) and in Cochaba, a town on the *east* side of the Jordan river (quoted in Eusebius, *Ecclesiastical History* 1.7.14).

The Jerusalem Church in Exile

The failed Jewish revolt against Rome (66–74) was a critical event in the history of Jewish Christianity. Josephus, with perhaps only some exaggeration, said that the Jewish war was "the greatest of all those, not only in our times, but, in a manner, of those that were ever heard of" (*Wars*, Preface). The destruction and bloodshed were immense. It is the primary reason that the Jerusalem church virtually disappears from the scene after this time.

Eusebius, Epiphanius, and *Recognitions* 1.39 all say that the church survived the catastrophe of the year 70: the church received a divine revelation and fled from Jerusalem. According to Eusebius (*Ecclesiastical History* 3.5.3) and Epiphanius (*Panarion* 29.7.8), the place of refuge was Pella, a city on the other side of the Jordan near the Sea of Galilee. The *Recognitions* doesn't specify a location, but just indicates that those who believe will be kept in safety from the impending destruction.

Given the huge destruction and deaths due to direct and indirect effects of the war, it would not be necessary to postulate the complete destruction of the church to explain the relative lack of accounts of the Jerusalem church. The simplest explanation is just that Jewish Christianity was severely affected by the war, just because everyone was severely affected.

The revolts could not help but weaken the influence of the Jerusalem church. The Jerusalem church may have been unable to maintain regular contact even with any sympathetic gentile churches that existed. They had other things on their mind—like just surviving.

The difficulties the church faced were political as well as physical. The outcome of the revolt, and of two later failed Jewish revolts in the second century, undercut the ability of the church to function either as a Jewish sect or within the Christian movement.

On the Jewish side, these failed revolts erased the multitude of Jewish sects and allowed the ancestors of rabbinic Judaism, the Pharisees, to attain almost universal supremacy. Ironically, because of the destruction of the temple, one of the chief grievances of the Ebionites was eliminated. The Jewish protest of the sacrifices, going back nearly a thousand years to Amos and Hosea, almost completely disappears in the Talmud, written down after the destruction of the temple. "One could go through passage after passage which in the Bible seems to bear an anti-cultic meaning without finding one which the Rabbis used in such a way" (Sanders, p. 162–163). However, Jewish use of some of these passages has re-emerged in the modern Jewish vegetarian movement (Schwartz, p. 106–109).

Possibly late in the first century, Jewish Christians were likely excluded from the Jewish synagogues and condemned as Jewish heretics, since they didn't accept the "rabbinic" reforms which united Judaism after the first revolt. The alleged purpose of the *birkat ha-*

minim, the benediction against the heretics (discussed in chapter 8), was precisely to exclude Jewish heretics such as the followers of Jesus, as well as any other heretics. These might have been other followers of John the Baptist not in the Jesus movement; for example, the Mandaeans (non-Christian followers of John the Baptist) also date their separation from Judaism to the first century. No longer were the Ebionites tolerated as one among countless other sects.

Gentile Christianity, by contrast, was relatively untouched by the trauma of the Jewish revolts. Even before the first revolt, some gentile churches—under Paul's influence—were likely suspicious of the Jerusalem church, and Paul's arrest and disappearance probably didn't enhance their feelings. "Look out for the dogs, look out for the evil-workers, look out for those who mutilate the flesh," warned Paul from his jail cell (Philippians 3:2–3).

In gentile Christian eyes, the catastrophic destruction of Jerusalem and the temple appeared as a divine judgement against *all* Jews, including Jewish Christians. Ignatius, at the beginning of the second century, says that "where there is Christianity there cannot be Judaism" (*Letter to the Magnesians* 10). Eusebius concludes that "the judgment of God at length overtook those who had committed such outrages against Christ and his apostles, and totally destroyed that generation of impious men" (*Ecclesiastical History* 3.5.3). While this is a fourth century judgment, it is probably reflective of the general opinion that had prevailed for some time previously. It is a natural and obvious conclusion that Judaism itself was condemned by the catastrophic outcome of the revolt, and thus the Jewish Christians were condemned as well for still "clinging" to this religion.

At some time in the second century, Jewish Christianity re-emerges in the historical record, as the heresy of the Ebionites, as described by Irenaeus. Are we talking about the same group here? Aren't the Jewish Christian Ebionites of the late second century, nothing more than the successors of the Jewish Christians in the Jerusalem church led by James and Simeon?

From Jewish Christian accounts, it sounds as if this was a perfectly natural progression. The later Ebionites inherited the mantle of the Jerusalem church. How could the rest of the gentile church affirm their allegiance to the primitive church and claim to be the true followers of Jesus, and yet reject the successors of the primitive church, the Ebionites? To the Ebionites, this must have seemed an incredible, ludicrous claim, hardly even worthy of a reply.

And yet, this is precisely what gentile Christianity was doing, and modern scholars have almost universally swallowed this claim with hardly a thought. To modern scholars, getting from the Jerusalem church following James in apostolic times, to the gentile Christianity centered in Rome a century later, seems a natural and obvious progression. But getting from the Jerusalem church following James in apostolic times, to those second century Christians who are also Jewish, who honor James as the leader of the whole church, and who lived and worked in the same area that Jesus and his first followers lived and worked, appears to be some kind of extraordinary claim requiring extraordinary evidence.

Suddenly, within the space of a few decades, Jewish Christianity became a sect excluded by both Jews and Christians. Or, in the words of Jerome, "but while [the Ebionites] desire to be both Jews and Christians, they are neither the one nor the other" ("Letter 112").

Part V:
The History of the Ebionites

19. The Origin and Geography of the Ebionites

After the destruction of Jerusalem, the Jerusalem church essentially disappears from the history books so far as the orthodox are concerned. The connection between Christian believers and the church goes through Rome, rather than Jerusalem or Pella. When the successors of the Jerusalem church re-emerge in the written records, they have changed both their name and their location. They are now known as "Ebionites" and are found just outside of Judea.

The Origin of the Ebionites

Irenaeus' work *Against Heresies* contains the first definite mention of the Ebionites. This was written late in the second century, about a century after the destruction of the temple.

We don't know precisely when this group of Jewish Christians took the title of "Ebionites." Hans-Joachim Schoeps says that it was likely sometime after they fled from Jerusalem during the first Jewish revolt against Rome (Schoeps, p. 10–11). There are snatches of references to "the poor" in Paul's letters (e. g. Galatians 2:10) and the gospels (e. g. Luke 6:20). But there is no evidence that this was a title referring to the church, rather than a literal description of those who were poor, during apostolic times.

What happened to Jewish Christianity in between the destruction of Jerusalem and their appearance in *Against Heresies*? The orthodox connected the Jerusalem church to the larger church by postulating that Peter came to Rome and founded a church there. It was Peter, not James, who was the leader of the whole church, and James was just a "local" bishop in Jerusalem. After Peter founded a church in Rome he became a martyr there, being crucified by the order of the Emperor Nero, probably around the year 64.

Historically, this story is *possible*, but rather doubtful. In the first place, the statement that Peter was the leader of the whole church is incorrect. James, not Peter, was the head of the Jerusalem church, so even if Peter did somehow get to Rome, he would still have thought of himself as answering to James or to Simeon, James' successor after the year 62 (see chapter 12).

If we assume that Peter (answering either to James or Simeon) did set out on a missionary journey, it is difficult to believe that Peter got all the way to Rome. He presumably traveled to Antioch, as that is where his celebrated confrontation with Paul occurred. If he had traveled further, he might have found himself repeating the confrontation at Antioch in other gentile churches, trying to combat Paul's explanations over and over again and explain why he "refused to eat with the gentiles."

After the year 70, the Jerusalem church had a lot of other things to worry about, so missionary work probably took a back seat. The destruction of the temple and the reconfiguration of Judaism under the direction of the Pharisees quickly isolated the Ebionites. And in case that wasn't enough for Jewish Christianity, some decades later there was another Jewish revolt against Rome, the Bar Kokhba revolt of 132–135 CE.

Hadrian, the Roman emperor from 117–138, had initially promised to rebuild the Jewish temple, but when these expectations and others were dashed, the Jews rose up in a third Jewish revolt against Rome. (A second Jewish revolt had taken place outside of Judea, in north Africa, 115–117.)

Justin, an early second-century Christian writer, briefly and indirectly refers to the Ebionites sometime after this revolt:

> They [the Jews] kill and punish us whenever they have the power, as you can well believe. For in the Jewish war which lately raged, [Bar Kokhba], the leader of the revolt of the Jews, gave orders that Christians alone should be led to cruel punishments, unless they would deny Jesus Christ and utter blasphemy. (Justin, *First Apology* 31)

While Justin doesn't lay it out explicitly, the Christians whom Bar Kokhba tortured were not gentile Christians but almost certainly Jewish Christians, just because those were the Christians whom Bar Kokhba found in the area. The Jewish Christians were opposed to temple worship in the first place, and would have no interest in seeing it rebuilt; and their pacifist tendencies did not lend themselves well to the spirit of the revolt either.

However, interestingly, Justin does not imply that these Jewish Christians were heretics. Elsewhere Justin says that Jewish converts to Christianity who continue to follow Jewish rituals such as circumcision and Sabbath, but do not insist on observance of Jewish rituals by the gentiles, should be accepted as legitimate Christians (*Dialogue with Trypho* 47). Many church writers say that the Ebionites observed circumcision and the Sabbath (Irenaeus and Epiphanius, for example); but none of these state that the Ebionites *required* circumcision and Sabbath observance as a condition of salvation, and *Homilies* 8.6–7 seems to meet Justin's concerns on this point. Evidently the idea that Jewish Christianity was a *Christian* heresy had not yet emerged when Justin wrote.

At the conclusion of the revolt, the Romans expelled all Jews (including Jewish Christians) from Jerusalem. The Jewish Christians fled Jerusalem yet again, and this time they left for good. After this point the Jerusalem church was permanently in exile, inhabiting areas on the periphery of Palestine.

As noted previously, Irenaeus gives the Ebionites just a few sentences in his *Against Heresies*, which is hundreds of pages long. This may in part simply be due to the fact Irenaeus is writing about what he knows. He lived in Gaul and may not have been very familiar with Palestine or the Ebionites. His brief dismissal of the Ebionites may also indicate not a decline in the absolute strength of the Ebionites, but rather a decline in their *relative* strength. The gentile church was rapidly expanding and the Ebionites were stagnant in their membership. But in any event Jewish Christianity experienced a rapid decline in influence relative to the church outside of Palestine, due in no small part to two devastating wars in the region and their persecution by and isolation from the orthodox Judaism of the day. In the meantime, gentile Christianity was almost completely untouched by these events.

Marcion

In roughly this same time period, Marcion emerged as a threat. Marcion was a famous gentile gnostic Christian heretic who not only opposed the orthodox point of view, but that of the Ebionites as well.

Marcion was born late in the first century in Sinope, in present-day Turkey on the Black Sea, and lived until about 160. He came to Rome in 140, but he was expelled from the church there because of his heresies. He was in some ways the antithesis of the Ebionites, the logical conclusion of the most radical followers of Paul. In fact, from the point of view of the Ebionites, Marcion was probably a bigger threat than the orthodox. In the *Recognitions* and *Homilies*, Peter is often more interested in refuting views that sound like Marcion's, than in combating the "orthodox" point of view or even that of Paul.

Marcion wanted to completely divorce Christianity from Judaism. He postulated two Gods, not one. The Jewish God, the lesser God, created the world. It was an evil world of an ignorant Creator. The highest God was the God of Jesus Christ, who rejected Judaism by rejecting the Jewish God altogether and the wicked world which the Jewish God created. Jesus' kingdom was not of this world, and in fact Jesus never physically incarnated at all; he was like a spirit or ghost, seeming to exist but never actually having a material existence.

Moderns typically pronounce Marcion's name, by the way, with a "soft c" rather than a "hard c"—like the "c" in "piece" rather than the "c" in "cake." The Greek transcription of his name is *Markion Sinopon*, Marcion of Sinope. While we can debate the "correct" pronunciation of various names from the ancient world, in this case it would seem that the "hard" pronunciation is more logical.

For Marcion, Paul was the hero—he alone had truly understood Jesus, which the Jewish disciples like Peter had completely misunderstood. He also came up with the first version of the New Testament, which was Luke plus 10 of the letters of Paul (omitting the "pastoral epistles," I and II Timothy and Titus). This was the first attempt by anyone to establish a collection of New Testament books as a "canon."

The versions of Luke and of Paul's letters that Marcion published, however, were not always identical to the canonical versions of these same texts. We don't have a copy of Marcion's "New Testament," but because of the polemical attacks on Marcion, which mention the discrepancies between Marcion's version and the standard New Testament, we do have a good idea of the text which he used. Marcion's Luke, for example, did not have the story of Jesus' birth in it. Also, his version of Galatians evidently omits Galatians 3:6–9 and 3:15–25, where Paul starts out saying, "Thus Abraham believed God, and it was counted to him as righteousness" (Manen, 1887). However, all of the really interesting passages from our point of view, where Paul denounces Peter, are left intact.

Marcion had a profound effect on second-century Christianity. Marcion greatly helped popularize the letters of Paul. According to Gerd Lüdemann, "without Marcion there would have been no New Testament; without this heretic, no letters of Paul" (*Heretics*, p. 167). Marcion understood the problem that the Jewishness of Jesus really posed and saw that Paul was clearly taking Christianity in the general direction that Marcion wanted to go. Like Marcion, Paul broke with the "Jewish" apostles. Like Marcion, Paul complained about the subservience to Jewish customs and rituals.

What would Christianity have been without Marcion? Paul might be completely unknown or have disappeared into history. In that case, Christianity might have gone in a completely unpredictable direction. It might have become a smaller religion in which the Ebionites had a much larger influence, perhaps a religion in which Paul was a minor figure, or that never even knew about Paul.

These speculations are quite interesting and could be argued at some length, but essentially we don't know the answers. Because Marcion was such an overwhelming presence, it is hard to identify any surviving Christian writings, written after the destruction of the temple, that were not either written or edited in the light of Marcion. Even the gospels show this effect: Luke 24:42–43 is clearly an attempt to show that Jesus was physically resurrected, and is an answer to Marcion. How much else is either changed or missing? We can't say.

Jewish Christianity and Marcion

The primary enemy that Jewish Christianity faced in the second century was not the orthodox church, but Marcion. In fact, while it probably can't be proven either way, orthodoxy could be essentially a secondary reaction to Marcion. That is, Marcion was a reaction to Jewish Christianity, and orthodox Christianity was a reaction to

Marcion, thus making orthodoxy a "heresy of a heresy," as Charles Vaclavik puts it.

All we have to do is read the *Recognitions* and *Homilies* to understand this dynamic. Peter is presented as debating someone (Simon Magus) who often talks a great deal like Marcion. Peter is *not* presented as debating someone who talks like Ignatius or Justin Martyr. Who were the Jewish Christians more concerned about?

Hans-Joachim Schoeps therefore credits the Ebionites with having a palpable and hitherto unnoticed effect on Christian history (Schoeps, p. 129). Without the help of the Ebionites, what we know as "orthodoxy" might have disappeared from history. Marcion would have likely been the victor in this struggle and Christianity would have grown into a group that literally worshiped a different God from the Jewish God. The Ebionites best preserved the knowledge that Christianity had, after all, originally been a Jewish sect. Even though the later victorious church substantially modified or rejected the Ebionite interpretation of events, they did acknowledge the religion's Jewish foundations.

The Geography of Jewish Christianity

We can also discover something about the origin of the Ebionites by looking at where they lived. The Ebionites were strongest around where Jesus grew up and first preached, and also in the areas to which the Jerusalem church fled during the first Jewish revolt against Rome—the area on the other side of the Jordan in and around Pella.

Epiphanius provides a lot of information about the location of the various Jewish Christian sects, with Eusebius providing some supporting details. When we put these on a map, we can see that Jewish Christianity remained a largely local or regional affair. It is very plausible that the Ebionites were closely related to Jesus' family, who were found in just the same area. During the several centuries of its existence, Jewish Christianity never really went beyond a few days' journey from its point of origin near the sea of Galilee. Epiphanius says that Ebionism began in Cochaba, and he locates the Nazoraeans there as well.

Three towns stand out, all of them on the east side of the Jordan: Pella, Banias, and Cochaba. Pella and Cochaba are both mentioned by Eusebius as well as Epiphanius as a location of Jewish Christianity.

We have already encountered Pella, the town to which the Jerusalem church fled before the destruction of the temple in the year 70 and which Schoeps describes as a "chief center" of the Ebionites. Banias, also known as "Panias" and as "Caesarea Philippi," is a city not only strongly connected with the Ebionites but also with several episodes in the ministry of Jesus in the gospels—Peter's confession, the "transfiguration" (probably on Mount Hermon), and the healing of the boy seized by a demon (Mark 8:27–9:29 and parallels).

Cochaba is harder to locate. According to Schoeps, Cochaba is likely between Abila and Adraa (*Jewish Christianity*, p. 28), though others put it almost as far north as Damascus. Eusebius quotes Julius Africanus as saying that many of the relatives of Jesus (the "Desposynoi") lived in Cochaba (*Ecclesiastical History* 1.7.14). The Ebionites evidently got as far west as Cyprus but no further.

Placing these names on a map (see figure 19–1) shows that there is a definite geographical pattern to the distribution of Jewish Christianity—it is on the east bank of the Jordan, and north and south of Judea, forming a crescent shape around Judea.

Why this distribution just *outside* of Judea? Almost certainly this is where any Palestinian Christians would have needed to flee to escape the double catastrophe of persecution by Jews and destruction by the Romans in the two Jewish revolts in Palestine. As soon as the Jewish Christians found safety, they stopped, choosing to remain as close as possible to their traditional homes.

There is further evidence that the believers escaped just east of the Jordan. Matthew refers to Capernaum as "across the Jordan" (Matthew 4:15) and to Judea as "beyond the Jordan" (Matthew 19:1). Since Capernaum and Judea are on the *west* side of the Jordan, this implies that the writer is on the *east* side; if the writer were on the west side, one wouldn't speak of these locations as being "across" (or "beyond") the Jordan. This would put Matthew in the region of the southwestern corner of present-day Syria, or modern Jordan. This is exactly the area where the Ebionites were the strongest, thus making the Ebionite claim to have the original gospel of Matthew considerably stronger.

There do not appear to be competing traditions about the family of Jesus. Jesus' family was likely the organizational glue that held the Palestinian Jewish Christian groups together through much of this time. This somewhat wide distribution of Jewish Christian groups, plus their endurance for three centuries, suggests that the Jewish Christian churches were a substantial presence in Palestine. It is entirely possible, or likely, that Jewish Christianity was the *primary* form of Christianity in these areas for several hundred years.

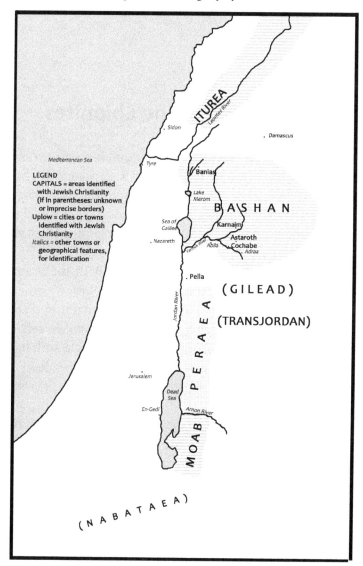

Figure 19–1. The geographical distribution of Jewish Christianity in Palestine.

Sources: Epiphanius, *Panarion* 18.1.1, 19.1.2, 29.7.7–8, 30.2.7–8, 30.18.1, 53.1.1. Beroea, Cyprus, and Arielis are mentioned by Epiphanius but not on the map. Beroea is a town in northwestern Syria, near present-day Aleppo. Cyprus is an island in the Mediterranean just south of modern-day Turkey.

20. Our Knowledge of the Ebionites

Throughout this book we have been using sources for our knowledge of the Ebionites—the church fathers and the pseudo-Clementine literature, mostly. We now come to the point in the narrative, in the second through fourth centuries, when our sources on the Ebionites were actually written, and so we now want to examine these in more detail.

The most interesting source of knowledge about the Ebionites is the "pseudo-Clementine literature": mostly, the *Recognitions* and the *Homilies*, as well as two much shorter letters written by Peter and Clement to James. The *Recognitions* and the *Homilies* reflect the Ebionites' own experience and struggles—their struggle with Judaism, their conflict with Simon Magus (who puts forward the views of Paul and Marcion), and their own experience of Jesus Christ, the true prophet.

These writings themselves report directly on nothing beyond the first century, even though they were written after that. When we leave Peter and Clement in the *Recognitions* and *Homilies*, Peter has finished debating Simon Magus, whom he has completely refuted in a succession of debates, and Clement has been miraculously reunited with his family.

In this chapter and the next two, we will look at the substance of Ebionite theology.

Our Sources: Irenaeus and Hippolytus

The church fathers Irenaeus, Hippolytus, and Epiphanius all discuss the Ebionites. There are other writers, but they mostly seem to be copying from them and don't seem to add very much that is new. Jerome, Eusebius, Origen, Augustine, Clement of Alexandria, and Theodoret are some of the better known of these early writers, and from time to time I have quoted from them. There is a catalog of references to Jewish Christianity in *Patristic Evidence for Jewish-Christian sects* (Klijn and Reinink).

But all church fathers are not equal. The contribution of Epiphanius swamps that of the others. If you go back and look at Tables 3–1 and 3–2 (in chapter 3), you can immediately infer from Table 3–1 that Epiphanius says much more than Irenaeus or Hippolytus. Of the 15 beliefs I have set out as Ebionite, Epiphanius has 11 of them, whereas Irenaeus and Hippolytus only have 5 and 4.

If you actually read these authors, you immediately see the reason. Irenaeus and Hippolytus provide us with just about a paragraph *each* on the Ebionites. Irenaeus (*Against Heresies* 1.26.2) takes just three sentences to say that the Ebionites believed that God created the world, denied the virgin birth, used the Gospel of Matthew only, "repudiate the apostle Paul," observed the Jewish law, and expounded the prophets "in a somewhat singular manner." Further down (*Against Heresies* 5.1.3), he repeats this information, adding the information that the Ebionites reject using wine in the Eucharist.

Hippolytus takes a little longer to repeat most of this information in a single paragraph (*Refutation of All Heresies* 7.22; very briefly summarized at 10.18). Hippolytus adds one new idea, that the Ebionites believed that *anyone*, by observing the law, could be Christ. This is very similar to *Recognitions* 1.45, which says that pious believers are anointed with similar oil to that with which God anointed Jesus. We might refer to this idea as "the Christhood of the believer."

This is virtually the *entirety* of what Irenaeus and Hippolytus have to say on the Ebionites. That the Ebionites "persevere in the observance of those customs which are enjoined by the law" (Irenaeus) might mean that the Ebionites practiced animal sacrifice (commanded by Leviticus) except for one problem: the temple was destroyed, so they couldn't practice animal sacrifice even if they wanted to. This statement, therefore, implies nothing about their views on animal sacrifice. There is no indication that they thought that these Jewish customs were *required*, by the way, just that they observed them. The main point of the section is that the Ebionites did not follow the "unknown God" followed by Marcion and Valentinus.

There is no reference in Irenaeus or Hippolytus to Ebionite vegetarianism, opposition to animal sacrifice, voluntary poverty, pacifism, and so forth, but this doesn't prove very much, for several reasons. In the first place, Irenaeus and Hippolytus give only brief descriptions and give no indication that they have seen either actual Ebionites or Ebionite documents. Neither of them is that interested in the subject—the Ebionites are a digression in a lengthy work.

Secondly, though, in the time frame we are talking about (second and third centuries), none of these things were either heretical or even that distinctive. Most early Christians were pacifists as a matter of course at that time, including Irenaeus and Hippolytus themselves, as well as such figures as Origen, Tertullian, Justin, Arnobius, and Lactantius. Many were vegetarians as well, likely including Origen, Tertullian, Clement of Alexandria, and Jerome. Even Irenaeus himself recalls the prophecies of Isaiah about the future world without any killing and without eating animals (*Against Heresies* 5.33.4). Augustine said in the fifth century that the number of Christian vegetarians was "without number" (*Of the Morals of the Catholic Church* 33). Irenaeus and Hippolytus were not concerned with detailed descriptions but with the refutation of *heresies*, so their attention was drawn specifically to the heretical elements.

Epiphanius

Epiphanius is a very important source on the Ebionites. Epiphanius lived and wrote in the second half of the fourth century, about 50 years or so after the Council of Nicaea. By contrast with earlier church writers, Epiphanius has a lengthy description of the Ebionites which amounts to over 24 pages in a modern translation. This is found in his *Panarion* (or "the Medicine Chest"—medicines, that is, to be used against the "disease" of heresy).

Epiphanius not only talks about the Ebionites, he also talks about related Jewish or Jewish Christian groups such as the Nazoraeans, Nasaraeans, Ossaeans, Sampsaeans, and Elkasaites. Moreover, Epiphanius makes it clear that he has copies of Ebionite literature in front of him, and he quotes from their gospel at several points. He has talked to individual Ebionites, and he quotes from conversations he has had with them. He is better informed, and he says a lot about it.

Scholars sometimes are reluctant to cite Epiphanius and make the excuse that Epiphanius is unreliable. Well, he *is* unreliable in a sense. Epiphanius is a person whom we might refer to colloquially today as a "big mouth." Such people have a lot to say, talk all the time, have an exaggerated sense of their own self-importance, and repeat things they have heard indiscriminately. Epiphanius does not evaluate different sources and draw conclusions, as a modern scholar would; he just writes. He often doesn't tell us what his sources are, and he cites them uncritically. His rhetoric is often arrogant and overblown, and we get a lot of comments like this: "What frightful shrieks and snake-like hisses from the horrid serpents! How poisonous their nonsense is!" (*Panarion* 30.25.3)

On the other hand, we never get the impression that Epiphanius is making anything up. He is quoting from *someone*, he has heard it *somewhere*. A good example of this can be found in his insistence that the founder of the Ebionites was a fictional person named "Ebion." Curiously, he also cites the Ebionites' *own* views of where their name came from, which with characteristic arrogance he dismisses. The Ebionites themselves knew nothing about any "Ebion" but rather derived their name from their voluntary (or possibly, not so voluntary) poverty. And in fact, we find several references to "Ebion" in Tertullian (*On the Flesh of Christ* 14, 18, 24), which is possibly where Epiphanius got the idea. This is typical Epiphanius: he just writes down everything.

In some cases, this actually makes Epiphanius a better source than other church writers. If he had used more "critical thinking" or actually *thought* about what he was saying, we might have a more readable text, but he might have filtered out a lot of really interesting information.

For example, he describes the name of the Nazoraeans, a heretical Jewish Christian sect, as the *earliest* name used by all Christians. Other church fathers might have been embarrassed by this, since they were typically at pains to show that heresies had an origin *later* than orthodox Christian doctrine, and if possible to trace the heresy to a particular heretic. Likewise, Epiphanius feels no shame at locating the heretical Jewish Christian sects in exactly the same location that the Jerusalem church fled to after the destruction of Jerusalem.

Epiphanius just blurts it out without thinking. So for our purposes, a "big mouth" church father isn't necessarily a bad thing.

It's true that Irenaeus and Hippolytus are writing from a much earlier time—a century or two earlier, in fact. But nothing that Irenaeus or Hippolytus say in the *few sentences* they devote to the Ebionites indicates that they have either seen the Ebionite literature or have ever talked to any actual Ebionites; and none of it, moreover, contradicts anything in Epiphanius.

There is simply no contest between Epiphanius and any other early church father. Ignoring Epiphanius is not much different from ignoring what the church fathers say about the Ebionites entirely. We should certainly read Epiphanius critically; we need an argument, another source, something to convince us that Epiphanius isn't just repeating something unreliable. But in the case of Jewish Christianity that is usually fairly easy to do, because of the *Recognitions* and *Homilies*, which are completely independent sources.

The *Recognitions of Clement* and *The Clementine Homilies*

The second category of sources is the pseudo-Clementine literature, which consists of several documents. Most importantly, there are the lengthy *Recognitions of Clement* and *The Clementine Homilies*, which occupy 137 and 124 pages, respectively, in volume 8 of the *Ante-Nicene Fathers*. But there are also two much briefer documents, the *Epistle of Peter to James* and the *Epistle of Clement to James*, which are 3 and 5 pages each.

All of this is important because, unlike the writings of the church fathers, it comes (mostly) from the hands of the Jewish Christians themselves, and so gives us a chance to hear them in their own voice, rather than mediated through the eyes of their opponents. There is the possibility of hostile or indifferent editing, so we can't just assume that these entire documents are straight from the hands of the Ebionites and quote chapter and verse to prove a particular view of what the Ebionites thought.

Typically, if we find an idea in the *Recognitions* and *Homilies* and attributed to the Ebionites by Epiphanius, it is likely that it really was an Ebionite idea. If we also find the same idea attributed by Paul to his Jewish Christian opponents in the church, that further adds to its credibility. Epiphanius may not have been capable of critical thinking, but we are.

These writings are called "pseudo-Clementine" because the purported author, Clement of Rome, is almost certainly not who actually wrote them—just as I and II Timothy and Titus in the New Testament, though attributed to Paul, are almost certainly not really written by Paul. However, we are not interested in proving anything about the "historical Clement," but about Jewish Christianity; and as Jewish Christian sources, there's nothing "pseudo" about them, they are extremely useful.

The constant reference to this literature as *"pseudo*-Clementine" is, probably, in no small part an attempt to denigrate Jewish Christian literature. No one calls I and II Timothy and Titus (in the New Testament) the "pseudo-Pauline literature," that would be an insult to believing Christians! But since there aren't any believing Ebionites still around (or not in any significant quantity), no one has any compunctions about such references to the pseudo-Clementine literature.

Virtually everything of significance that Epiphanius says about the Ebionites is duplicated in either the *Recognitions*, the *Homilies*, or both. Chapter 3 contains two tables, Table 3–1 and Table 3–2, which gives a list of some of the more obvious Ebionite doctrines I have referred to throughout the book.

Epiphanius attributes to Jewish Christians a number of ideas which are found only rarely anywhere else in early Christianity at all, and certainly not in combination: Jesus is the "true prophet," vegetarianism, rejection of animal sacrifice, "false texts" in the scriptures, Christ was in Adam and appeared to the patriarchs such as Abraham and Moses. And surprise, surprise: these rare and unique views also turn up in the *Recognitions* and *Homilies.* As a consequence, there is a consensus among the scholars that have studied the subject, going back to the nineteenth century, that the *Recognitions* and *Homilies* reflect Jewish Christian ideas.

In fact, the correspondence is *so* remarkable that one is tempted to say that maybe copies of the *Recognitions* and *Homilies* have fallen into Epiphanius' hands and that Epiphanius is just reading them as Jewish Christian documents. However, this appears quite unlikely. Epiphanius, who seems just to dump everything in front of him onto the reader, mentions the Ebionite documents he has seen—their gospel (*Panarion* 30.3.7), "The Travels of Peter" (30.15.1), an Ebionite "Acts of the Apostles" (30.16.6), and "the Ascents of James" (30.16.7). All of these documents are lost to history. But most likely the *Recognitions* and *Homilies* are based on, or copy from, these Ebionite writings. After all, they do mention James, they do describe some of Peter's travels, and they do contain lots of Ebionite ideas. It's quite likely that the documents Epiphanius knows about have somehow been incorporated, wholly or in part, into the *Recognitions* and *Homilies*.

The literary situation with regard to the *Recognitions* and *Homilies* is quite complex. The *Recognitions* and *Homilies*, generally considered third-century documents, are very similar to each other. They both feature the same basic plot line. Clement searches for knowledge and finds Peter; Peter and Clement travel together while Peter debates Simon Magus, the arch-enemy of the Jesus movement; and Clement in the end is reunited with his long-lost family—his father, his mother, and his two brothers, all of whom had been separated not only from Clement but also from each other. And, as befits a religious romance, they all convert to Christianity. The *Recognitions* and *Homilies* look very much like two different versions of the same original.

The current prevailing view is that there was an original or "basic" writing which is the core of both the *Recognitions* and *Homilies*. Later, a second writer (the author of the *Recognitions*) modified this basic writing and a third writer (the author of the *Homilies*) modified it in a different way. Of course, there may be other editors who got their fingers in the pie, too, but that's roughly the situation. This isn't the only theory; some scholars have postulated that the *Recognitions* (or the *Homilies*) was written first, and then the author of the other document copied parts of it and made modifications. But the theory of a single basic document developed in two different ways seems intuitively stronger. Jones (2007) makes the "Circuits of Peter" (or "Travels of Peter") the basic writing, and traces two of the sources of this document, in turn, back to the Book of Elxai and to a Counter-Acts of the Apostles (found in *Recognitions* 1.27–1.71).

Fortunately, we don't have to resolve all (or even most) questions relating to the *Recognitions* and *Homilies* to figure out their relevance to the Ebionites. There is material that is unique to the *Recognitions* which seems to be clearly Ebionite—e. g. *Recognitions* 1, containing the famous description of the confrontation between James and Saul (Paul) in the temple. There is also material unique to the *Homilies* which is clearly Ebionite—e. g., the idea of false texts in the scriptures put forward in *Homilies* 2.

Two things follow from all this.

1. The *Recognitions* and *Homilies* are probably based on earlier Jewish Christian documents, to which Epiphanius refers. This "multiple attestation" validates much of what Epiphanius says; it means that anything mentioned by Epiphanius, that is also found in the *Recognitions* or *Homilies*, is almost certainly an Ebionite idea.

2. The *Recognitions* and *Homilies* are third or fourth century documents, and the "ancestor documents" which they in turn have been copied from (such as the "Travels of Peter" to which Epiphanius refers) may be even earlier, ultimately going back as early as the second century. Therefore, we can push our knowledge of the Ebionites back at least a century or two. Most likely, this is not just what the fourth-century Ebionites were like, but also the Ebionites of the second and third centuries as well.

How far can we take these correspondences? What about all the things in the *Recognitions* and *Homilies* which are *not* mentioned by Epiphanius? Can we read the *Recognitions* and *Homilies* as Ebionite texts, quoting chapter and verse to prove a particular theory of the Ebionites? We can't do this automatically, even within the same chapter. *Recognitions* 1.33 and 1.34, for example, contain the Ebionite idea that Christ ("the true prophet") appeared to Abraham and Moses—a belief also mentioned by Epiphanius. But *Recognitions* 1.49 and 1.69 say that Christ will come exactly twice—once in humbleness in first-century Palestine, and the second in glory to judge the world. This seems to contradict what is clearly said elsewhere; it may, in fact, to be the insertion of an orthodox editor, since this is the only place this orthodox idea is mentioned.

So we need to be cautious about using the *Recognitions* and *Homilies*. If we find an idea in the *Recognitions* or *Homilies*, it certainly *could* have been an Ebionite idea, but we need some sort of argument (agreement with Epiphanius or some other source, or logical coherence) in order to reasonably say that it *was* an Ebionite idea.

Conclusions

Epiphanius and the *Recognitions* and *Homilies* are our major sources for Ebionite beliefs. We can't quote them chapter and verse, but when they agree with each other or seem to cohere with other things we know about the Ebionites, they form a consistent picture of what the Ebionites believed.

Irenaeus and Hippolytus are earlier sources with less information. But they do prove that a group known as the "Ebionites" existed in the second and third centuries, and was already distinguished by "deviant" ideas about Jesus (that he was human and had human parents) and a dislike for the apostle Paul.

21. Ebionite Theology in a Nutshell

In this chapter, we will examine the *Recognitions* and *Homilies* looking for an overall Ebionite theological framework. As we mentioned much earlier, the basic point of view of the *Recognitions* and *Homilies* is simple and similar in outline to that of the orthodox:

1. God is the creator of everything that is.
2. Jesus is the messenger of God.
3. Jesus brings both a moral code and a warning of a future judgement.

When we get to the details, however, we see that the *Recognitions* and *Homilies* had a peculiar "twist" on each of these points.

Which Ideas are Ebionite?

How do we know that anything in the *Recognitions* and *Homilies* is authentically Ebionite? We cannot be certain. However, when this theology supports and is consonant with other known Ebionite elements, we gain confidence that this is not in the *Recognitions* and *Homilies* by accident; it's there because the same Jewish Christian ideas underlie all of them. We are looking for *coherence*.

However, there is a problem here, and that is that the *Recognitions* and *Homilies* are not always internally consistent—sometimes we see blatant contradictions that will leave us scratching our heads. Is this because an Ebionite doctrine has been "corrupted" by non-Ebionite editors? Or is it because the Ebionites themselves were sometimes contradictory? Here are several examples of this dilemma:

1. At many times it is asserted that baptism is a necessary prerequisite for salvation, no matter how many righteous deeds

you have done (*Recognitions* 6.8–9, *Homilies* 11.26–27), but when it gets down to cases, Peter appears to relax this requirement (*Homilies* 13.20).

2. *Recognitions* 5.7 asserts that those who sin through ignorance are not condemned, but *Recognitions* 5.18 says that those who sin through ignorance *will* be condemned.

3. *Homilies* 2.38–44 rejects the commands to offer animal sacrifices in the Old Testament as falsehoods which Moses never uttered; but *Recognitions* 1.36 says that Moses *did* wisely make such commands, as a concession to human weakness.

4. A variety of ideas about "Christ" and the "true prophet" are put forward; sometimes the true prophet manifests physically (*Homilies* 3.20) but at other times he manifests spiritually, "within the mind of every one of us" (*Recognitions* 8.59).

5. *Recognitions* 4.15 states that demons will suffer torment in hell; but *Homilies* 9.9 argues that the demons will feel pleasure, being in their natural element.

6. Throughout most of the *Recognitions* and *Homilies*, it seems that Christ appears throughout history. But there are two passages, *Recognitions* 1.49 and 1.69, which assert exactly two appearances of Jesus.

What is going on here? We have to look at each problem on a case-by-case basis. It's possible, for example, in the last case—the two passages asserting exactly two appearances of Jesus—that this is an insertion by a non-Ebionite editor, since it seems to conform so closely with orthodox theology and contradict the Ebionite ideas of the "eternal Christ" maintained elsewhere.   On the other hand, for the other problems mentioned above, such as whether Moses ever made commands to offer animal sacrifices, the answer is likely very different. Both contradictory positions are individually compatible within an overall Ebionite framework. In this case we may have contradictory ideas which are both Ebionite in some sense.

Based on Epiphanius, we have reason to say that the Ebionites sometimes contradicted themselves. Epiphanius says the "Ebion" was like a "many-headed hydra" (*Panarion* 30.1.1). Rather than referring to factionalism within Jewish Christianity, this most likely refers to the fact that Epiphanius would get different answers to the same question from people all sharing the same basic framework. "They get all giddy from supposing different things about [Jesus] at different times," says Epiphanius about the Ebionites (*Panarion* 30.3.6).

So the presence of inconsistencies in themselves (and there are quite a few), does not *necessarily* imply the corrupting influence of a non-Ebionite editor; it may also mean that the Ebionites just hadn't quite figured out what they really believed themselves. In fact they, like we, often just said different things at different times without always working out the implications.

Radical Monotheism and the Doctrine of Opposites

Interestingly, one of the key beliefs of the Jewish Christians—one which is central to understanding their history—is not a heretical belief, but an orthodox belief: that the God of Jesus is the creator of the heavens and the earth. The Ebionites denied the Marcionite doctrine that there were two Gods, a Jewish Creator God and the Father-God of Jesus. The *Recognitions* and *Homilies* are filled with statements of and arguments for radical monotheism (*Recognitions* 1.25, 2.41–42, 2.44, 2.45, 5.2, 5.13, 7.29, 8.12, 8.14, 8.20, 8.34, 8.39, and 9.1; *Homilies* 2.12, 2.45, 7.2, 8.9, 8.10, 9.19, 10.10, 10.19, 10.20, and 16.5).

Citing evidence of monotheism in a Jewish Christian group might seem redundant, but the issue was not trivial for the Ebionites. They were in competition with groups that were *not* monotheistic, such as those following Marcion, who held that there was both a "Christian" God and a "Jewish" God. In the *Recognitions* and *Homilies*, the opposing views are put forward by Simon Magus, who quotes scripture to prove his point that there is more than one God (e. g. *Recognitions* 2.38–39, *Homilies* 16.6). "Simon Magus" in the *Recognitions* and *Homilies* may just be a convenient mouthpiece in which to put some of Marcion's views, but he is likely also an historical figure (see chapter 25); Simon Magus represented the powerful anti-monotheistic forces with which the Ebionites were struggling.

The Ebionite argument is often (so to speak) more orthodox than the orthodox, because God is responsible for so much more. In orthodox theology, God presides over a universe in which (by virtue of free will) some beings, human and angel, have consciously deviated from God's will. But in the *Homilies* (and to a lesser extent the

Recognitions), this picture is substantially modified. God presides over a monistic universe *in which, in effect, true evil does not exist.*

The devil and demons act in accordance with the laws God gives them. This is not rebellion, but loyalty (*Recognitions* 4.16–17; *Homilies* 8.20). It is a relative and temporary evil. God created and presides over both realms, but he delegated this world to the devil, and the next to Jesus (*Homilies* 20.2, *Panarion* 30.16.2).

In contrast to a dualism of two co-eternal forces of good and evil, like that of Marcion, this is a dualism deliberately set up and controlled by God. Monotheism is reconciled with evil through the doctrine of opposites, sometimes called "the law of conjunction." God created pairs of opposites for our benefit and instruction (*Recognitions* 3.59, 3.75, *Homilies* 2.15, 2.33, 3.16, 3.22–24, 3.27, 3.59, 19.23, 20.2). In the *Homilies* they include such pairs as Ignorance and Knowledge, World and Eternity, Female and Male, etc.; in the *Recognitions*, the opposites are more historical in character—Pharaoh and Abraham, Magicians and Moses, Simon Magus and Peter, etc.

The doctrine of opposites is modeled after or based on the Pythagorean idea of opposites (see table 6–2), which is itself a monotheistic or even monistic system. God created these opposites for our spiritual realization (*Homilies* 19.23). Suffering is temporary and is for our spiritual realization (or the spiritual realization of others). Peter adds enigmatically, "But the humiliations and exaltations of men take place according to lot; and he who is not pleased with his lot can appeal" (*Homilies* 19.23). He never explains what the "lot" is, by which humans are assigned either positive or negative experiences in this life, but it seems to be an allusion to the "myth of Er" in Book 10 of Plato's *Republic*, in which the dead are reborn in circumstances determined partially by lot. *Homilies* 15.8 contains another reference to the myth of Er, so the Ebionites were evidently aware of this Platonic reference and perhaps held a theory of reincarnation.

Both Marcion and the Ebionites were opposed to the violence and evil which had come to overrun the world; both were pacifists, and both were vegetarians. Marcion saw the world as inherently flawed, a creation botched from the beginning. The Ebionites, by contrast, did not see the world as flawed. They wanted to simultaneously explain that they were loyal to the one true God who created the world, and yet also opposed the violence and evil which had come to overrun the world. Evil only seemed to be a power, but this was an illusion—"Evil, then, does not exist always, yea, it cannot even exist at all substantially" (*Homilies* 19.20). The Ebionites saw evil as something to be opposed, but also in a certain sense something to be reconciled with.

Jesus, the True Prophet, and the Christ

For the Ebionites, Jesus is both the "true prophet" and also the "Christ." Both of these concepts are clearly Ebionite in origin, yet are sometimes taken in rather different directions.

On the one hand, the "true prophet" continually returns throughout history (*Recognitions* 1.33, 1.34, 1.52, 2.22, 2.48, 8.59; *Homilies* 3.20). Indeed, Adam himself had this spirit of Christ or of the true prophet (*Homilies* 3.20, *Panarion* 30.3.5), and the true prophet appeared to Abraham and Moses (*Recognitions* 1.33, 1.34). This is in contrast to the orthodox concept of Christ who appears exactly twice, the first time in first-century Palestine and the second time on the judgment day.

But on the other, there is a historical figure Jesus who was the "true prophet" predicted by Moses (Recognitions 1.57, *Homilies* 3.53, etc.). These do not *necessarily* contradict each other, but the prophet predicted by Moses is not obviously someone who continually appears throughout history.

"Christ" is likewise used in different ways; sometimes "Christ" is a title that applies to Jesus and evidently to others as well (*Recognitions* 1.45), but sometimes sounds like a single entity (*Recognitions* 1.43). So the Ebionite concepts of "true prophet" and "Christ" are hard to define in a precise way.

The Ebionites invoked different scriptures than the orthodox did to discover a prophecy about Jesus. In orthodox theology, many writers go back to Isaiah 53, the image of the "suffering servant," to find a prophecy on which to base Jesus' claim to be the Messiah. The Ebionites did not take this path, instead going to a different scripture with different overtones. At *Homilies* 3.53, Peter quotes Deuteronomy 18:15–19—Moses' prediction of a future prophet—and says that Jesus applied this prophecy to himself.

In Deuteronomy, Moses says "The Lord your God will raise up for you a prophet like me from among you, from your brethren—him you shall heed" (Deuteronomy 18:15). Deuteronomy 18:20–22 adds the unhelpful information that if a prophet claims to be the true prophet, but doesn't deliver on the prophetic part because his prophecies fail, you can disregard him; he is a false prophet.

This is a case in which it is not clear whether there are two contradictory Ebionite ideas (Jesus appearing twice, versus Jesus appearing throughout history), or one very complex idea (Jesus appearing twice, but "Christ" occurring throughout history, including as Jesus). But in either case, "Jesus" and "Christ" are not synonymous. Many people can be called "Christ"; Jesus was just the most important (*Recognitions* 1.45, *Refutation of All Heresies* 7.22).

In the *Recognitions* and *Homilies* the figure of the true prophet is considerably more exalted than one would expect from Deuteronomy. Deuteronomy would lead one to believe that the "true prophet" will be a figure somewhat like Isaiah or Jeremiah, or at most like Moses himself. But in the *Recognitions* and *Homilies*, the true prophet—while still not quite the incarnation of the Almighty—is much more powerful than that. Nowhere in the *Recognitions* and *Homilies* is Jesus quoted as saying, "Before Abraham was, I am" (John 8:58); but the concept of the true prophet seems to be modeled after this and similar sayings.

The exact ways in which the true prophet manifests are also unclear. *Homilies* 3.20 implies that the true prophet incarnates or materializes *physically*, saying that the true prophet has taken on various shapes and forms since the beginning of the world. Epiphanius explicitly says that the Ebionites believed that Christ appeared *bodily* to the patriarchs (*Panarion* 30.3.5). This appears to straightforwardly support the idea of reincarnation, at least for Jesus.

Interestingly, the New Testament states that some people thought of Jesus as a reincarnation of a previous holy figure—"some say John the Baptist, others say Elijah, and others Jeremiah or one of the prophets" (Matthew 16:14). In fact this verse is likely a polemical reference to the Ebionite idea of the true prophet. This would indicate that this idea goes back to the first century, so this element of Ebionite theology is quite old, since it was known to the gospel writers as well as to the Ebionites.

But at another point the Ebionite Peter says that the true prophet "is within the mind of every one of us" (*Recognitions* 8.59), which implies not so much a physical appearance as a "spiritual" appearance. Peter also speaks of the "true prophet" as a spirit who, in effect, whispers in the ear of the righteous, even in countries which have never heard of Jesus (as in *Recognitions* 9.20–31)! This seems to be consonant with the Ebionite idea that all believers are "Christs" (Hippolytus, *Refutation of All Heresies* 7.22).

The Message: Against Blood

In the *Recognitions* and *Homilies*, Jesus brings a radical ethical message of the virtue of poverty, of vegetarianism, of the rejection of animal sacrifice, and the rejection of war (see Table 21–1). A key doctrine of Jewish Christianity is nonviolence, the refusal of "blood," whether that is the blood of a human or an animal. There is also a rejection of wealth and private property, as suggested by the term *ebionim* ("the poor").

	Recognitions	*Homilies*
Vegetarianism, Rejection of Animal Sacrifice	1.36, 1.37, 1.39, 1.54, 1.64, 2.71–72, 4.36, 7.6, 8.48	2.44, 3.24, 3.26, 3.45, 3.52, 3.56, 7.3, 7.4, 7.8, 12.6, 8.19, 9.7, 18.19
Pacifism, rejection of war and bloodshed	1.71, 2.25, 2.27, 2.30, 2.36, 3.42, 4.31	2.44, 3.19, 3.62, 4.20–22, 9.2, 11.19, 12.26, 12.32
The virtue of poverty or simple living	2.29, 5.9, 7.6	3.69, 7.4, 11.4, 12.6, 12.32, 15.8–9

Table 21–1. Some references to simple living and nonviolence in the *Recognitions* and *Homilies*.

Epiphanius also emphasizes their opposition to bloodshed, and says that the Ebionites were vegetarian (*Panarion* 30.15.3). In the Ebionite gospel, Jesus indignantly rejects eating meat at the Passover (*Panarion* 30.22.5). Epiphanius relates a conversation in which he questions an Ebionite about their rejection of meat-eating and animal sacrifice, citing the cases of these practices among the patriarchs. The Ebionite responds "Christ revealed it to me" (*Panarion* 30.18.9). It is apparent that the Ebionites were also pacifists and didn't kill humans, but the striking thing is that they didn't kill animals either, being vehemently opposed to animal sacrifice—their gospel quoting Jesus as saying, "I have come to destroy the sacrifices, and if you do not cease from sacrificing, wrath will not cease from you" (*Panarion* 30.16.5).

The warnings against wealth are not as prominent or frequent as the warnings against blood, but do appear at several places. *Homilies* 15.9 contains the startling statement, "possessions are sins," which is similar to the nineteenth century French socialist Proudhon's statement—echoed by Marxists—that "property is theft." Evidently the only private property allowed is bread, water, one garment, and whatever is necessary through work to sustain life. *Recognitions* 7.6 and *Homilies* 12.6 emphasizes Peter's simple lifestyle and vegetarian diet, adding olives and pot-herbs to the list of allowed foods.

Something very close to a Jewish Christian credo appears in *Homilies* 7.4. The "things which are well-pleasing to God" are enumerated: (1) "to pray to Him"; (2) "to abstain from the table of devils, not to taste dead flesh, not to touch blood"; (3) "to be washed from all pollution" (baptism, we presume), and (4) the Golden Rule: "be of one mind in many bodies," and do unto others as you would have them to unto you. This is all repeated at *Homilies* 7.8, with some minor additions—washing after intercourse, being "sober-minded" (avoiding alcohol), and avoiding suffocated animals (although this seems redundant, since we are already avoiding "dead flesh").

Ritual Observance

Ritual observances do not seem to play a major role in salvation in the *Recognitions* and *Homilies*. The Ebionites seemed to downplay specifically Jewish observances. The main ritual which *does* receive emphasis is not any of the "Jewish" rituals that we normally think of, but baptism.

Even those who are totally righteous in every other way, still need to be baptized. "Unless a man be baptized in water . . . he can neither receive remission of sins nor enter into the kingdom of heaven" (*Recognitions* 1.69; cf. 1.63, 6.8–9, *Homilies* 11.26–27, 13.21). As mentioned above, though, Peter appears to relax this requirement when given a specific question. When Mattidia, Clement's mother who lived righteously but without knowing Jesus, comes to be baptized, Peter adds that had she drowned on her trip to Palestine, the sea itself would have baptized her for her salvation (*Homilies* 13.20). Peter likewise says that if Niceta's father dies without being baptized, he may yet be saved, "For those who have lived righteously, for the sake of God alone and His righteousness, they shall come to eternal rest, and shall receive the perpetuity of the heavenly kingdom" (*Recognitions* 10.2). Peter seems to be willing to improvise a bit with this requirement.

Epiphanius says that "Ebion" (the fictitious leader of the Jewish Christian Ebionites) was attached to "the Sabbath, circumcision, and all the other Jewish and Samaritan observances" (*Panarion* 30.2.2). He says that the Ebionites are "proud" of circumcision and advocate circumcision (*Panarion* 30.26.1–2), but stops short of saying that they thought that circumcision was required for salvation.

Looking at the *Recognitions* and *Homilies* suggests that the Ebionites viewed circumcision as the default cultural practice, but was definitely not a requirement, and in any event not nearly as important as baptism. Circumcision is only explicitly mentioned in the *Recognitions* in order to deny that it is a requirement (5.34); the true Jew need not be circumcised. This agrees with *Gospel of Thomas* 53: if circumcision were useful, they would have been born circumcised.

Homilies 8.6–7 says that the teachings of Moses and Jesus are the same. God accepts anyone who has believed *either* of these and acted accordingly, as long as they do not condemn the Jews or gentiles who follow the other teacher. *Homilies* 8.7 adds a conclusion that seems to refer to the Ebionites' own revelation: "Moreover, if any one has been thought worthy to recognize both as preaching one doctrine, that man has been counted rich in God, understanding both the old things as new in time, and the new things as old." This, again, explicitly opens salvation up to those who are gentiles.

The *Epistle of Peter to James* does contain the one favorable reference in the pseudo-Clementine literature to circumcision. James, after reading Peter's letter, maintains that the books of Peter's preachings should only be communicated to "one who is good and religious, and who wishes to teach, and who is circumcised, and faithful"; and those receiving the books must further agree only to give these writings to someone else "judged worthy, as I myself have been judged, or more so" (*Epistle of Peter to James* 4). This does not require circumcision for salvation, only for being a teacher.

The *Epistle of Peter to James* is distinctive for two other reasons. It regards the preachings of Peter as something to be kept *secret,* rather than declared to the world. It is not to be communicated to the gentiles, or even other Jews not yet determined worthy. Secondly, prospective teachers must make a lengthy declaration which is sanctified by the elements of heaven, earth, and water; at the end, the ceremony is sealed with a sharing of bread and salt. This sounds more like the Elkasaites (see chapter 24) than the Ebionites. The Elkasaites had an element of secrecy in their teachings, and invoked the elements of heaven, earth, water, bread, and salt (*Panarion* 19.1.6).

Epiphanius does not give details about other Jewish festivals or rituals, and the *Recognitions* and *Homilies* don't provide much more information. Sabbath observance is not discussed in the *Recognitions* and *Homilies*—perhaps it was taken for granted. There are some brief injunctions "to keep the law of purification" and "to wash after intercourse" at *Homilies* 7.8, but there is no elaboration on this. The Mandaeans, interestingly, have a similar command to immerse after intercourse (see chapter 25).

The Word of God

How did the Ebionites interpret the sacred texts of Judaism? The Ebionites had an obvious problem here; the Old Testament contains numerous texts which support exactly the sorts of things that the Ebionites condemned. One could open the book of Leviticus almost at random and find commands to offer animal sacrifices. Warfare and murder is also sanctioned in the Jewish scriptures; Joshua and I Samuel have God commanding the slaughter not only of enemy combatants but of civilians as well.

The Ebionites felt that there *was* a law of God, but different from the written texts handed down by tradition. "God," says *Homilies* 8.10, "appointed a perpetual law to all, which neither can be abrogated by enemies, nor is vitiated by any impious one, nor is concealed in any place, but which can be read by all"—rejecting the need for scholars, scribes, traditions, or texts to explain it to us.

The *Homilies* explicitly rejects "false texts" in the scripture: "For the Scriptures have had joined to them many falsehoods against God on this account" (2.38), and *Homilies* 2.43–44 gives a whole catalog of specific objections that could easily apply to a wide variety of scriptures. *Homilies* 3.50 and 3.51 quote Jesus as saying some critical things about the scriptures as well (see discussion in chapter 5).

The opponents of the Jesus movement accused the Christians of controverting the scriptures. This is the charge leveled against Stephen in Acts 6:13–14, that he "never ceases to speak words against this holy place [the temple] and the law" and will "change the customs which Moses delivered to us" (see chapter 12). Of course, changing the customs about animal sacrifice is *precisely* what the Ebionites intended.

In ancient times, as in modern times, the scriptures commanded a lot of respect, thus complicating the Ebionite position. Peter wants to avoid the appearance of making a public issue out of the truth of the Bible (*Homilies* 2.39). He adds, "wherefore every man who wishes to be saved must become, as the Teacher [Jesus] said, a judge of the books written to try us. For thus He spake: 'Become experienced bankers'" (*Homilies* 18.20).

"Become experienced bankers" means to become like a banker who is able to tell the true coins from the false—the true and false coins being the true and false scriptures in the economy of salvation. This is a saying of Jesus not in the Bible, but quoted by other early church fathers such as Clement of Alexandria (*Stromata* 1.28). This saying may then have a very early origin, possibly from the original Christian community or before. It was likely one of the teachings of the early community which was dropped in the rush to fight Marcion, who objected to the scriptures as well, though for different reasons. In Marcion's view, the scriptures were the true teachings about the imperfect God, while for the Ebionites, the scriptures were the imperfect teachings about the true God.

We also have testimony to their attention to the scriptures outside of the *Recognitions* and *Homilies*. Symmachus was a late second-century Ebionite scribe whose translated the Old Testament into Greek (*Ecclesiastical History* 6.16–17), a translation greatly admired by Jerome. Alas, Symmachus' translation doesn't tell us much about the Ebionite view of the Old Testament; he evidently translated the "false texts" along with everything else (Schoeps, p. 84), though it was a great help to Jerome. The bulk of the surviving translations of Symmachus have come down to us when quoted by Origen, according to Schoeps, who also notes: "Since Symmachus was a polished translator and stylist, his influence extended beyond the Ebionite circle to Jerome's Latin vulgate" (Schoeps, p. 15).

This rejection of Old Testament scriptures that seem to contradict the message of the true prophet is largely absent from the *Recognitions*. *Homilies* 3.45 say that there are false texts in the scripture, and that God *never* made commands regarding animal sacrifice (echoing Jeremiah 7:22, "I said not a word about them"). But *Recognitions* 1.36 implies that Moses, "that faithful and wise steward," *did* make commands regarding animal sacrifice as a concession to human weakness. Moses wanted to eliminate the worst aspects of animal sacrifice, by getting rid of its idolatrous aspects, leaving it to another later prophet (namely, Jesus) to eliminate animal sacrifice entirely. This could be the consequence of a non-Ebionite editor, but most likely it was an ambiguity among the Ebionites themselves. Both views support the Ebionite position of opposition to animal sacrifice, just in somewhat different ways.

Conclusion

In a nutshell, the Ebionites thought that there was one God, the creator of heaven and earth, and that Jesus was his prophet, bringing a moral code and a warning of future judgment. The moral code is a simplified but quite strict version of the law given to Moses. The *Recognitions* and *Homilies* develop these themes in a way that is not only consistent with what we already know about the Ebionites, but appears to support or elaborate on the Ebionite position. It is likely that many of the ideas come directly from the Ebionites themselves.

They are often muddy or contradictory in developing these themes; sometimes they will support one idea, then another. Does this perhaps betray the influence of a hostile or indifferent editor of the *Recognitions* and *Homilies*, who thereby distorted Ebionite ideas? Certainly we need to be cautious before attributing any idea in the *Recognitions* or *Homilies*, unsupported by any other evidence, to the Ebionites. But a close reading suggests a simpler explanation: the Ebionites just hadn't fully worked out their theology.

22. Ebionite Demonology and the Problem of Evil

The first followers of Jesus, if the gospels can be allowed as a guide, believed that demons were a real and tangible force in the world. The gospels are full of struggles between Jesus and his disciples on one hand, and the demonic forces they found all around them on the other. Jesus drives out demons himself (Matthew 8:16, 9:32, 12:22, etc.), and gives authority to his disciples to cast out demons (Matthew 10:1, 10:8, etc.).

The Ebionite approach to food makes heavy use of their understanding of demons; they based their rejection of eating with unbelievers not on concepts such as ritual purity or observance of kosher laws, but rather on the struggle against demons. The *Recognitions* and *Homilies* can help us here by giving us insight into the "demonology" of the Ebionites, and provides a link between the Ebionites and the first followers of Jesus. To an outsider, not eating with unbelievers might *look* like a ritual observance issue, but what they were really doing was avoiding demons.

The Spread of Evil

The "problem of evil" was as perplexing to the Ebionites as it was to any of the other ancient or modern thinkers. For the Ebionites, God created the world and presides over all of existence, but has given this world to the devil; so evil is all-pervasive, and yet ultimately unreal (*Homilies* 20.2, *Panarion* 30.16.2). Evil spreads through demon possession. The view of demons and evil in the *Recognitions* and *Homilies* can be summarized as follows:

1. Demons can enter someone through bloodshed—either of humans, or of animals. (They can also enter through other immoderate actions.) One participates in bloodshed obviously by murder of a human or killing an animal, but one can also be implicated merely by eating an animal which has been killed or sacrificed to demons (*Recognitions* 1.30, 2.71, 4.19, 4.36, 5.32, 8.51; *Homilies* 7.3, 8.20, 9.13–14, 9.23). We see here the centrality of vegetarianism and pacifism for Jewish Christian belief (see also table 21–1).

2. Demons may also enter someone who shares the same table with someone already demon-possessed. Anyone who eats at a table where one person is already demon-possessed, is eating at the table of demons, regardless of what is being eaten (*Recognitions* 1.19, 2.3, 2.71-72, 7.29, 7.34; *Homilies* 1.22, 13.4).

This theory explains the *spread* of evil very vividly. It expands like a contagious disease, either by evil action or evil association. Demons are sometimes explained as real creatures with an independent will; but in contradictory fashion, demons are sometimes referred to in metaphorical ways—as in the aphorisms that "ignorance . . . is the worst of all demons" (*Recognitions* 2.25) and that "all evil springs from ignorance" (*Recognitions* 4.8, 5.4).

The devil and demons are presented in the *Homilies* as *loyal* angels (8.19–20, 9.9–10, 9.21, 20.9). God gave a law to the demons, just as he gave a law to humans; and the law to demons is that they cannot enter into human beings unless those humans do the will of demons and commit acts of bloodshed or some other gross form of immorality. But in the *Recognitions* the demons are not loyal angels; they are supernatural beings who have freely chosen evil. Epiphanius ascribes the view of the *Homilies* to the Ebionites, saying that the Ebionites thought that the present world has been given to the devil, at the request of *both* Jesus and the devil (*Panarion* 30.16.2)! According to this idea, as we will see below, the devil and demons are operating as part of God's plan and their presence is actually key to our spiritual awakening.

Since bloodshed is the key way in which demons increase their power, it is the demons who demand, and benefit by, animal sacrifice and warfare. These actions grant demons the right to possess someone, and demon possession in turn leads to other kinds of violent or immoral actions (*Recognitions* 5.32–33).

The Origin of Evil

While this explains the *spread* of evil, it does not explain nearly as well the *origin* of evil. If the world was created by a good God, and was itself good, then how did evil get mixed up in the world? Here we get two rather different answers, a philosophical answer and a mythological answer.

The philosophical answer is the doctrine of opposites, modeled on the Pythagorean idea of opposites (discussed in chapter 6 and chapter 21). God created everything in pairs—first the worse (or evil), then the better of the two. In the *Recognitions*, the opposites are such figures as Cain and Abel, Aaron and Moses, Antichrist and Christ; in the *Homilies*, the pairs are contrasting realities such as dark and light, female and male, and ignorance and knowledge.

God created these opposites for our spiritual benefit (*Recognitions* 3.58–59, 3.75; *Homilies* 2.15, 2.33), since without any experience of evil, people lacked gratitude to God, so what was provided was "a certain arranged harmony, removing from them good things as having hurt them, and introducing evil things instead, as advantageous" (*Homilies* 8.11). *Consciousness of God requires experience of evil.*

The other answer was the mythological answer, which is found in the Ebionite rewrite of Genesis (see chapter 5). The *Recognitions* and *Homilies* having nothing corresponding to the idea of "original sin" as orthodox Christianity understood it. Adam did not sin (*Homilies* 3.20), nor did the first seven generations of humans (*Recognitions* 1.29). When humanity did start going bad, it was in the eighth and ninth generations when meat-eating, violence, and cannibalism were introduced. In the *Homilies* 8, even this was not directly a consequence of human sin, but a result of the actions of giants, who were the offspring of angels and human women. Evil is a fact, but it is not a consequence of sin so much as of ignorance. Indeed, evil seems to have been created by God as a way to dispel ignorance.

The End of Time

The *Recognitions* and *Homilies* also display a similar dichotomy of answers about the judgment at the end of time. The mythological answer is that souls which are possessed by demons are bound to the demon which they possess. When that demon departs for hell at the end of time, the soul which is bound to it must follow it to hell (*Homilies* 9.9). The demon, however, will be pleased by this, being in its own element of fire, while the soul will be tortured. In *Recognitions* 4.15, by contrast, both the demon and the soul it possesses will be tortured, because in the *Recognitions* demons are disobedient spirits rather than loyal spirits.

However, the philosophical response to this question makes it impossible for anyone actually to *get* to hell, or at least impossible to get there and stay there forever. In the *Homilies*, at least, God creates the devil for his own purposes (*Homilies* 20.2, 20.8), which suggests that evil is part of the divine plan, rather than the result of disobedience. Punishment must be proportional *(Recognitions* 2.20), suggesting the impossibility of an eternal damnation. Those who are ignorant will not be condemned (*Recognitions* 5.7)—and recall that ignorance is the source of all evil. Hell really would be evil, but evil has no substantial existence, and evil will not always exist (*Homilies* 19.19, 19.20), a set of statements which when taken together imply that hell, if it exists, is not eternal.

Peter later mentions the story in Exodus 7 in which Aaron's rod is turned into a serpent to impress the Pharaoh, and then the next day it turns back into a rod; he takes this story as a hint that the devil himself may be saved (*Homilies* 20.9). If the devil is saved, then by Ebionite logic that binds souls to the demons they have served, the souls and demons who are bound to the devil must also be saved.

The Table of Demons

The main practical application of the Ebionite idea of evil is to the issue of bloodshed and the table of demons. God does not want animals to be killed (*Homilies* 3.45). This is the starting point for the Ebionite idea of the table of demons, a critical focus of controversy in the early church described by Paul in Galatians and I Corinthians.

Peter in the *Recognitions* and *Homilies* urges everyone not to eat at the table of demons. This means, of course, not to eat meat or eat animals sacrificed to idols, but Peter also urges his hearers not to eat with those who are themselves possessed by demons (*Recognitions* 1.19, 2.3, 2.71–72, 7.29, 7.34; *Homilies* 1.22, 13.4). Both activities risk demon possession and carry risk for one's soul. If you eat with someone who is themselves possessed by a demon, then the demon is present at the table, regardless of what you are eating.

When Peter declines to eat with Clement (before Clement's baptism), Clement is technically Peter's guest, and therefore it would not seem to be a problem for Peter to determine the menu. If only the menu were the problem, Peter could just say "sorry, we're not eating the meat of sacrificed animals today." Rather, it is the table-companions *themselves* who make it the table of demons and who make such a meal a dangerous one.

The *Recognitions* and *Homilies* do not always express the restriction against eating at the table of demons in this way. There is clearly a difference between refusing to eat *something* which is objectionable (e. g. meat sacrificed to idols), and refusing to eat with *someone* who is objectionable (e. g., a pagan who eats meat sacrificed to idols). At times the *Recognitions* and *Homilies* provide a criterion which pertains to *what*, rather than *who*, is objectionable (*Homilies* 7.4, 7.8, 8.19). It's possible that the difference between these two formulations may explain Peter's change of heart in Galatians; initially, he may have believed that complicity with demons only resulted from *what* you ate, but now he believes after hearing from James that it is *who* you ate with, as well.

Peter sometimes advises his hearers not to eat with the unbaptized (*Recognitions* 1.19, *Homilies* 1.22), but sometimes the advice is not to eat with "gentiles" (*Recognitions* 7.29, *Homilies* 13.4). But baptism expels the demons (*Recognitions* 2.71), so once someone is baptized, Peter is willing to eat with them.

Peter cites as a text Jesus' own command, that when they should enter into a city, they should first find out who in it is worthy, and eat with *them* (*Recognitions* 2.3), referring to Matthew 10:11: "And whatever town or village you enter, *find out who is worthy in it*, and stay with him until you depart" (emphasis added). Someone who is "worthy" is evidently someone who already has been baptized and has put demons out of their lives completely. Notice that the New Testament parallels to Matthew 10:11 (Mark 6:10 and Luke 9:4) omit the requirement to stay only with the "worthy," so it is possible that editors of the New Testament were aware of this issue and weighed in on one side or the other. Only the story in Matthew supports the Ebionite version of this command.

The way the issue is framed is remarkably analogous to the situation in Galatians 2, when Paul complains bitterly about the fact that Peter at first ate with the gentiles, but now refuses to eat with them. Peter in the *Homilies* certainly seems to be defending Peter in Galatians. It seems clear that this is the Ebionite understanding of the controversy Paul reports in Galatians 2:11–14 ("until certain men came from James, he ate with the gentiles; but when they came he drew back and separated himself").

We can't say definitely that the "historical Peter" had exactly this concern, just that he acts as if he was worried about eating at the table of demons. At the least, given the animosity between the Ebionites and Paul, it appears that this was the later Ebionite understanding of the issues at stake. Peter in the *Homilies* does not object to eating with gentiles based on concerns about the Jewish kosher laws or about ritual impurity, but rather because of *demons*.

Conclusions

Many of the arguments in the *Recognitions* and *Homilies* appear not only consonant with what we already know about the Ebionites, but seem to be designed to wrestle specifically with problems posed by Jewish Christian theology. So while we may not be sure that all of the precise arguments or details offered by the *Recognitions* and *Homilies* are Ebionite, it appears likely that the outline offered here expresses the general sense of Ebionite understanding.

For the *Recognitions* and *Homilies*, sin originates in ignorance, and spreads through demons. Jesus came to destroy the wicked animal sacrifices which contaminated ancient Israel and led to war, adultery, and all other kinds of wickedness. The Ebionite church struggled not only against the violence of much of the pagan world, but also against those who would diminish the message of Jesus and advocate complicity with violence, thus aiding the influence and spread of demons.

Part VI:
The Influence of Jewish Christianity

23. *Gnosis* and Christ

Whatever happened to the Ebionites? All we know is that after the church fathers' references, we know nothing more of the Ebionites. They are just gone from the historical record.

The Ebionites resembled and sometimes interacted with several other movements in the ancient world. These other movements may have been allies, competitors, or even spiritual heirs of the Ebionites—or perhaps, a combination of these. The Ebionite message probably was altered in stages until at some point it stopped being recognizable as "Ebionite." After the fourth and fifth centuries, we never find explicit references to the Ebionites or to Jewish Christianity, with the possible exception of the Elkasaites (depending on whether we count them as Jewish Christian). But in some cases we can see traces of clearly Ebionite ideas which last for a thousand years. In other cases, we find evidence for the survival of Ebionite ideas down to the present day, albeit in "non-Christian" groups.

None of these other groups or ideologies is more problematic than gnosticism.

What is Gnosticism?

If we can credit Irenaeus, who wrote his book *Against Heresies* in the second half of the second century, then gnosticism was the major internal threat to Christian orthodoxy.

The gnostics whom Irenaeus describes subscribe to views like those of Marcion (indeed, Marcion is a major theme of *Against Heresies*). For these gnostics, the creator God described in the Bible is not the true or highest God. They posited a dualism in which two Gods exist—the God who actually created the world (but didn't do a very good job), and the highest, true, spiritual God, the "Father" of Jesus Christ. Judaism made a fundamental mistake by following this lesser Creator God. Christ did not partake of this imperfect world or follow this imperfect God. He only *seemed* to have a physical body, he was actually just a spirit—a doctrine known as the idea of the "docetic" Christ (from *dokeo*, to appear).

This description accurately represents the views of at least one very famous heretic, Marcion. There are modern "gnostics," such as Stephen Hoeller, who echo this definition: "the world is flawed because it was created in a flawed manner" (Hoeller, 2011).

But is ancient gnosticism a movement with a common origin and common ideas, and if so, what are those ideas? Or is Irenaeus lumping together groups under the rubric of "gnosticism" which are really rather different? Even before the discovery of the Nag Hammadi manuscripts in the mid-twentieth century, some scholars had already questioned this assumption. The distinguished scholar Adolf Von Harnack said that Marcion was *not* a gnostic, because Marcion did not subscribe to the elaborate creation myths (Harnack, 1901). For Harnack, it was the creation myths (such as those of Valentinus) which made a thinker "gnostic" and Irenaeus' usage of the term was too broad. It is not helpful that Irenaeus seems to be one of the few ancient writers who talk about the gnostics, and that we know of no groups that actually described themselves as "gnostic"; so there's no obvious way to resolve the problem of what exactly gnosticism is.

The Nag Hammadi manuscripts discovered in the mid-twentieth century in Egypt further complicated the situation. Irenaeus attacks a "gnosticism" in which there is dualism, more than one God, a "docetic Christ" who only appears to have a body, and stresses that the world is an evil place. But many of the Nag Hammadi mansucripts don't manifest the kind of "gnosticism" which Irenaeus attacks at all. In *The Gospel of Truth* there is no dualism; there is one God; Christ appears physically; and the material world is not evil. The *Apocryphon of James* and the *Treatise on the Resurrection* both agree on Jesus' physical nature. *Gospel of Thomas* 113 seems to reject any sort of cosmic dualism, saying that the kingdom of heaven is already here. Is all of this "gnostic"? If so, then Irenaeus' definition is not too broad, as Harnack thought, but much too narrow.

So do we say that some or all of the Nag Hammadi documents are not gnostic? Or do we change our concept of gnosticism, and if so, how? If we broaden the definition of "gnosticism" to include all of the

Nag Hammadi documents as "gnostic," then there is the danger to have *so* muddied the usage of the term that it will become useless.

If the term "gnostic" has just become an arbitrary label, wouldn't it be easier to stop talking about gnosticism altogether, and instead talk about specific historical persons or groups? Karen King wrote a book titled *What is Gnosticism?* which lays out the problems very well.

We cannot solve a historical problem by definition, and it's totally beyond the scope of this book to come up with a suitable definition of "gnosticism." What we can do is look at two different but likely concepts of gnosticism and see how helpful they are in understanding the influence of the Ebionites. I would suggest that any such definition can *only* be defended if (a) the "gnostics" so defined *include* the figures attacked by Irenaeus as "gnostic," or at least most of them, and (b) the definition is not so broad that orthodoxy could be labeled as "gnostic." There are two possible definitions I would propose:

1. Gnosticism = Marcionite dualism
2. Gnosticism = Right knowledge is essential for salvation

The Arguments of Hans-Joachim Schoeps

The most straightforward definition of gnosticism assumes that Irenaeus knew what he was talking about, and equates gnosticism with dualistic views like those of Marcion. In fact, the primary evidence that Irenaeus *does* know what he's talking about, and therefore that this idea of "gnosticism" has some merit, comes from consideration of the Ebionites. The Ebionites seemed to view Marcion and allied thinkers in much the same way that Irenaeus does, although they obviously disagree with Irenaeus on other issues.

Hans-Joachim Schoeps, probably the most distinguished twentieth-century scholar on the Ebionites, maintained that "it can be demonstrated with certainty that the Ebionites offered front-line opposition to the powerful movement of pagan gnosticism" (*Jewish Christianity*, p. 121). Schoeps has offered convincing evidence that the Ebionites were opposed to the system of Marcion and allied thinkers. He presents five themes in the *Recognitions* and *Homilies* which are polemical responses to these particular "gnostics" (*Jewish Christianity*, p. 121–130).

1. Monotheism versus polytheism—Peter maintains that there is one God, in contrast to his opponent Simon Magus who maintains the Marcionite thesis that in addition to the creator God there is a different, higher, unknown God.

2. False texts—when Simon Magus produces various Old Testament texts to prove his Marcionite thesis, Peter responds by denouncing these as falsehoods.

3. The problem of evil—the ideas in *Homilies* 19 and 20 seem devised to counter the gnostic idea of an "aboriginal principle of evil" which leads to a cosmic dualism of two *independent*, eternal, and co-equal forces of good and evil.

4. The idea of opposites, created by God—this is an attempt to argue against Marcion's idea that good suddenly entered the world when Christ preached a previously genuinely unknown Father-God. According to the idea of opposites, everything proceeded from God but it entered the world in contrasts—with "evil" actually coming first and essentially heralding the coming of the "good" (see chapters 6 and 21).

5. Jesus as the "true prophet"—Marcion wanted to oppose Jesus to the God of the Old Testament, but the "true prophet" idea relates Jesus to a prophecy in Deuteronomy as well as to the figures of the Old Testament, who in Ebionite thought responded to the holy spirit (or "Christ") just as Jesus did.

6. To Schoeps' arguments we might add a sixth point, the conflict with Paul: the Jewish Christians despised Paul and felt he was an apostate from the law. Marcion and other gnostics not only turned Paul into a hero, but contrasted him with Peter whom Marcion regarded as a false apostle.

Under this definition, gnosticism did have a further history within Christianity, such as the Bogomils and the Cathars, who were still operating during the Middle Ages. These groups had obvious affinities with Marcionite dualism. However, it is hard to connect the Ebionites to these groups, since they were obviously their ideological opponents.

"Gnostic" Elements in the Ebionites

It is clear that the Ebionites were opposed to Marcionite gnosticism. We might then ask, are there any *similarities* between the Ebionites and Marcion, or the Ebionites and other so-called "gnostics"? It turns out that there are several.

1. *Common ethical focus.* Both the Ebionites and the Marcionites (among others) were pacifist and vegetarian. Marcion ridicules the "Creator God" because this God relies on warfare and violence (Tertullian, *Against Marcion* 1.6, 3.12, 3.14, 4.20). Marcion also was vegetarian (Hippolytus, *Refutation of All Heresies* 7.18), though he may have occasionally eaten fish (Tertullian, *Against Marcion* 1.14). Pacifism and vegetarianism are both widespread among all the various Christian factions, orthodox and heretical. It is likely that both of these tendencies go back at least to Jesus himself and to pre-Christian Nasaraeans.

2. *Common origin.* If Simon Magus is a historical figure and a spiritual ancestor of Marcion, and Simon was also a follower of John the Baptist, then both Marcion and the Ebionites could share a common spiritual ancestor in John the Baptist. This would put the debate between Peter and Simon Magus in a different light—as a debate between different followers of John the Baptist.

3. *The spiritual nature of the resurrection. Recognitions* 3.30 and *Homilies* 17.16 agree with Paul's statement, "flesh and blood cannot inherit the kingdom of God" (I Corinthians 15:50)—for which Paul himself puts forward the testimony of Peter and James to the resurrected Christ. The Jewish Christians recognized that Jesus *incarnated* physically, but believed that at the final resurrection all humans (and he) will be spiritual beings, like the angels in heaven.

4. *Salvation through right knowledge.* There is another possible link to gnosticism, and that is to go to the root meaning of gnosticism, which lies in "gnosis" or knowledge. In the *Recognitions* and *Homilies*, there is a constant emphasis on knowledge as the key to salvation, and ignorance as the root of all evil. "All evil springs from ignorance" (*Recognitions* 5.4). "Hear *them*, He [Jesus] said, as

entrusted with the key of the kingdom, which is knowledge, which alone can open the gate of life" (*Homilies* 3.18).

Schoeps acknowledges some "gnostic" elements within Ebionism, but protests that "after all, syncretism [combination of elements from opposing belief systems] is not the same as Gnosticism" (p. 130). He correctly protests that "the whole controversy . . . would collapse if we could agree upon a *uniform* terminology" (p. 129, emphasis in original).

The Ebionites were certainly opposed to the views of Marcion, Valentinus, Cerdo, and Simon Magus on a number of very important points. But they also seem to have a number of similarities. What accounts for these similarities? One possibility is that the Ebionites and the gnostics are drawing on the same pre-Christian sources. Indeed, this source might be John the Baptist and his movement.

However, the orthodox obviously *also* shared these pre-Christian origins and ethical focus. The Ebionites and the gnostics share pacifism and vegetarianism, but many in the orthodox community were also pacifist and vegetarian: Origen, Clement of Alexandria, Basil the Great, Jerome, and others. Orthodox Christianity claimed John the Baptist as a predecessor. And while the Ebionites and the gnostics both believe in the spiritual resurrection, this by itself would not seem to precipitate a major division in the church. This is especially true given that the Ebionites agreed, contrary to Marcion, that Jesus incarnated physically and that the God of Jesus created the world.

This leaves us with one final idea which might link the Ebionites to gnosticism, the concept of "right knowledge."

What is "Right Knowledge"?

If there is a clear connection between the Ebionites and "gnosticism," which the orthodox do not share, it runs through the idea of "right knowledge."

Now on the face of it, all religions, including all the various sects of Christianity, stress the importance of "right knowledge." But for most of them, this is not a fundamental problem. You consult the appropriate scriptures, priests, oracles, or other authorities, who have the knowledge you need. So what makes gnosticism different is not that they stress the need for right knowledge, but that they see "right knowledge" as a *special* problem, because the knowledge is hidden or obscured from view. In this sense of gnosticism, "gnosis" has to do with mysteries and secrets.

However, in this sense, it is not clear that "gnosticism" is a specific belief or idea, so much as it is a more general attribute of doctrines. To make an analogy, we might today describe a certain religious group as "monastic," because they had a community, a common discipline, common dress, sometimes common housing, and so forth. However, describing a group as "monastic" tells us nothing about what they *believed* or even what they practiced. There are Christian monks and Buddhist monks. There are nuns like the late Mother Teresa who are helping the poorest of the poor in Calcutta, but there are also the Knights Templar in the Middle Ages who rode off to the Holy Land to slaughter the infidels.

The same applies to the concepts of knowledge, mysteries, and secrets. What are the secrets? And why are they secret? The answers could be completely different. Obviously different groups which are "gnostic" in this sense could have utterly opposed ideas, depending on what the secrets are. And the reason the knowledge is obscured could be as simple as "the religious authorities are against us" to a Marcionite explanation that the material world is inherently corrupt.

Sometimes in a religious context, there are mysteries which are *intrinsically* mysterious. Many mystics (Plato in *Letter VII*, Zen Buddhists, etc.) would say that the ultimate truth cannot be written down because it cannot be put into words; it is beyond conceptual understanding. In other cases, something is a mystery just because it is not widely disseminated or is actually obscured by the prevailing religion.

Why did the Ebionites emphasize "right knowledge"? What is obscuring the truth? The answer is that the world is like a house filled with "the darkness of ignorance and the smoke of vices," and that this obscures God's will, which otherwise would be naturally revealed. We need outside aid to open the door of the house and let the smoke out, and the light in (*Recognitions* 1.15). This outside aid is provided by the true prophet.

Not only is the established religion not helping, it is part of the problem. The scriptures are also filled with darkness and smoke—the idea of "false texts." The priests, through their animal sacrifices, are actually adding to ignorance and vice. Because one can become afflicted with demons just by eating with people who are themselves possessed by demons, the whole world can be inundated with false things—false religion, false delusions of imperialism, false reliance on wealth, and so forth. Finding the truth becomes much more difficult.

In this sense, the Ebionites did have a place for "mysteries." Peter says "keep the mysteries for me and for the sons of my house" (*Homilies* 19.20). The Ebionites saw the overt forms of Judaism as part of the problem. After seeing how gentile Christianity was developing, they likely saw the overt forms of Christianity as part of the problem as well. Put in this way, "gnosticism" has nothing to do with specific doctrines like cosmic dualism or ideas about a creator God. It has to do with access to divine truth. For the gnostics, knowledge by ordinary straightforward means had been blocked, and thus they lay an unusual stress on the need for special attention to spiritual knowledge. "Enter by the narrow gate," advises Jesus (Matthew 7:13, see also *Homilies* 7.7), indicating that following the obvious path does not take you to salvation, for "broad is the path that leads to destruction."

In this sense, you could argue that John the Baptist and Jesus were both "gnostics." They saw the path to truth blocked, not just by temptations or sins, but by religion itself. They rejected the overt forms of religion, such as animal sacrifice and the sacred scriptures, and advocated a special path to God.

The similarities between Marcion and the Ebionites are not entirely due to syncretism. They both saw the corruption of the prevailing religion; it was just that Marcion thought that this corruption was *inherent* in the nature of existence. Which movement is "syncretistic" depends on one's point of view.

Conclusions

The relationship between the Ebionites and "gnosticism" depends on the meaning of gnosticism. Ultimately this is a question of definitions. We have looked at two possible definitions of gnosticism, a "broad" definition of gnosticism (gnosticism = salvation through right knowledge) and a "narrow" definition (gnosticism = Marcionite dualism).

The narrow definition of gnosticism, as pertaining to a specific set of dualistic ideas, is helpful in understanding the Ebionites, but in this case the Ebionites were completely opposed to gnosticism. The phenomenon Irenaeus describes was real and politically important, and did form a coherent body of opinion in early Christianity.

In the broad definition, there are "gnostic" ideas which both Marcion and the Ebionites took. However, in this sense, probably Jesus and John the Baptist were "gnostic," and this says nothing about their actual ideas, just about their views of how divine knowledge is to be accessed. The door to knowledge is closed: but "knock, and the door will be opened." Tracing these ideas or their influence further, though, is not that helpful in terms of understanding the influence of the Ebionites, because "gnosticism" (in this sense) does not imply any particular beliefs or even a common continuous community, just a characteristic posture of the group towards the issue of how to access divine knowledge.

24. The Revelation of Elxai

The Elkasaites are an early religious group often classed as "Jewish Christian." They are remarkably similar to the Ebionites in many ways. They are vegetarian, against animal sacrifice, believe that Christ was in Adam and appears throughout history, and reject "false texts." This certainly sounds a lot like the Ebionites.

Two other groups, the Ossaeans and the Sampsaeans, are only mentioned by Epiphanius; but these two groups turn out to be Elkasaites under different names. Epiphanius identifies Elxai as a revered figure of the Ossaeans, which are now called "Sampsaean" (*Panarion* 19.2.1). The Sampsaeans are also known as Elkasaites (*Panarion* 53.1.1).

But are the Elkasaites in fact Jewish Christians? There is a significant problem here, because while there are a lot of doctrinal similarities with the Ebionites, it is not clear that they follow Jesus. The Elkasaites (Sampsaeans) do talk about "Christ," and use the book of Elxai, as do the Ebionites, Nazoraeans, and Ossaeans. Epiphanius doesn't see anything distinctively Jewish or Christian about the book of Elxai; and he says that he is not clear that, after looking at their book, they believe that *Jesus* is the Christ (*Panarion* 19.3.4). He describes Elxai as Jewish, rather than Jewish Christian (*Panarion* 19.1.5).

Hippolytus says they believe that Christ was reincarnated throughout history and that his appearance as Jesus was one of these reincarnations (*Refutation of All Heresies* 10.25). Indeed, Christ not only has appeared many times in the past, but will continue to appear in the future (*Refutation of All Heresies* 9.9).

Was there a schism between the Elkasaites and the Ebionites, and if so, what was at stake? We have no direct accounts from Epiphanius or Hippolytus. Broadly speaking, there are two possibilities. The first is that the Elkasaites are a Jewish Christian group which broke away from "mainstream Jewish Christianity" (the Ebionites?) early in the second century, following the book of Elxai instead. The second is that they didn't break away because they were never in the same movement in the first place, but followers of a pre-Christian group from which, perhaps, both they and the Jesus movement sprang. This could be the "Essenes," the "Ossaeans," the Jewish "Nasaraeans" which Epiphanius talks about, or other followers of John the Baptist—thus accounting for their similarity to the Ebionites, yet their reluctance to acknowledge Jesus.

That would mean that the many distinctive beliefs shared by the Ebionites and Elkasaites actually belonged to a group which *preceded* Jesus. If the Elkasaites did spring from such a group, but subsequently did not follow Jesus, this creates a further terminological issue concerning "Jewish Christianity." We are willing to countenance the idea of a Jewish Christianity *before* Jesus. We might also need to deal with the idea of a Jewish Christianity *after* Jesus, but without him.

Hippolytus and Epiphanius—our sources for the Elkasaites

Two early church figures wrote extensively on the Elkasaites: Hippolytus in the third century (*Refutation of All Heresies* 9.8–12, 10.25) and Epiphanius in the fourth century (*Panarion* 19, 53). Thanks to them, we may have an almost exact date for the origin of the Elkasaites: the third year of the emperor Trajan, when the new remission of sins preached by Elxai was to occur (Hippolytus, *Refutation of All Heresies* 9.8). Hippolytus says that the book of Elxai was written in Parthia; and the year 116 was the third year the Roman armies under Trajan had been in Mesopotamia, which one distinguished scholar thinks is the date the book was written (Luttikhuizen, p. 190–192). The alternative date would be the third year that Trajan first became emperor in Rome, which would be the year 100. Either way, at the time the Elkasaites began, Paul, Peter, and James were long dead.

But who was Elxai? To start with, no one is sure of the spelling of the name of the founding prophet of the Elkasaites. There are references to "Elxai," "Elchasai," "Elci," "Elcesaei," "Alchasaios," and even "al-Hasi" (Luttikhuizen, p. 179–180). These are not differences in spelling due to different systems of transcriptions of ancient alphabets—they are different in the original languages also. In fact, we do not know much about this prophet, not even whether he existed at all, which seems a rather nebulous point.

While we don't know much about a prophet "Elxai," there are numerous references to the *book* of Elxai and to the Elkasaites. According to Epiphanius, "Elxai" means "hidden power" (*Panarion* 19.2.1). Indeed, the term "hidden power" in Aramaic, *"hayil kesai,"* may be the source of the term "Elxai" (Luomanen, p. 96). Just as Epiphanius thought there was a fictitious person "Ebion" who was the leader of the heretical Ebionites, there may be no prophet "Elxai" at all, just a book and some followers of the book describing "hidden power." In this book I will follow Epiphanius and spell the prophet's name Elxai and the name of the group Elkasaites, but this is somewhat arbitrary given the diversity of spellings in the original documents.

Hippolytus knew about the Elkasaites through his encounter with a rival in the church at Rome, Alcibiades, a follower of the Elkasaites who used the book of Elxai. Elxai had proclaimed a new forgiveness of sins, even serious sins after baptism, in the third year of the emperor Trajan (probably the year 116). Thus the Elkasaites thought that forgiveness was possible even after denying the faith during persecution, that most dreaded of sins. While many Christians may have looked askance at a church which welcomed apostates back to the fold, obviously any apostates might be rather interested in such a church.

Epiphanius describes the Elkasaites in similar terms to Hippolytus. Epiphanius does not have a separate chapter for the Elkasaites in the *Panarion*; rather, references to the Elkasaites are spread out through a number of chapters dealing with various Jewish or Jewish Christian groups. He has a chapter on the Nasaraeans (*Panarion* 18), Ossaeans (19), Nazoraeans (29), Ebionites (30), and Sampsaeans (53); but he has no separate chapter about the Elkasaites. In the chapter on the Ossaeans, he casually mentions that Elxai joined the Ossaeans and evidently was their leader. He then goes on to say virtually nothing about the Ossaeans per se, instead talking about Elxai and his book, saying that the Ossaeans are now called the Sampsaeans (19.2.1). Later, in his chapter on the Sampsaeans, he repeats a lot of the same information and says that the Sampsaeans are also called Elkasaites (53.1.1), so all three of these groups are the same group. Chronologically, though, the name "Ossaeans" seems to come first.

Could the "Ossaeans" be the same group as the "Essenes"? At first this may seem unlikely, since Epiphanius also describes another group named the "Essenes." These "Essenes," according to Epiphanius (*Panarion* 10), are an obscure Samaritan group engaged in calendar disputes with other obscure groups. But as we saw in the case of the Nazoraeans and Nasaraeans, when Epiphanius sees two groups with the same name which he perceives have different doctrines, he will give them slightly different names. Moreover, we gather from Hippolytus (see chapter 7) that there *were* different groups, with wildly different doctrines, all known as "Essenes." The description of the Ossaeans and Elkasaites is just close enough to that of the Essenes of Philo and Josephus so that we suspect that the "Ossaeans" of Epiphanius are one of the groups of "Essenes" described by Philo, Josephus, and Hippolytus.

Doctrines of the Elkasaites

Epiphanius discusses several ideas of the Elkasaites which we would quickly identify as Jewish Christian doctrines: loyalty to the Jewish law (*Panarion* 19.5.1), the rejection of animal sacrifice, vegetarianism, rejection of the texts on animal sacrifice (*Panarion* 19.3.6), and honoring God through "baptisms of some sort" (*Panarion* 53.1.4). They also believe that Christ appeared in Adam, and periodically appears in the world (*Panarion* 53.1.8). Hippolytus affirms all of this, mentioning briefly that the Elkasaites thought that "Christ was not for the first time on earth when born of a virgin" (*Refutation of All Heresies* 9.9). He adds that their views were like that of Pythagoras—presumably referring to the doctrine of transmigration of souls, which Hippolytus had earlier described. All of these ideas are attributed to other Jewish Christian groups and are found in the *Recognitions* and *Homilies*.

But there are other distinctive beliefs of the Elkasaites, *not* shared with other Jewish Christian groups, and generally *not* found in the *Recognitions* and *Homilies*—so whoever wrote the *Recognitions* and *Homilies* was probably *not* an Elkasaite. What are these distinctive beliefs?

1. *The family of Elxai.*

There were women leaders of this group as late as the fourth century—Marthus and Marthana. Marthus and Marthana were "worshiped as goddesses" because they were descended from Elxai himself (*Panarion* 19.2.3). Here we have some sort of religious dynasty being founded, evidently organized by a family entity and passed on through their biological descendants. This is similar to the Ebionite reliance on the family of Jesus. Evidently this group, at least, did not consider being female a bar to leadership.

2. *A really enormous Christ and a really enormous Holy Spirit.*

The Elkasaites declare that "Christ is the Great King" (*Panarion* 19.3.4), though even Epiphanius is unsure whether they mean that *Jesus* is the Christ, or someone or something else. The Elkasaites had fantastic ideas about Christ: they thought that Christ was 96 miles high and that his sister, the Holy Spirit, was of a similar size.

It is hard to know what to make of this. What about the Christ who is ninety-six miles high? Do they mean that *Jesus* is ninety-six miles high? The ninety-six mile high Christ is probably not Jesus, but some sort of angel or spirit, and it is not clear what possible relationship there might have been between Jesus and this Christ. Did the Elkasaites follow Jesus?

Since Hippolytus holds that the Elkasaites made Jesus one of the many incarnations of Christ, it is also possible that they were willing to accept Jesus into their pantheon without attributing undue importance to him, just as some Hindus today are willing to grant that Jesus was an avatar of God without describing themselves as Christians. The Elkasaites might have originally been independent of the Jesus movement (as, say, followers of John the Baptist) but had "adopted" Jesus as part of their outreach to gain new converts.

3. *The elements to swear by.*

The Elkasaites introduced seven elements to swear by: salt, water, earth, bread, heaven, ether, and wind. Alternatively, this list is given as sky, water, "holy spirits," the "angels of prayer," olive, salt, and earth (*Panarion* 19.1.6). A few of these elements are found in the *Recognitions* and *Homilies*. Bread and water are elements of the Ebionite Eucharist, and water is the means of baptism. Salt is used by Peter twice; at *Homilies* 14.1, it is part of the Eucharist, and as part of the meal at *Homilies* 19.25. Olives are part of Peter's sparse vegetarian diet (*Recognitions* 7.6, *Homilies* 12.6).

However, the *Recognitions* and *Homilies* do not discuss any of these seven elements in a way that suggests undue reverence for them. The whole concept of oath-taking seems to be foreign to the Ebionites; *Homilies* 3.56 specifically precludes swearing by heaven, and Jesus in the gospels says, "do not swear at all" (Matthew 5:34). Swearing, even by a holy object or name, isn't the kind of thing that Ebionite Christianity would seem predisposed to accept, and swearing by forces of nature or inanimate objects seems positively pagan.

The *Epistle of Peter to James*, though, really does ask people to "adjure" to carry out certain actions, using the witnesses of heaven, earth, water, and air (*Epistle of Peter to James* 4). Even though the epistle quickly adds that this is not an oath, saying that oaths are unlawful, this certainly sounds like an "oath" given another name in order to comply with the letter of Jesus' command not to swear. Because this affirmation also invokes four of the seven "witnesses" mentioned by Epiphanius, this letter may actually be an Elkasaite document.

4. *Apostasy under duress is acceptable.*

For the Elkasaites, lying about one's beliefs in time of persecution is acceptable. Temporarily renouncing one's faith allowed one to avoid martyrdom. Incidentally, a similar view is found in Islam. Someone's uttering unbelief incurs a terrible penalty, "except under compulsion, his heart remaining firm in Faith" (*Qur'an* 16:106).

Martyrdom does not seem to be a major theme for the Ebionites, although acceptance of apostasy seems to be foreign to Ebionism. Jewish Christian martyrs include James, who was killed at the instigation of the high priest in the year 62; the Jewish Christians who (according to Justin) were persecuted during the Bar Kochba revolt (132–135); and, if one counts arrest as a form of martyrdom, the relatives of Jesus interrogated by Domitian, James and Zoker.

Apostasy was a particularly dreaded sin for early Christians. Baptism (a public declaration of faith) was seen as uniquely powerful and washed away the contaminations of idols, but then apostasy (a public renunciation of faith) essentially undid the baptism. On the other hand, the Ebionites practiced daily baptism (*Panarion* 30.15.3). The Ebionite attitude towards baptism may have worked hand in hand with a relaxed attitude towards apostasy, a dynamic also found in the Mandaeans, non-Christian followers of John the Baptist who also practiced frequent baptisms and tolerated temporary apostasy.

5. *Pray towards Jerusalem.*

The Elkasaites prayed toward Jerusalem. Thus, if they were northeast of Jerusalem (say, in Pella or Cochaba) then they would pray towards the southwest. This reminds us of the Islamic prayer towards Mecca. The Ebionites *might* have done this as well; Irenaeus says that they "even adore Jerusalem as if it were the house of God" (*Against Heresies* 1.26.2). But there is no suggestion in the *Recognitions* or *Homilies* that prayer in a particular direction is any more effective for that reason.

6. *Circumcision.*

Hippolytus says that the Elkasaites think that "believers ought to be circumcised" (*Refutation of All Heresies* 9.9). From this single reference it is hard to say whether Hippolytus really thought they *required* circumcision of adult male converts, but this seems to be the implication. This is unlike the views put forward in the *Recognitions* and *Homilies*, but having some support in the *Epistle of Peter to James*, where teachers are required to be circumcised (see chapter 21). Epiphanius says that the Elkasaites practiced circumcision but does not say that they required it (*Panarion* 19.5.1).

This suggests that circumcision was an issue *within* Jewish Christianity, rather than simply a conflict *between* Jewish Christians and gentile Christians. The Elkasaites may have attracted more of those favorably disposed towards the "circumcision party" which so annoyed Paul in the first century, in contrast to the more liberal views of the Ebionites, who thought of gentiles who followed Jesus and Jews who followed Moses as both worthy of admiration. These liberal views of the Ebionites may have attracted notice within mainstream gentile Christianity. John Chrysostom (in the fourth century) complained in lengthy and bitter sermons about some gentile Christians in close contact with the Jews of Antioch; these gentile Christians, like the Ebionites, seemed to be willing to accept Jewish followers of Moses as roughly equivalent to gentile followers of Jesus.

7. The book of Elxai.

The Elkasaites based their ideas on the book of Elxai. This book does not survive and we do not even have any quotations from it in other authors, except Epiphanius, who seems to be reading from it and basing his other ideas about the Elkasaites on it in *Panarion* 19. Epiphanius cites one statement, which might be from the book of Elxai, as "Children, go not unto the sight of fire . . . but go rather unto the sound of water" (*Panarion* 19.3.7), which is perhaps an invitation to avoid the fire of animal sacrifice and instead be baptized.

However, according to Epiphanius, this book got a friendly reception from *all* the other Jewish Christian and allied groups (*Panarion* 19.5.4, 53.1.3), including the Nazoraeans, Nasaraeans, and Ebionites. While "Ebion" knew nothing about Elxai, some Ebionites who later "became associated" with Elxai adopted the Elkasaite idea of a really enormous Christ and Holy Spirit who were 96 miles high (*Panarion* 30.17.5–7). If Epiphanius is correct, this would imply that these groups "traveled together" on their spiritual journey, even though they did not necessarily accept all of the Elkasaite ideas.

The absence of any polemics or evidence of friction between Ebionites and Elkasaites does not necessarily prove there was no split between them; these may have existed but are now lost to history. But if in addition the other Jewish Christian groups really did favorably receive the book of Elxai, then it becomes more plausible that these were just followers of John the Baptist who never attached much importance to Jesus.

Conclusions

The Elkasaites really pose several mysteries about Jewish Christianity. Their views and their theology are remarkably like those of the Ebionites: they reject animal sacrifices and "false texts," accept the idea of Christ reappearing throughout history, and so forth, so there is *some* relationship. But how did they come to be separate from the Ebionites? Were they originally part of the Jesus movement, and then split off to follow the book of Elxai? Or were they spiritual descendants from some pre-Christian group such as the Essenes, the Nasaraeans, or John the Baptist, of which the Ebionites and the Elkasaites were both independent spiritual descendants?

To investigate this further, we now turn to another group, the Mandaeans, which clearly is *not* Jewish Christian, and whose origins will shed further light on the Elkasaites.

25. The Mystery of the Mandaeans

The Mandaeans are the least well understood of the groups related to Jewish Christianity.

What sort of connection might there be between any of the forms of Jewish Christianity and the Mandaeans? The Mandaeans claim to be followers of John the Baptist, and yet do *not* follow Jesus, rejecting him as a false Messiah. Potentially, they provide evidence for what Jewish Christianity was like before or without Jesus.

The Mandaeans are not obviously a spiritual descendant (or a splinter group) of the Ebionites, because they reject Jesus. Even over a space of many centuries, it is hard to explain how a group thinking Jesus was the "true prophet" appearing throughout history could evolve into a group that thought Jesus was a lying prophet and that John the Baptist was the truly pivotal figure. Perhaps we should take them at their word, that they really are completely independent of the Jesus movement and always have been.

All our information about the Mandaeans is fairly late in the day—the earliest reference to the Mandaeans is about the eighth century. The Ginza, one of their holy books, could be from the seventh century. Lady Ethel S. Drower, an early twentieth-century British independent scholar, writer, and traveler, has done more than any other single person to bring to light the history and culture of the Mandaeans. She has written several books on the Mandaeans which even today are the starting point for anyone looking into this subject.

Like the Ebionites, the Mandaeans trace themselves back to the first century and John the Baptist. Unlike most of the other groups discussed in this book, they still exist today—living in present-day Iraq and Iran, with some few followers outside that area. They are a small baptismal sect, practicing frequent baptisms in flowing water.

They hold that there is a world of light into which the soul, following the correct rituals and suitably purified, may ascend at death.

While they claim to have sprung from Judaism and to have migrated later to Mesopotamia, the Mandaeans also reject Judaism, saying that the Jewish God is a false God—somewhat analogous to Marcion, who said that the Jewish God and the God of Jesus were two different Gods altogether. They also reject Jewish customs such as circumcision and observance of the Sabbath. In several ways they are quite different from Ebionite positions, so different that it is difficult to imagine that the two groups ever had a common origin.

The Mandaean liturgies say that the leaders of the Mandaeans appeared before the Muslim authorities in the early days of Islam (639–640 CE). They appealed to the Muslims for protection as "people of the book" and cited their own holy book, the Ginza, as well as their allegiance to John the Baptist, a figure also highly regarded by Muslims (Buckley, p. 5). *Qur'an* 5:69 says that Jews, Christians, and Sabians ("baptizers") shall not fear or grieve, and Muslims counted them as a protected minority under Muslim rule.

When the Mandaeans encountered Christians many centuries later, they of course trotted out their allegiance to John the Baptist; some Christian missionaries even referred to them as "Christians of St. John"—not at first realizing that the John which the Mandaeans referred to was John the Baptist rather than John the apostle, and also not realizing that the Mandaeans were in fact not Christians at all.

Ideological Connections to Jewish Christianity

There are a number of interesting parallels between the Mandaeans and any Jewish Christians; the evidence is circumstantial, but suggestive.

1. *Baptism.* Epiphanius describes the Ebionites as recommending daily baptism (*Panarion* 30.15.3). The Mandaeans also regularly baptize; it is not a one-time initiation, but a frequently repeated ritual. After baptism, the Mandaeans take a bread-and-water ritual meal, which is very similar to the bread-and-water communion which the Ebionites practiced. The Mandaeans believe that baptism helps cure diseases, which is remarkably analogous to *Homilies* 9.19: "washing in a flowing river, or

fountain, or even in the sea, with the thrice-blessed invocation . . . you shall drive out evil spirits and dire demons, with terrible diseases, from others." The Mandaeans and the Ebionites both emphasize baptism in *flowing* water, rather than baptism in standing pools of water as at Qumran (the Qumran pools may have been technically "flowing," but the water would be replaced only very slowly, to conserve water in the desert).

2. *Jewish origin.* In their own accounts, the Mandaeans originated as Jews but then left the Judaism and migrated eastward in the first century. However, they forbid circumcision and attack the Jewish religion in other ways. We don't know why the Mandaeans prohibited circumcision; it may have had something to do with forbidding the shedding of blood, along the lines of the prohibition of blood in the apostolic decree. The Elkasaites and the Dositheans, two possible spiritual "ancestors" of the Mandaeans, evidently practiced circumcision, so there's no clear precedent for this prohibition.

3. *Adam speculation.* Both the Mandaeans and the Ebionites have a high regard for Adam. In Mandaean cosmology, there is a secret Adam (Adam Kasia) who is the prototype of all humanity, as well as of the physical Adam (Adam pagria). After the "fall of the soul," or the fall of the "inner Adam" or "secret Adam" into the physical Adam, Adam becomes a living soul. Manda d-Hiia then comes from the Light World and teaches Adam about the ritual of baptism and tells him of his true celestial nature. This is very similar to the Ebionite theme "Christ was in Adam" (a heavenly being descending into an earthly one). There is no suggestion that Adam commits a "sin" along the lines of the Garden of Eden.

4. *Nasoraeans.* The Mandaeans have three levels of initiation. At the first level, there are ordinary Mandaeans, who are lay people. At the second level, there is the priesthood; priests are entrusted to carry out the Mandaean rituals of baptism, weddings, and the rites for the dying, which are often quite complex. At the third and highest level, there are those initiated into the inner mysteries of the religion: these are called "Nasoraeans." This is a slight variation in spelling from the Jewish Christian or related sects which we investigated earlier—the Nasaraeans and Nazoraeans. There is even an indication that this name was

originally taken from the Christian movement; in one Mandaean text the term *nasuraiia* is used to refer to Christians, the *opponents* of Mandaeism, rather than to the Mandaean elite (Lupieri, p. 9–10). It is worth mentioning also that the general Arabic name for Christians is *Nasara* (Drower, 1937, p. 4).

One of the strongest arguments that the name "Nasaraean" or "Nasoraean" (in whatever spelling) refers to those who are entrusted with secrets (see chapter 8) is the name of this Mandaean elite. They really *are* entrusted with secrets: they are not to reveal the secrets of their religion even to other Mandaeans.

5. *Rejection of blood, vegetarianism.* The Mandaeans are generally not vegetarian; animal sacrifice is part of some of their rituals. On the other hand, there is also a kindly attitude towards vegetarianism as the highest ideal. Blood is forbidden. Meat not ritually slaughtered is forbidden, as well as killing an ox or a buffalo. One Mandaean told Lady Drower that "To kill, even according to the rites for slaughter, is a sin," while other Mandaeans say that "a deeply religious man forswears meat and fish," and some Mandaean legends represent the Nasorai—the Mandaean elite—as vegetarians (Drower, 1937, p. 48).

6. *Apostasy acceptable.* The Mandaeans, like the Elkasaites (but probably not the Ebionites), seem willing to accept apostasy; the Ginza states, "If oppressed (persecuted), then say: We belong to you. But do not confess him in your hearts . . ." (Drower, 1937, p. 15). The Mandaeans carry many memories of persecution in their history.

Connection to the Elkasaites
Lady Drower postulated a connection between the Mandaeans and Jewish Christianity, and the Elkasaites in particular. In addition to the similarities cited above, she gives these arguments (Drower, 1960, pp. 88–106):

1. Like the Mandaeans, the Elkasaites invoke witnesses at baptism. The Elkasaites summon the witnesses of heaven, water, holy spirits, the angels of prayer, oil, salt, and earth (Hippolytus, *Refutation of All Heresies* 9.10). The Mandaeans summon the

witnesses of pihta (bread made with salt), the Jordan (running water), Habsada (personified day of the week Sunday), and Zidqa (oblation).

2. The Elkasaites had a strong cult of Adam. Christ was first formed in Adam, and puts Adam's body on when he chooses (Epiphanius, *Panarion* 53.1.8; compare *Panarion* 30.3.5 for the Ebionites). The Mandaeans also believe in the centrality of the heavenly Adam. Indeed, there is even an etymological connection: "Adam Kasia" (heavenly or secret Adam) could be rendered "El Kasia," with the first syllable "El" meaning "power." The name of the prophet of the Elkasaites, "El Kasia," the heavenly Adam, could be the basis of the name "Elkasaites" (cf. *Panarion* 19.2.1).

Drower also mentions the Elkasaite emphasis on early marriage and disapproval of celibacy (*Panarion* 30.2.6, 30.18.2) and immersion following sexual relations (*Homilies* 7.8, *Panarion* 30.2.4), as items in common with the Mandaeans—though these seem to be similarities of the *Ebionites* with the Mandaeans, rather than of the Elkasaites with the Mandaeans. Further, she discusses the statement in Aramaic which Epiphanius takes from the book of Elxai, "I will be your witness on the great Day of Judgment" (which appeares, untranslated by Epiphanius, at *Panarion* 19.4.3), which "to a Mandaean, sounds like a quotation from the Ginza [a Mandaean holy book]." She quotes from the Ginza to demonstrate her point. References to the Day of Judgment, of course, also sound very much like the *Qur'an*.

There are two other documents where references to "Elxai" (in variant spellings) occur, both of which place the Elkasaites in the same general area as the Mandaeans. The first is in Manichaean literature. The Cologne Mani Codex, a parchment discovered in 1969 from the fourth or fifth century, speaks of Mani's life in a baptismal sect in southern Babylonia—a sect which Mani eventually broke with to form his own group, the Manichaeans. In this text, the leader of this baptismal sect is referred to as "Alchasiaos"—who certainly might be "Elchasai" or "Elxai."

The second is in Islamic literature. The Muslim scholar al-Nadim completed an encyclopedia, the "Kitab al-Fihrist," in about the year 988. He gives a brief account of the "Mughtasilah" who were also called the "Sabians of the Marshlands" (both terms referring to "baptizers"). He states, "Their head is known as al-Hasih and it is he who instituted their sect." He identifies the "Mughtasilah" as the group with which Mani spent his youth, in agreement with the Cologne Mani Codex. This suggests that a baptizing sect which still recognized Elxai existed in the fifth and the tenth centuries, located in the same general area in which the modern Mandaeans are found. Neither of these references necessarily *proves* that these groups were the predecessors of the modern Mandaeans or were even related to them at all, but it certainly puts the Elkasaites in the right area for this to happen.

Dositheus and Simon Magus

The similarities between the Mandaeans and Jewish Christianity are intriguing, but circumstantial and quite late. No ancient church writers mention the Mandaeans. Is there a way to push back further in time the evidence for a group of non-Christian followers of John the Baptist?

It turns out that there is evidence of just such a group, the Dositheans. We know from the New Testament and the *Recognitions* and *Homilies* that the Jesus movement did not absorb all of John's followers (see chapter 9, "John the Baptist") and that there was tension between the followers of Jesus and of John after the two had left the earth.

The *Recognitions* and *Homilies* describe the Ebionites' arch-enemy, Simon Magus, as either a follower of Dositheus or John the Baptist or both. Epiphanius adds other significant details about Dositheus. He says that Dositheus was a vegetarian, believed in the resurrection, and observed Jewish customs such as circumcision and keeping the Sabbath (*Panarion* 13.1–2).

Incidentally, both Epiphanius (*Panarion* 14.2.1) and the *Recognitions* (1.54) seem at times to confuse Dositheus the follower of John, with a much earlier Dositheus who was the teacher of Zadok, the founder of the Sadducees, but this is completely wrong, both of them clearly have got the wrong "Dositheus." It doesn't make sense chronologically, because that would date the origin of the Sadducees some time *after* the death of John the Baptist!

The character of "Simon Magus," the successor of Dositheus, in the *Recognitions* and *Homilies* might be just a convenient mouthpiece for views that the Ebionites wanted to refute. But he also appears to be a historical figure. Simon Magus is mentioned also in Acts (8:9–24), by Irenaeus (*Against Heresies* 1.27, 2.Preface), and by Hippolytus (*Refutation of All Heresies* 10.8). In these documents Simon Magus is described variously as a magician who has performed miracles and advocates various Marcionite ideas—sometimes polytheism, sometimes a secret or unknown God, sometimes other ideas.

What these other church fathers leave out, and what is interesting to us, though, is that Simon is a follower of John the Baptist. After the death of John the Baptist, Dositheus succeeded to the leadership of John the Baptist's group, and then Simon Magus followed after Dositheus (*Homilies* 2.23–24). From this, we can conclude that there was a split among the followers of John the Baptist—some following Jesus, some following Dositheus. Saul, when he was persecuting the early church, evidently thought that the Jesus movement and Simon Magus were in the same group (*Recognitions* 1.70), which tends to add authenticity to this suggestion.

The fact that Simon Magus is related to Marcionite views, as are the Mandaeans, provides further evidence that all of these groups share a common origin. Could the Dositheans and Simon Magus, therefore, be the spiritual ancestors of the Elkasaites and the Mandaeans? And, by all being followers of John the Baptist, would they not then be "spiritual cousins," so to speak, of Jewish Christianity? Did not the Mandaeans, John the Baptist, Jesus, and the Ebionites all trace themselves back to a single pre-Christian group?

There is no clean way to resolve these questions. The only things which are relatively probable are (1) that there was a pre-Christian group (probably called "Nasaraeans" in some spelling) which is the ancestor of all of them, (2) some followers of John the Baptist were either independent of or hostile to Jesus.

There are a lot of possibilities and not a lot of hard evidence one way or the other. The Mandaeans may be spiritual descendants of the Elkasaites. There are some similarities between the Mandaeans and the Elkasaites, and the Elkasaites were known to have been in the same area as the Mandaeans are today, as late as the tenth century. The Elkasaites may have originally been followers of John the Baptist independent of the followers of Jesus, although they seem to be willing to fit Jesus into their system.

But the Mandaeans might also be spiritual descendants of Simon Magus. The Mandaeans seem to have a decidedly "Marcionite" bent, rejecting both the Jewish God and Jewish customs, matching up quite well with the description of Simon Magus in the *Recognitions* and *Homilies*. The Elkasaites resemble the Ebionites more than they resemble the Mandaeans: they are strict vegetarians, reject animal sacrifice, honor the law, honor Jerusalem, practice circumcision, and observe the Sabbath. Figure 25–1 illustrates one possibility.

The Mandaeans remain a mystery. There are enough similarities between the Mandaeans, the Ebionites, and the Elkasaites, so that it is fairly clear that there is a connection somewhere, but you could plausibly argue for any of several possible hypotheses. In any event, though, the existence of another baptismal sect admiring Adam, John the Baptist, and "Nasoraeans" strengthens the hypothesis that there was a pre-Christian group of some sort—identified as "Nazoraeans" in some spelling or other—which is the common ancestor of the Ebionites, Elkasaites, and Mandaeans. We have seen this idea before; the history of the Mandaeans simply undergirds it.

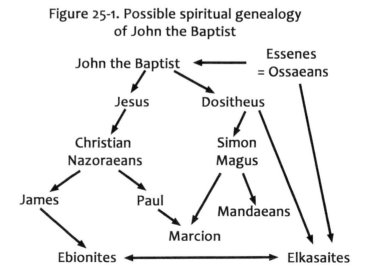

Figure 25-1. Possible spiritual genealogy of John the Baptist

26. Into The East

Thus far, we have only seen evidence for movements parallel to the Ebionites, but not of any movements influenced by the Ebionites. Did the Ebionites disappear without a trace? We see some Ebionite views reflected in China, India, Persia, and Arabia. This is not proof, but it is certainly evidence that the Ebionites left a considerable imprint on disparate religious groups throughout Asia.

The Impact of the Ebionites on Islam
The strongest evidence for a continuing influence of Ebionite Christianity is in Islam. It is likely that Islam absorbed any remaining influence of Ebionism in the seventh century, as there is clear evidence of Ebionite views in Islam (see *The Lost Religion of Jesus*, p. 203–215).

The evidence, as with most of the other groups we have described, is all circumstantial. As far as we know, no Islamic writers explicitly discuss the Ebionites at all. (The Muslim scholar al-Nadim wrote in 988 about a sect which was probably Elkasaite—see chapter 24 above).

Islamic views about Jesus are strongly reminiscent of the Ebionite Jesus, sharply divergent from orthodox Christian views, and even divergent from orthodox Islam. This Islamic Jesus comes closest to expressing the point of view of the Sufis, a mystical branch of Islam, who often said that they wanted to go beyond what was merely expected of all Muslims in their love of God. In this "going beyond" they were able to re-introduce Ebionite ideas as hyper-orthodox Islam.

How do we know what Muslims thought about Jesus? For anyone who isn't fluent in Arabic, there is a problem; very few of the "classics" of Islam have been translated into English. From time to time various English collections of Islamic sayings about Jesus have come out. In 2001 a much more complete book of 303 sayings and

251

stories was published by Tarif Khalidi, entitled *The Muslim Jesus*. I will refer to the sayings in this collection by the number of the saying.

1. *Voluntary poverty*. Jesus disdains the world and the things of this world (Khalidi, sayings 41, 62, 105, 115, 116, 299). Jesus says that wealth is a sickness (62), making your home in this world is like building a house on the open sea (41), and that seeking worldly things is like drinking sea water (115). Twice Jesus advises: "the world is a bridge. Cross this bridge, but do not build upon it" (99, 220). In the Islamic Jesus, as in Jewish Christianity, Jesus adopts an ideal of voluntary poverty which is taken much further than it is in either orthodox Christianity or orthodox Islam.

2. *Vegetarianism and a simple diet*. Sayings from the Islamic Jesus emphasize the simplicity of Jesus' diet, and its basis not just in vegetarian food but the barest and simplest sort of food. Jesus' food is the plants of the field and the produce of the earth (135, 189), he advises us to eat wheat bread and pure water (42), to eat barley with joy (136), to combine the eating of barley with fasting (146). Jesus even eats the leaves of trees (78). Jesus explicitly condemns meat-eating when he says, "Flesh eating flesh? How offensive an act!" (176). (Cf. *Gospel of Thomas* 87: "Wretched is the body that is dependent on a body.")

3. *This world given to the devil*. Jesus frequently gets into conversations with or about Satan and the devils. The world is Satan's farm (Khalidi, saying 82), Satan is the pillar of the world (118), Satan always accompanies this world (72). After Jesus comes into the world, Satan despairs of tempting humans through idol worship (207). Satan accuses Jesus of loving the world because Jesus uses a stone for a pillow, whereupon Jesus throws the stone at Satan and tells him to take the stone and the world with it (119).

4. *Pacifism*. Jesus says that we should never return wrongdoing for wrongdoing (143), answers insults against him with pleasant words (80) and blessings (100), advises his followers to keep silent, or at least speak only good, to enter paradise (125), and to forgive those who do them evil (65). This of course comports with the pacifism of the early Christians, but not with the attitude of the orthodox Christian church at the time of Islam,

nor with orthodox Islam, as the *Qur'an* explicitly permits warfare (2:216).

5. *Respect for animals*. Jesus has many nice things to say about animals. Jesus takes care of a grey donkey, commenting that nobility implies kindness to all creatures (Nurbakhsh, p. 107). He prays that a cow struggling to give birth to a calf will be delivered of the calf (Khalidi, saying 103); he says to a pig whom he passes, "pass in peace" (128); he even speaks admiringly of the white teeth of a dead dog, in order not to speak slander even of a dead dog (127).

6. *Adam*. There are two sayings which relate to Adam. At one point, Jesus prefaces various commands taken roughly from the Sermon on the Mount with the words, "If you desire . . . to be the light of the children of Adam . . ." (65). This is reminiscent not only of the Ebionite and Elkasaite attitude to Adam, but of the Mandaean references to the light-world from which the original or secret Adam comes. When Mary the mother of Jesus is explaining her virginal conception to Joseph, she says that God has previously created Adam and Eve without pregnancy and without a male or a mother (264). The Ebionites rejected the virgin birth, but this story gives the virgin birth an Ebionite twist by comparing Jesus to Adam.

7. *Rejection of alcohol*. Jesus also rejects wine (61) as the key to every evil. Jesus speaks of bread and water as his mother and father—which is perhaps an Islamic recasting of the Eucharist (139). Jesus desires a bread and water meal, just like the Ebionite Eucharist, as well as omitting the wine which is forbidden both to the Ebionites and to Muslims.

The Islamic Jesus is very similar to the Ebionite Jesus. Where did Islam get these ideas? Mohammed became a prophet in a warlike, meat-eating society. It is likely that many of these ideas came neither from Mohammed himself nor from the culture around him, nor from orthodox Christianity, nor from any attempt to manufacture a Jesus compatible with Islam. They most likely came from a pre-existing tradition about Jesus—in this case, the tradition of the Ebionites.

Early Chinese Christianity and the Ebionites

Ebionite Christianity exerted influence even further to the east in the case of Chinese Christianity. The early Chinese Christians were not orthodox and have no relationship to the modern orthodox Christians in China; rather, they belonged to a Chinese Christianity that arrived in the seventh century, flourished for several centuries, and then gradually died out. This Chinese Christianity was probably influenced by the Ebionites.

We know about this early Chinese Christianity largely due to two discoveries: (1) in 1625, the Chinese discovered a gigantic stone monument, dated 781, which describes the arrival of Christians at the court of the Chinese emperor, where they found a very favorable reception. (2) In the late nineteenth century, a number of Christian manuscripts were found in Dunhuang (in Western China, along the old Silk Road). These manuscripts show evidence of a Chinese Christianity which is both vegetarian and pacifist. Martin Palmer's book *The Jesus Sutras* gives a fresh translation of these manuscripts, and due to his research we know a great deal more about the state of early Chinese Christianity.

The Chinese officially supported Christianity (along with Buddhism and Taoism) from 635, when a delegation of Christians came from "a far land" to visit the Chinese emperor, until the year 845, during the great persecution of "foreign religions" in China—which fell primarily on the Buddhists, but also affected the Christians. This non-orthodox Chinese Christianity continued in a weakened form after 845, but had gradually died out by the time that orthodox Christianity came to China many centuries later.

The "Jesus Sutras" (as Palmer calls the Dunhuang manuscripts) are Christian, but the terminology has been thoroughly re-arranged to conform to Chinese sensibilities. Instead of references to God, Christ, the Holy Spirit, Satan, angels, saints, and prophets, we have instead references to "the One Sacred Spirit," the "World-Honored One" (a title given to the Buddha in some Buddhist texts), "the pure Wind," the "Great Evil Ghost," "flying immortals," and "Buddhas." But this appears to be a change in terminology rather than in substance.

The most remarkable similarity of the "Jesus Sutras" to Ebionite Christianity concerns commands not to kill sentient beings. This applies to animals as well as humans, directly implying vegetarianism and pacifism. Vegetarianism is embedded in their version of the ten commandments, in the Sutras rendered as the "ten covenants"—which roughly corresponds to the "ten commandments" found in Exodus and Deuteronomy, with some significant variations.

In this list, the fourth and fifth covenants (relating to kindness and not killing) both directly support vegetarianism and pacifism. The fourth covenant advises us to "be kind and considerate to everything, and to do no evil to anything that lives." The fifth says "not to take the life of any living being," and teaching others to do likewise (Palmer, *The Jesus Sutras*, p. 164), which has a strong parallel in the first precept of Buddhism.

It is striking, also, that this section is introduced by the statement, "The Messiah taught the laws of God" (p. 159), thus framing Jesus' statements in the framework of the Jewish law. Jesus insists that "everything that exists needs the True Law" (p. 189), and that this law has always existed: "this Teaching has existed in Heaven since the beginning" (p. 191). This very much resembles *Homilies* 8.10 which refers to the "perpetual law" which was present since the creation and can be read by anyone, an idea not found in orthodox Christianity. Animal sacrifice is specifically rejected: "it is forbidden to take a life even for a sacrifice" (p. 165).

John the Baptist is also vegetarian. John is not named, but is described. Jesus came to the Jordan, a place of "running water" so that he might receive a name. He meets "the Brother" who had dwelt in the wilderness, had never eaten meat or drunk wine, and ate only vegetables and honey. It is not explicitly stated that "the Brother" baptizes Jesus, but when he emerges from the waters, a voice from Heaven describes Jesus as "my son." This is clearly a description of John the Baptist; and corresponding to the gospel of the Ebionites and the "Slavonic" version of the writings of Josephus, John is also strictly vegetarian and does not eat locusts (p. 166). The Ebionite emphasis on the poor emerges in the suggestion that the followers of this path renounce desire, don't hoard goods, and don't own slaves (p. 226).

The Ebionites denied "original sin" in the Garden of Eden. In the "Jesus Sutras," the law of God is something natural, "you gravitate naturally to these teachings and through them you will come to Peace and Happiness." Indeed, even animals know it: "Animals practice true faith and live by these laws," declares Jesus (p. 193).

In the earlier Sutras (but not in the later ones) there is an apparent denial of the orthodox trinity, or the divinity of Jesus:

> Anyone who says 'I am a god' should die. The Messiah is not the Honored One. Instead, through his body he showed the people the Honored One . . . What he brought was not from being human, but came directly from the Honored One (Palmer, p. 63).

In this text, "the Honored One" seems to refer to God and would indicate that Jesus was not God, indicating support for Ebionite, Nestorian, or some other non-orthodox theology. However, the text is confusing (and possibly confused), because there is no real equivalent for the western idea of God in Chinese religions. Most likely, this passage is an inexact attempt to translate Christian terms into their Chinese equivalent.

"World-Honored One" in Buddhist terminology refers to the Buddha, which is a totally different concept from God. "Honored One" may also refer to Taoist or Confucian deities. In any event, though, in context the intent of the passage seems to be denying that Jesus is God, in accordance with Ebionite and other non-orthodox Christian beliefs, with the translators doing the best they can with the Chinese terms at hand.

There are a number of distinctive Ebionite ideas embedded in the "Jesus Sutras," most notably, vegetarianism, pacifism, opposition to animal sacrifice, John the Baptist's vegetarianism, and belief in an eternal "true law" from which these ethical teachings sprang. While vegetarianism and pacifism occurred in other forms of early Christianity, it is hard to identify Christian sects other than the Ebionites in which *all* of these views were also held. Early Chinese Christianity does not seem to be primarily under the influence of Chinese Buddhism, Taoism, or Confucianism; while there is an obvious influence on terminology here, there does not appear to be a systematic inclusion of any particular Chinese philosophy, only Chinese terms.

The text of one of the early Sutras itself gives a date of 641, a mere six years after the initial reception of Christians at the court of the Chinese emperor. This seems too soon to be a new creation of

Chinese Christians under the imprint of Chinese philosophy and religion. The stone stele of 781 speaks of the emperor commanding that the manuscripts be *translated* into Chinese, suggesting that the "Jesus Sutras" are in fact translations of books which are lost in their original tongue (probably Syriac) and exist today only in the Chinese version.

Overall, this does not appear to be a Christianity which has come under the sway of Chinese philosophy. It is not a question of Chinese Christianity modifying Christian ideas to conform to Chinese ideas, but rather simply a question of the gospel seed from a heretical Christianity falling on fertile ground in China.

"A Far Land"

From where exactly did the mission to China come? The only direct evidence in the Dunhuang manuscripts is that it came from "a far land." It is probably not a mission from the orthodox Christianity of the Byzantine Empire, since the Sutras are so unorthodox. It could conceivably be an Ebionite mission from Syria, Arabia, or elsewhere, but this also seems unlikely, as the mission to China seems to have been well organized and the emperor knew about his visitors some time in advance—a feat which the presumably much-weakened Ebionites would have been hard put to mount, even if they still existed in the seventh century.

Persia in 635 was the home to the Church of the East or "Nestorian" churches who refused to accept the Council of Ephesus in 431. The Nestorians believed that Christ is two persons, each with its own nature, a man Jesus and the divine Logos which dwells within him, acting in harmony (Atiya, 1980 and Vine, 1937). By this time there were also monophysites in Persia as well, who rejected the Council of Chalcedon in 451. The monophysites believed that Christ is one person with one semi-divine nature, a position slightly different both from that of the orthodox and from that of the Nestorians.

Unfortunately, we know very little about the practice of Christianity in Persia at this time. Much of the literature of this time was destroyed during the Mongol invasions many centuries later, so it is hard to relate the "Jesus Sutras" to anything in Central Asia. If any of the "Jesus Sutras" are truly from the Church of the East, they tell us substantially more about the Church of the East than we already knew.

One single clue we have is the cryptic statement "The Messiah [Christ] is not the Honored One [God]," which seems to be a replication of Peter's denial at *Homilies* 16.15, "nor did [Jesus] proclaim Himself to be God." It could conceivably also be monophysite, or more likely, "Nestorian." Thus, the "Jesus Sutras" could have been brought from a non-orthodox Persian Christianity. If it did, though, this was a Persian Christianity which had a number of distinctively Ebionite views.

The St. Thomas Christians of India

There is another possibility here, and that is that the authors of the "Jesus Sutras" came from India or churches which derived from India. There is a strong tradition that St. Thomas, one of the apostles mentioned in the gospels, went to India and founded a church there.

As with Christianity in Persia, we have little manuscript evidence about early Christianity in India. Christianity in India had evidently already existed in India for centuries when it established friendly relations with the Nestorian Church of the East around the eighth century. In 1599, orthodox Christian authorities recently arrived in India, in a chilling act of cultural vandalism, burned all the manuscripts of the native church which they found there, to eliminate the "Nestorian" influence.

This leaves us with two documents associated with Thomas possibly of interest: the *Gospel of Thomas* and the *Acts of Thomas*. Because both of these invoke the name of St. Thomas, and because St. Thomas is connected with India, this suggests that these documents (or ones like them) were part of the message first taken to India by early Christians.

The famous *Gospel of Thomas*, a sayings gospel, is very early, possibly from the first century, and shares a number of verses with the canonical gospels. It also shares some ideas both with the "Jesus Sutras" and with the Ebionites.

One similarity between the *Gospel of Thomas* and the "Jesus Sutras" is the reference to "light." Chinese Christianity invoked the idea of light in the name it gave itself: "This truth cannot be named . . . when forced to give it a name, we call it The Religion of Light"

(Palmer, p. 226). This sounds strikingly as if it were invoking Thomas 50: "Say to them, 'We have come from the light, where the light has originated of itself.'" This interest in the light, of course, is also manifested by John 1:9 ("the true light that enlightens every man was coming into the world") as well as the Mandaean Light-World.

Though there is nothing which clearly marks *The Gospel of Thomas* as an Ebionite gospel, there are several Ebionite-leaning verses. Saying 12 makes James the leader of the early church, and saying 71 has Jesus saying "I will destroy this house" (probably the temple). Some passages suggest an underlying vegetarian message.

> Jesus said: Wretched is the body which depends on a body, and wretched is the soul which depends on these two. (*Gospel of Thomas* 87)

Stevan Davies comments on this passage:

> How does a body depend on a body? By eating it. A human body eats animal bodies for food. Therefore, a soul, we hear, is wretched if it depends on a carnivorous mode of life. (Davies, p. 90).

Davies also cites these sayings:

> When you ate dead things, you made them alive. When you arrive into light, what will you do? (*Gospel of Thomas* 11)

> Anyone living from the living will not die (*Gospel of Thomas* 111).

Davies comments (p. 10): "Such sayings support a vegetarian criticism of meat-eating, because eating 'dead things' or animal flesh seems to be a practice that is ended when one begins to live from the living." The meaning of the sayings is not crystal clear, but suggest that Jesus had an underlying vegetarian message, something that would be well received in an India that was increasingly vegetarian.

The *Acts of Thomas*, a third-century document, talks about Thomas and relates several stories about Thomas and his mission to India. In one charming story, King Gundaphorus of India finds that Thomas knows how to build palaces and orders him to do so. But the money, provisions, and food which the king sends to build the palace are distributed by Thomas to the poor. When the king asks to see the palace, Thomas says that he cannot see it now, but he will see it when he dies.

The king is angry and throws Thomas into prison with a view to torturing and killing him. But at that time the king's brother Gad becomes ill and dies. When Gad arrives in the next life he is shown the very palace Thomas promised the king, and begs the angels to let him return to life. The angels allow Gad to be revived, whereupon he tells Gundaphorus, and they all convert to Christianity (*Acts of Thomas* 17–25).

The feature in the *Acts of Thomas* of greatest interest is Thomas' attitude towards animals. Thomas has an extremely strict vegetarian diet: bread, salt, and water (*Acts of Thomas* 20, 104). Thomas advises that there is no need of sacrifices (*Acts of Thomas* 36), and in fact the devils are comforted by sacrifices made with wine (76). Moreover, animals not only talk with Thomas but actually preach (39, 68–81)! This reminds us of Jesus' statement in the "Jesus Sutras" cited above, "Animals practice true faith and live by these laws." Thomas also has a bread-and-water Eucharist, even though the preparation for the Eucharist had water mixed with wine (120–121). All of these relate both to the Ebionites and to the theme of kindness to all beings found in the "Jesus Sutras."

The one theme that is not particularly Ebionite in the *Acts of Thomas* is the theme of celibacy. Thomas advises a new married couple that they will achieve salvation if they abstain from all sexual relations (12–13). This sounds like the Encratites, who advocated abstinence from meat, wine, and marriage, while the Ebionites were said to repudiate celibacy (*Panarion* 30.2.6). It is not clear that Thomas implies that abstaining from "foul intercourse" is a requirement for salvation—in fact, the wild beasts, when they preach, imply that "one wife" is acceptable (79).

Some of the features of Christianity emphasized by the *Gospel of Thomas* and the *Acts of Thomas* could manifest Ebionite influence. It is certainly possible, therefore, that the "Jesus Sutras" originated in India, where the gospel of nonviolence towards animals would also have fallen on fertile ground, as vegetarianism was being practiced among growing numbers of Indians at that time.

Conclusions

Where is the "far land" from which those missionaries bearing the "Jesus Sutras" came? Like so many other aspects of ancient Christianity, we can't reach a definite conclusion. Geographically, it seems to make the most sense to say that they came from eastern Persia, as Palmer suggests, but it might have been India. In any case, there certainly seems to have been an Ebionite influence on early Chinese Christianity: vegetarianism, pacifism, non-orthodox Christology, the vegetarianism of John the Baptist, inclusion of animals as living under the law, and the counsel against hoarding goods or owning slaves.

The Ebionites also had an influence on the image of Jesus in Islam—even more striking than the case of Chinese Christianity, since many of the elements of the Islamic Jesus are not only different from orthodox Christianity, but from orthodox Islam as well. The exact connections are probably lost to history, but Jewish Christianity exerted some kind of clear influence on the religions to the east of Judea which lasted, in some cases, down to the present day.

27. The Significance of the Ebionites

What is the significance of the Ebionites? The Ebionites have both a historical and a spiritual significance.

Historical Significance
What do the Ebionites tell us about history?

Jesus was an integral part of a larger movement. Jesus did not create his movement from scratch; this movement already existed and Jesus emerged as its leader. John the Baptist, Jesus, and James the brother of Jesus were all martyred; and though they could not have fully understood it during their lives, were all spectacularly successful as leaders. They each brought their own unique personality and ideas to bear on the struggle in front of him; but what these three shared was of much greater import than how they differed. Whatever James the brother of Jesus was, Jesus was as well. And whatever Jesus was, John the Baptist was as well. And whatever John the Baptist was, he was not acting alone.

When the gentile churches rejected the Jerusalem church and Jewish Christianity, they were rejecting the core of the primitive religion. This was not so much a *split* in the church into two or more factions, so much as it was a *shattering* of the church into countless groups.

This shattering of early Christianity resulted in a period of chaos—a period which is actually unusual in the history of religion. This shattering did not mean that all early teachings of Jesus or the first disciples were suppressed by some strong, authoritarian church. Quite the contrary; for well over a century after the destruction of Jerusalem in the year 70, there was effectively no central Christian authority *at all*. Rather, there was a period of chaos in which churches continued to spread.

What is striking about early Christianity after the destruction of Jerusalem is its absolutely baffling nature, which is evident not just to us, but to the participants themselves. Many of the early Christian writings are just polemics against heretics. Origen remarks that "many" Christians have disputes with each other on "subjects of the highest importance" (*De Principiis*, Preface, Section 2). Irenaeus spills a lot of ink describing and denouncing myriad groups in early Christianity; Hippolytus and Theodoret both chime in with their own lengthy treatises. Epiphanius counts 80 different heretical groups. Tertullian describes heresy as widespread, spends a lot of time refuting Marcion, but eventually finds himself outcast as a heretic.

All of the major religions have some sort of factionalism. Within Buddhism, you have Theravada, Mahayana, and Vajrayana; within Islam, there are Sunni and Shia; within Judaism, there are Orthodox, Conservative, Reform. But early Christianity is really quite different, as a comparison with other religions quickly shows.

In the case of Buddhism and Islam, you have a dispute between just a handful of groups, sharing a clear core of teachings, but differing over more detailed teachings or practices. For example, the issue of vegetarianism between Theravada and Mahayana revolves around several disputed sutras and the Buddha's (alleged) instruction to his monks that they may eat meat if they do not suspect that the animal was killed specifically for them.

But this occurs against a background of a shared core of teachings. In the case of Buddhism, for example, you have the four noble truths and the noble eightfold path, which includes at least five basic precepts (against killing, lying, stealing, sexual immorality, and intoxicants). All the various groups accept these and seek enlightenment and release from suffering, though with varying interpretations. In the case of Islam, you have the entire Qur'an, which is accepted by all Muslims. The Sunni-Shia split is more over questions of authority with some rituals and prayers being observed differently, leaving the ethical and theological core of the religion broadly similar.

Christianity is quite different. In the first two Christian centuries there are dozens of different groups, and there is no coherent body of shared beliefs *at all*. There is nothing corresponding to the five precepts of Buddhism; there is scarcely even one universally accepted precept. There are myriad views of God, Jesus, the Bible, and ethics; even monotheism itself is disputed.

It isn't until the council of Nicaea in the fourth century that a coherent "core" of the religion emerges. Even then this core has numerous factors (the virgin birth and the divinity of Jesus, for example) which are fundamental to the religion but which can't really be traced back to the first few decades of Christianity, despite centuries of rhetorical efforts.

Why did this happen? It's because the core of the primitive religion was found only in the Jerusalem church—James and his successors. Paul was not a peer of the Jerusalem church and never knew the earthly Jesus. But after both Paul and James were gone, the whole world of Jewish Christianity was turned upside down, and the Jerusalem church was left behind in the wake of the devastating defeat of the Jewish revolt against Rome. It became easy to ignore what was left of the Jerusalem church, and in fact ignoring it may have become a practical necessity. The entire Christian religion, cut off from its source, had to be interpreted second-hand, and they did it with what was at first a complete vacuum in leadership.

This improvisation led ultimately to a church which discarded much of the original teaching. The church rejected simple living, pacifism, and vegetarianism except as exercises of an ascetic elite. In the beginning, Christianity really was a fairly radical religion; but in the end, it became a "secular" and conventional religion, and the world was only marginally distinguishable from what it would have been had Judaism, Islam, or even paganism taken Christianity's place.

To make Christianity comparable to Islam, you would have to imagine that Jesus wrote or dictated the entire New Testament. To make Christianity comparable to Buddhism, you'd have to imagine that Jesus at least wrote or dictated the Nicene Creed and perhaps founded a few monasteries. But Jesus did none of this. All he left were his Jewish followers and the Jerusalem church, which gentile Christianity brushed aside within a century.

Working in the other direction, to make Buddhism comparable to Christianity, you'd have to imagine dozens of different Buddhist groups, with some having 3, some 4, and some 18 noble truths. To make Islam comparable to Christianity, you'd have to imagine that there were, a century after Mohammed, dozens of different versions of the Qur'an, all claiming to be from Mohammed.

When the gentile church rejected Jewish Christianity, it essentially was starting over. The result of this controversy was not that Christianity was split into two or three factions; it was shattered into countless factions. That's what makes the history of Christianity different from the history of other religions. Neither Christians nor scholars have acknowledged the reality of these divisions. A religion that does not know where it came from, does not understand where it is going, either; and that is exactly the problem of modern Christianity.

Spiritual Significance

The spiritual significance of the Ebionites is that they saw that simple living and nonviolence were essential to spiritual understanding and living. They also saw that vegetarianism was an integral part of simple living and nonviolence. There is an essential connection between all sentient creatures. One kind of violence cannot easily be separated from another.

The environmental crisis we face today is also a spiritual crisis. We don't so much need new technologies, as a different idea of what it means to be human. Modern civilization fosters an economy of "more" and accustoms us to a lifestyle of "more." Whatever we have, it is not enough, and this excuses all the violence towards nature and the domination of people in far away lands who are different from us. All of our intellectual structures, from social morality to religion, are bent towards service of this ideology of domination.

The classic defense of the materialism of the modern world is from Genesis 1:26, in which God gives humans "dominion" over all the other life on earth. And how far as this dominion gotten us? Every human discovery or invention is bent to human domination of the planet. This kind of "dominion" over the earth means death, not just a spiritual death but a physical death for humanity. We are facing an earthly apocalypse of our own making. Meat-eating seems natural, but it is only natural in the context of the social order in which we find ourselves, which rewards precisely those things which Jesus preached against—aggression, violence, and bloodshed. The Ebionites saw that wanton destruction of animals is the pillar on which all other violence rests. Remove this pillar, and the whole structure collapses. Most of contemporary Christianity seeks to leave this pillar in place, but ameliorate the inevitable results.

It should not be surprising that Jesus and the first Christians knew of and considered the question of eating animals. It is a familiar question directly addressed by the great Eastern religions such as Buddhism, Hinduism, and Jainism, as well as western thinkers such as Pythagoras, Plato, and some of the great Hebrew prophets such as Hosea, Amos, and Isaiah.

Jesus and the Ebionites were neither the first nor the only ancient peoples to deal with these kinds of questions. The idea that Jesus had something important and totally original to say is a hangover from the idea of the divine origin of Jesus. Jesus sought to *recover* the original law, rather than to reveal something completely new. Jesus was likely not to emphasize the newness of his ideas, but rather to emphasize how his ideas were embedded in something *already* revealed.

There was a Jewish religious baptismal movement which *preceded* Jesus, in support of simple living, nonviolence, and vegetarianism, and in opposition to inequality, war, and animal sacrifice, claiming this revelation as the law of God. Jesus was its most spectacularly successful leader and was killed after creating a public disturbance in the temple in defense of one of his key beliefs, rejection of animal sacrifice. Jesus probably found the truth already at hand—as old as the prophets, as old as the patriarchs, as old as creation. When he seized on it and started preaching, he was not advancing a completely new system of thought, but simply giving voice to eternal truth.

Bibliography

Numeric dates are cited in mm/dd/yyyy format.

MODERN WORKS

Achtemeier, Paul. "An Elusive Unity." *The Catholic Biblical Quarterly* 48: 1–26, 1986.

Akers, Keith. *The Lost Religion of Jesus: Simple Living and Nonviolence in Early Christianity*. New York: Lantern Books, 2000.

Atiya, Aziz S. *A History of Eastern Christianity*. Millwood, New York: Kraus Reprint, 1980.

Bauckham, Richard. "The Relatives of Jesus." *Themelios* 21.2 (January 1996): 18-21.

Borg, Marcus and Crossan, John. *The Last Week*. HarperSanFrancisco, 2006.

Buckley, Jorunn. *The Mandaeans*. New York: Oxford University Press, 2002.

Carroll, Lewis. *Alice's Adventures in Wonderland* and *Through the Looking Glass*. New York: The Modern Library, 2002.

Crossan, John Dominic. *Jesus: A Revolutionary Biography*. HarperSanFrancisco, 1994.

Crown, Alan and Cansdale, Lena. "Qumran: Was it an Essene Settlement?" in *Biblical Archeology Review*, 20(5):25 ff., September/October 1994.

Davies, Stevan. *The Gospel of Thomas*. Translation and Annotation. Boston and London: Shambhala, 2004. Note that there is another version of this in paperback published by Skylight Paths Publications (Woodstock, Vermont) in 2002 which has different pagination but seems to be the same text.

Drower, E. S. *The Mandaeans of Iraq and Iran*. Oxford University Press, 1937.

Drower, E. S. *The Secret Adam, a study of Nasoraean gnosis*. Oxford, Clarendon Press, 1960.

Eisler, Robert. *The Messiah Jesus and John the Baptist*. London: Methuen and Company, 1931.

Finkelstein, Israel and Silberman, Neil Asher. *The Bible Unearthed*. New York: Simon and Schuster, 2001.

"Hanina b. Dosa." Entry in *The Jewish Encyclopedia*.

Harnack, Adolf Von. *History of Dogma*, Vol. I, p. 266–281. Translated by N. Buchanan. Published by Boston, Little (1901). Cited at: http://www.gnosis.org/library/marcion/Harnack.html (12/24/2010).

Hartman, Gideon, Guy Bar-Oz, Ram Bouchnick, and Ronny Reich. "The pilgrimage economy of Early Roman Jerusalem." *Journal of Archaeological Science*, Volume 40, Issue 12, December 2013, Pages 4369–4376.   At   http://dx.doi.org/10.1016/j.jas.2013.07.001, accessed 10/18/2013.

Hoeller, Stephan A. "The Gnostic World View: A Brief Summary of Gnosticism." At http://www.gnosis.org/gnintro.htm, accessed 6/12/2011.

Isser, Stanley Jerome. *The Dositheans: a Samaritan sect in late antiquity.* (Studies in Judaism in Late Antiquity, Vol. 17.) xii, 223 pp. Leiden: E. J. Brill, 1976. Guilders 60. (This book is not cited in the text.)

Jackson-McCabe, Matt. "What's in a Name? The Problem of 'Jewish Christianity.'" In *Jewish Christianity Reconsidered: Rethinking Ancient Groups and Texts*, ed. Jackson-McCabe, Matt, p. 7–38. Minneapolis: Fortress Press, 2007.

Jacobovici, Simcha and Pellegrino, Charles. *The Jesus Family Tomb: The Discovery, the Investigation, and the Evidence That Could Change History*. Harper San Francisco, 2007.

Jewish Encyclopedia, The. New York and London: Funk and Wagnalls Company, 1907.

Jones, F. Stanley. "Hegesippus as a Source for Jewish Christianity." *Le Judéo-Christianisme Dans Tous Ses États: Actes du Colloque de Jérusalem*, 6–10 Juillet 1998, p. 201–212.

Jones, F. Stanley. "The Pseudo-Clementines." In *Jewish Christianity Reconsidered: Rethinking Ancient Groups and Texts*, ed. Matt Jackson-McCabe, p. 285–304. Minneapolis: Fortress Press, 2007.

Kahn, Charles H. *Pythagoras and the Pythagoreans: A Brief History*. Indianapolis and Chicago: Hackett Publishing Company, 2001.

Katz, Steven T. "Issues in the Separation of Judaism and Christianity after 70 C. E.: A Reconsideration." *Journal of Biblical Literature* 103(1): 43–76, 1984.

Khalidi, Tarif, editor and translator. *The Muslim Jesus: Sayings and Stories in Islamic Literature.* Cambridge: Harvard University Press, 2001.

Kimelman, Reuven. "*Birkat Ha-Minim* and the Lack of Evidence for an Anti-Christian Jewish Prayer in Late Antiquity." In *Jewish And Christian Self-Definition: Volume 2, Aspects of Judaism in the Graeco-Roman Period*, edited by E. P. Sanders with A. I. Baumgarten and Alan Mendelson (Philadelphia: Fortress Press, 1981).

King, Karen L. *What is Gnosticism?* Cambridge, Massachusetts: Belknap Press, 2003.

Klijn A. F. J. and Reinink, G. J. *Patristic Evidence for Jewish-Christian sects.* Leiden: E. J. Brill, 1973.

Lüdemann, Gerd. *Heretics: The Other Side of Christianity.* Translated by John Bowden. Louisville, Kentucky: Westminster John Knox Press, 1996.

Luomanen, Petri. "Ebionites and Nazarenes." In *Jewish Christianity Reconsidered: Rethinking Ancient Groups and Texts*, ed. Matt Jackson-McCabe, p. 81–118. Minneapolis: Fortress Press, 2007.

Lupieri, Edmondo. *The Mandaeans: The Last Gnostics*, trans. Charles Hindley (Eerdmans, 2002).

Luttikhuizen, Gerard P. *The Revelation of Elchasai.* Tübingen: J. C. B. Mohr, 1985.

Manen, W. C. van. "Marcions Brief van Paulus aan de Galatiers," *Theologisch tijdschrift*, Vol 21 (Leiden, 1887), pp. 528-533, transcribed into English by D. J. Mahar (1998). (Found at http://www.gnosis.org/library/marcion/Galatian.htm, and accessed 6/11/2012.)

Mason, Steve. "Did the Essenes write the Dead Sea Scrolls? Don't Rely on Josephus." *Biblical Archeology Review*, November/December 2008, pp. 61–65, 81.

McGowan, Andrew. *Ascetic Eucharists*. Food and Drink in Early Christian Ritual Meals. New York: Oxford University Press, 1999.

Morgado, Joe. "Paul in Jerusalem: A Comparison of his Visits in Acts and Galatians." *Journal of the Evangelical Theological Society* 37(1), March 1994, p. 55–68.

Nurbakhsh, Javad. *Jesus in the Eyes of the Sufis*. London: Khaniqahi Nimatullahi Publications, 1983.

Palmer, Martin. *The Jesus Sutras: Rediscovering the Lost Scrolls of Taoist Christianity*. New York: Ballantine, 2001.

Pines, Shlomo. *The Jewish Christians of the Early Centuries of Christianity According to a New Source*. Jerusalem: Israel Academy of Sciences and Humanities, 1966.

Pritz, *Nazarene Jewish Christianity*. From the End of the New Testament Period Until Its Disappearance in the Fourth Century. E.J. Brill and The Magnes Press, The Hebrew University, 1988. An excellent discussion of this book can be found at robertmprice.mindvendor.com/rev_pritz_nazarene.htm (accessed 10/26/2013).

Proctor, John. "Proselytes and Pressure Cookers: The Meaning and Application of Acts 15:20." *International Review of Mission* 85: 469–483, October 1996.

Renan, Ernest. *The Life of Jesus* (New York: Doubleday Anchor Books, n. d., but before 1970)

Riedweg, Christoph. *Pythagoras: His Life, Teachings, and Influence*. Translated from the German by Steven Rendall. Ithaca: Cornell University Press, 2005.

Salm, René. *The Myth of Nazareth: The Invented Town of Jesus*. Edited by Frank Zindler. Cranford, New Jersey: American Atheist Press, 2008.

Sanders, E. P. *Paul and Palestinian Judaism*. Philadelphia: Fortress Press, 1977.

Schoeps, Hans-Joachim. *Jewish Christianity: Factional Disputes in the Early Church*. Philadelphia: Fortress Press, 1967.

Schwartz, Richard H. *Judaism and Vegetarianism*. New York: Lantern Books, 2001.

Shires, Henry M. "The Meaning of the Term 'Nazarene.'" *Anglican Theological Review* 29(1): 19–27 (January 1947).

Simon, Marcel. "The Apostolic Decree and its Setting in the Ancient Church." *Bulletin of the John Rylands Library* 52(2): 437–460, 1970.

Skriver, Carl Anders. *The Forgotten Beginnings of Creation and Christianity* (Denver: Vegetarian Press, 1990).

Smil, Vaclav. "Eating Meat." In *Population and Development Review* 28(4): 599–639, December 2002.

Tabor, James. *The Jesus Dynasty*. The Hidden History of Jesus, His Royal Family, and the Birth of Christianity. New York: Simon and Schuster, 2006.

Tabor, James. *Paul and Jesus*. How the Apostle Transformed Christianity. New York: Simon and Schuster, 2012.

Tabor, James, and Jacobovici, Simcha. *The Jesus Discovery*. The New Archaeological Find That Reveals the Birth of Christianity. New York: Simon and Schuster, 2012.

Tyson, Joseph B. "Why Dates Matter." *The Fourth R* 18(2), March-April 2005, p. 8 ff.

Vaclavik, Charles. *The Origin of Christianity: The Pacifism, Communalism, and Vegetarianism of Primitive Christianity*. Platteville, Wisconsin: Kaweah Publishing Company, second edition, 2004.

Van der Horst, Pieter W. "The Birkat ha-minim in Recent Research." *The Expository Times,* September 1994, vol. 105 no. 12, p. 363-368.

Vermes, Geza. *The Changing Faces of Jesus*. New York: Penguin Books, 2001.

Vermes, Geza. *Jesus in his Jewish Context*. London: SCM Press, 2003.

Vine, Aubrey R. *The Nestorian Churches. A Concise History of Nestorian Christianity in Asia from the Persian Schism to the Modern Assyrians*. London: Independent Press, 1937.

Waterman, Leroy. *The Religion of Jesus*. Harper and Brothers, 1952.

Wilson, Barrie. *How Jesus Became Christian*. New York: St. Martin's Press, 2008.

Zwemer, Samuel M. *A Moslem Seeker After God*. New York: Fleming H. Revell, 1920.

ANCIENT WORKS

All translations from the Bible are from the Revised Standard Version, except for a few taken from the New English Bible, indicated "NEB".

Abbreviations:

ANF: *The Ante-Nicene Fathers*. Grand Rapids, Michigan: Wm. B. Eerdmans Publishing Company, 1995. The Rev. Alexander Roberts, D.D., and James Donaldson, LL.D., editors. 10 volumes.

Homilies: *The Clementine Homilies*.

NEB: New English Bible.

NPNF: *A Select Library of Nicene and Post-Nicene Fathers of the Christian Church*. 14 volumes. Buffalo: The Christian Literature Company, 1886. Philip Schaff, D.D., LL.D., editor. (Later reprinted by Wm. B. Eerdmans Publishing Company, Grand Rapids, Michigan)

NPNF–2: *A Select Library of Nicene and Post-Nicene Fathers of the Christian Church. Second Series.* Philip Schaff and Henry Wace, editors. 14 volumes. New York: Charles Scribner's Sons, 1905. (Later reprinted by Wm. B. Eerdmans Publishing Company, Grand Rapids, Michigan)

Recognitions: *The Recognitions of Clement.*

The Acts of Thomas. In *The Apocryphal New Testament*. Montague Rhodes James, Translator. London: Oxford University Press, 1924.

Al-Ghazali. *The Precious Pearl*. Jane Idleman Smith, translator. Missoula: Scholars Press, 1979.

Augustine. *Of the Morals of the Catholic Church*. NPNF, volume 4.

Augustine. *Against Faustus*. NPNF, Volume 4.

Aristotle. *The Metaphysics*, with an English Translation by Hugh Tredennick. Cambridge: Harvard University Press, 1961.

Arnobius, *Against the Heathen*. ANF, volume 6.

The Clementine Homilies. ANF, volume 8.

Diogenes Laertius. *Lives of Eminent Philosophers*, with an English Translation by R. D. Hicks (Cambridge: Harvard University Press, 1925), Volume 2, Book 8, pages 320–367.

Epiphanius. *The Panarion of Epiphanius of Salamis*, Book I. Frank Williams, translator. Leiden: E. J. Brill, 1987.

Epiphanius. *The Panarion of Epiphanius of Salamis*, Books II and III. Frank Williams, translator. Leiden: E. J. Brill, 1994.

Epistle of Clement to James. ANF, volume 8.

Epistle of Peter to James. ANF, volume 8.

The Gospel of Thomas. In Robinson, editor, *The Nag Hammadi Library in English*.

Hippolytus, *Refutation of All Heresies*. ANF, volume 5.

Iamblichus. *On the Pythagorean Way of Life*. Translated by John Dillon and Jackson Hershbell. Atlanta: Scholars Press, 1991.

Irenaeus, *Against Heresies*. ANF, volume 1.

Jerome, "Letter 112." NPNF, volume 1, pp. 333–343. (Note: this letter is styled "Letter LXXV" and is found in Augustine's collection of letters. Since Jerome and Augustine wrote letters to each other, the letter collections contain both parties' letters. Letter 75 in Augustine's collection, actually by Jerome, is 112 in Jerome's collection. NPNF only summarizes this letter in Jerome's collection, presumably to avoid duplication.)

Origen. *Contra Celsus*. ANF, volume 4.

Origen. *De Principiis*. ANF, volume 4.

Philo. F. H. Colson, translator. Cambridge: Harvard University Press, 1985. 10 volumes.

Philo. "Every Good Man is Free." In *Philo*, volume 9.

Philo. "On the Contemplative Life or Suppliants." In *Philo*, volume 9.

Plato. *The Collected Dialogues of Plato, Including the Letters*. Edited by Edith Hamilton and Huntington Cairns. Princeton University Press, 1961.

Pliny the Elder. *Natural History*. With an English translation by H. Rackham. Cambridge: Harvard University Press, 1969. In 10 volumes.

Porphyry. *On Abstinence from Killing Animals*. Translated by Gillian Clark. Ithaca: Cornell University Press, 2000.

The Qur'an. Translated by Abdullah Yusufali. Edited by Sayed A. A. Razwy. Elmhurst, New York: Tahrike Tarsile Qur'an, 1995.

The Recognitions of Clement. ANF, volume 8.

Robinson, James M., general editor. *The Nag Hammadi Library in English*. New York: Harper Collins, 1990.

Tertullian, *Against Marcion*. ANF, volume 3.

Vermes, Geza. *The Complete Dead Sea Scrolls in English.* Revised Edition. London: Penguin Books, 2004.

Wise, Micheal; Abegg, Martin; and Cook, Edward. *The Dead Sea Scrolls: A New Translation.* HarperSanFrancisco, 1996.

Subject Index

Modern authors are indexed here. For ancient sources, see the Ancient Authorities Index on p. 291.

Ancient Authorities Index

Classical Authors

Aristotle
Metaphysics
    Book 1, Part 5   69

Diogenes Laertius
Lives of the Eminent Philosophers

2.68	64
6.37	64
6.85	64
8.13	66
8.22	66
8.23	66
8.25	67
8.10	68

Iamblichus
On the Pythagorean Way of Life

11	59
13	66, 67
32	68
35	66
54	66
68	66
69	67
72	68
74	68
81	68
83	59
84	68
92–93	68
100	64, 67
107	66, 67
108	66
132	68
144	66
149	64, 67
154	59
155	66
168	66
188	67

Josephus
Antiquities of the Jews

14.2.1	45
15.10.4	71
18.1.5	71

Wars of the Jews

2.8.3	71
2.8.4	73
2.8.5	71
2.8.6	71
2.8.10	72
2.8.13	74
2.20.4	73

Philo
Every Good Man is Free
    75, 77–79, 84–86   71

Plato
Crito
    49c   60, 66
Laws
    955b–c   60
Letter VII
        57
        231
Lysis
    207c   60, 68
Phaedrus
    279c   60, 68
Republic
    372b-d   66
    449c   60, 68
    617e   58
    Book 10   57, 58, 208
Timaeus
    28c   58

Pliny
Natural History
    5.15.73   73

Porphyry
On Abstinence from Killing Animals
    4.12.3   72
    4.20.1   72

New Testament Apocrypha

New Testament

KEITH AKERS has been a writer and activist for three decades. In addition to *Disciples*, he is the author of *A Vegetarian Sourcebook* (G. P. Putnam's Sons, 1983) and *The Lost Religion of Jesus* (Lantern, 2000). His "Compassionate Spirit" blog can be found at http://www.CompassionateSpirit.com. He lives in Denver, Colorado.

Printed in the USA
CPSIA information can be obtained
at www.ICGtesting.com
LVHW022244250324
775504LV00040B/1168